George Herriman sketches for young fans. Date and source unknown.

# KRAZY & IGNATZ.

by George Herriman.

---

"Love in a Kestle or Love in a Hut."

Convening the Full-Page Comic Strips.

1916-1918.

Edited by Bill Blackbeard

---

Fantagraphics Books, SEATTLE.

# Krazy Kat By He

Published by Fantagraphics Books.
7563 Lake City Way North East,
Seattle, Washington, 98115, United States of America.

Edited by Bill Blackbeard.
Except where noted, all research materials appear courtesy of the San Francisco Academy of Cartoon Art.
Cover & endpapers design by Chris Ware.
Interior production by Alexa Koenings.
Production assistance and scanning by Paul Baresh.
Eric Reynolds, Associate Publisher.
Published by Gary Groth and Kim Thompson.


First Fantagraphics Books edition: April 2010.

ISBN: 978-1-60699-316-3.

Printed in Korea through Print Vision.

Special thanks to Derya Ataker, Warren Bernard, Marilyn Scott and Lucy Caswell at Ohio State University, Andrew Feighery, Dean Mullaney and Cat Yronwode, and Michael Tisserand.

iman KRAZY & IGNATZ.

# AND THE FIRST SHALL BE THE LAST: A HISTORY OF KAT REPRINTS

## A Word from the Publisher

### by Kim Thompson

Welcome to our very first collection of *Krazy Kat* Sundays. Or, if you want to look at it another way, our eleventh. (Or possibly even our thirteenth.)

Okay, you're getting confused. So let me back up a bit.

Ever since George Herriman laid down his pen for the final time on that sad day in April 1944, there have been many attempts to collect his masterpiece in a format more durable than the wisps of newsprint it had inhabited during its three-decade run. From 1946 (when Henry Holt & Co. released the very first Kat book collection) to the late 1980s these attempts were sporadic, and never amounted to more than a single collection here and there.

But in the 1980s the idea began to percolate that the wonderful work created by that first generation of cartoon geniuses ought not only to be preserved and presented to new generations of readers, but presented complete and intact. And so several publishers, including NBM, Kitchen Sink Press, and Fantagraphics, launched extensive reprints of such classic comic strips as *Prince Valiant*, *Thimble Theatre*, *Little Nemo in Slumberland*, *Li'l Abner*, *Terry and the Pirates*...and *Krazy Kat*.

The *Krazy Kat* reprint project came to be under the aegis of a consortium of comics lovers comprising Eclipse Comics, Turtle Island Press, and Bill Blackbeard. Using the complete collection of *Krazy Kat* tearsheets from Blackbeard's impossible-to-overvalue San Francisco Academy of Comic Art, they tackled what many consider the greatest strip ever created, launching what was intended to be a 29-volume set of books reprinting every single *Krazy Kat* Sunday strip (starting, in fact, with the episodes from 1916 you will find herein). In half a decade they managed to publish nine volumes, getting all the way up to 1924, before intractable (and non-Kat-related) business problems sank the good ship Eclipse in 1992.

And there matters rested until in 2002, the indomitable Bill Blackbeard decided to join forces with Fantagraphics Books, to finally complete the job Eclipse had begun.

And here is where things get slightly complicated. Reasoning that since the first nine volumes had been released recently enough that Kat Kollectors had most likely already gotten their newsprint-stained mitts on them (and someone with access to Amazon.com or eBay could still pick them up for reasonable prices — at least at that time), Blackbeard and Fantagraphics decided, rather than starting over again at the beginning, to pick up where Eclipse had left off — vowing eventually, should the venture be met with success, to loop back and reprint those first nine years.

Well, Sir, with last year's release of our tenth volume of *Krazy Kat* Sunday strips — covering the final two years, 1943 and 1944 — we finally ran out of never-reprinted Sunday strips. And so now we fill our promise and begin anew. And thus you ar holding in your hands the first collection of Sundays. Or, if you count the ten we've already released, the 11th. Or, if you add in the two hardcover "supercollections," each of which collects a decade's worth of strips, the lucky 13th. (And yes, there will be a third — or first! — hardcover supercollection of the 1916-1924 Sundays.)

The present volume collects, more or less, what was in the first three volumes of the Eclipse series. The three years of *Kat* Sundays, of course — newly scanned (and if some look better than the Eclipse ones it's not so much because our Eclipse friends were sloughing off, but because newfangled digital scanning has made possible retouching and cleaning of classic strips that was only dreamed of 15 years ago) — but also two Blackbeard articles from yore, and as the usual lagniappe, a set of Bill's inimitable "DeBaffler" entries (augmented with newly composed ones for 1916, a year previously un-deBaffled).

The original Eclipse edition illustrated Bill's article about pre-KK Kats with extensive samples of the relevant strips. We have chosen to spin this off into its own feature, "Before He Went 'Krazy': George Herriman's Aughts" (beginning on page 11), reprinting not only those Kat-starring strips but also a slew of never-before-reprinted vintage Herriman rarities from the nineteen-aughties. All of these come courtesy of the San Francisco Academy of Comic Art Collection, now housed at the Ohio State University Billy Ireland Collection Library and Museum.

Beginning on page 166, after the last strip from 1918, you'll find a special treat, a reprint of a June 1917 article about Herriman from the pages of *Cartoons Magazine*, an *avant la lettre* precursor of sorts to *The Comics Journal*. To be honest, the article, written by the impressively monikered Summerfield Baldwin, is not the most compelling or insightful of reads, but it's fascinating to see how early readers and critics began to respond to Herriman's artistry, and it does come with a few original Herriman illustrations done just for this piece.

Now it's time for thank yous. First a loud thanks to Chris Ware, who up to this point has designed each and every one of the first ten (or 12) books. With this volume, Chris, busy with his day job (apparently being The Most Acclaimed Cartoonist Of The New Century is time-consuming — who knew?), has had to pass along the job of designing the interiors (now most

IN THE SHADOWS OF A GREAT CITY
THE WEAKEST MEN ARE BRAVE WHEN TALKING OVER THE PHONE
WELL-FOR-
'TIS A BITTER RAIN
HUH, A LOADED CIGAR, I'LL SLIP IT TO THAT "KRAZY" KAT
HERE, KAT, IS A CIGAR FOR YOU
OH MANY THANKS TO YOU SIR
A DRIFTING BOAT
OR MAYBE A FAIR LADY
HELLO SIR
KRAZY KAT
AH, THERE'S MY SWEET-HEART'S SHIRT
KRAZY KAT
WELL, I DID IT, SIR-
KRUMMY KAT
SURE
FINE
HOW EXHILIRATING

capably handled by Ms. Alexa Koenings) but has graciously agreed to serve out his Coconino sentence by designing the final three covers.

Also thanks to go Paul Baresh, master scanner and retoucher, who has set the standard — particularly in the extra-challenging color Sundays, often scanned from out-of-register, faded, discolored pages with bleedthrough from the other side — in classic comic art restoration.

Thanks also to all the many Kat fans and kollectors who've helped us over the years, including the terrible trio of Derya Ataker, Jeet Heer, and Michael Tisserand (who is finishing up an actual full biography of Herriman for HarperCollins). And to Warren Bernard and Mark Newgarden, who provided us with the *Cartoons Magazine* article mentioned earlier. And also to comics megamogul Steve Geppi (whose Diamond Distribution insures that copies of these books go out to comics shops around the world), who generously provided us with scans from several original Kat pages in his possession. (This is why the strips for the July 29, 1917 and March 31, July 28, August 4, and October 28, 1918 are especially crisp and lovely.) And to the folks at Print Vision and Pac-Com (Korea), who have been responsible for the most excellent printing of the Fantagraphics Krazy books over the last several years.

Thanks also to the fine folks at Ohio State University, including especially Marilyn Scott and Lucy Caswell, to whom Blackbeard has bequeathed his collection but who graciously allowed us to hold onto the SFACA tearsheets used for this book (and many future Herriman collections) while we scanned them. They have nagged us only slightly for their return, and when you read this the strips should all be safely ensconced at Ohio State (Go Buckeyes!). OSU also generously and promptly provided us with all the scans we used for the accompanying "Herriman's Aughts" portfolio.

And of course an enormous tip of the perennial chapeau to George Herriman, without whom none of this would have been possible, and another to William Randolph Hearst, who whatever his other deeds and misdeeds may have been, generously and presciently gave Herriman that decades-long canvas upon which to paint his enduring masterpiece.

But the loudest and longest applause this time around, I think we can all agree, goes to Bill Blackbeard, who for decades dutifully compiled the greatest comic-strip resource the world has ever known, who edited (and provided strips) not just for these two series but also for a run of recent Pacific Comics Club *Krazy Kat* dailies reprints, but also, way way way back in 1977, Hyperion Press's collection of the *Family Upstairs* strips that introduced Krazy and Ignatz to the world. (Yes, Bill's been behind at least one Kat release in every one of the last five decades!)

Is it peculiar to dedicate a book to its own editor? Well, in that case, peculiar let us be: This one is for Bill!

*ABOVE: Back when Krazy Kat was a mere pendant to Herriman's* Family Upstairs *daily, the assiduous artiste used to draw out each strip in a sketchbook before redrawing it onto the* Family original. *Look for a facsimile edition of this remarkable archive of never-before-seen Herrimania from Fantagraphics Books later this year!*

# THE KAT'S KREATION

## by Bill Blackbeard

In the Beginning, there was the Squiggle. The Squiggle was lively and jet black and adorned with a white ribbon tied in a bow. Large goggly eyes made a burglar's mask out of a black cranium above a bewhiskered white muzzle. Usually set at a placid center amidst surrounding comic chaos, the squiggle was obviously a cat, a marginal visitor in many of the turn-of-the-century drawings of a young cartoonist named George Herriman.

Later, it was to become, forever, a kat.

Cat or kat, this masked feline was a figure Herriman clearly enjoyed drawing, turning up often enough in the artist's early work to justify being dubbed — one wonders if the thought occurred to Herriman — an actual mas-kat.

1

In and out of magazine gag panels and layouts, peeking from one-shot newspaper comic pages, the creature made its first full-fledged comic strip bow in Herriman's Will Rogers-inspired *Lariat Pete* Sunday half-page published by the T.C. McClure Syndicate in most papers on September 6, 1903 (p. 11).

2

In its first real adventure, the creature merely frolics on the outskirts of the central action, keeping serenely clear of the lunatic goings-on occurring at centerstage.

In the following week's episode (p. 11), however, it finds itself the focal point of the hero's lariat action, maintaining its essential calm nevertheless (aside from a briefly erected tail which rises in the second panel of the episode). The cat's bland indifference to the boy dropped on it — any actual cat would have bolted in terror and anguish — certainly foreshadows the attitude of the Coconino Kat to come when later brick after brick sparks loving hearts from its forever dizzy head.

3

A few months later, we find this cat again, this time stalking a dog — not yet a bull pup — in still another Herriman half-page strip called *Bud Smith*, drawn for the World Publishing Company, February 27, 1904 (p. 14). In this new strip, the taunting of the dog seems at first separate from the main action, but quickly comes to prove decisive to the climax of the episode as a whole.

4

Up to this point, the cat has appeared largely as a pantomime artist. Yet in another Herriman half-page from this period — *Rosy's Mama*, dated September 3, 1906 (p. 16) — we find the creature engaged in actual conversation.

"Cat, I have a presentiment," a small pup says in the third panel, anticipating the final outcome of Rosy's adventure.

"Me too, Oh," responds the Cat, breaking its previous silence.

Kicked around in the last panel as expected, the pup complains directly to Rosy's irate father: "Aah, wot did I do?"

Wot did I do, indeed.

Herriman's animals have learned how to speak.

Anthropomorphism has entered the Herriman cosmos, never to leave.

Three months after *Rosy's Mama*, Herriman tackled his first "cat" strip outright. The new cat was named *Zoo Zoo*, and it appeared in a panel under its own name on the editorial page of the *Los Angeles Examiner* in November, 1906. *Zoo Zoo* represented a fluffy reversal of a kind. Zoo Zoo, the cat, was snow white, with a black ribbon tied in a bow. The cat-who-will-be-krazy did not wait long, however, before also appearing in this strip.

5

In the episode which appeared in the *Examiner* on December 15, 1906 (p. 18),

Baron Mooch---He'll Eat Anything From Alfalfa to Gunpowder By Herriman
AM I ADDRESSING THE BEAUTEOUS MRS. LILLYDALE WHO HAS ADVERTISED FOR A HANDSOME BUTLER ?
YOU ARE SIR, WALK RIGHT IN.
BEING AS YOU'RE HUNGRY I'LL GIVE YOU SOME FOOD, NO BUDDY GOES HUNGRY IN THIS BOARDING HOUSE.
KIND LADY-
PRUNES
THREE PRUNES, AND I'M HUNGRY YET.
OI- ?
I'M NOT EXACTLY A PARROT - BUT —
BIRD FOOD
KWA-A-K
KWOK-
WHAT'S AILING MAMA'S ITTLE BITTSY, BIRDIE -?
OH SIR -
AH KAT, WERE YOU NOT SUCH A LOW BROW, I WOULD A TALE UNFOLD TO YOU -
GEO HERRIMAN.

Zoo Zoo's devoted owners have left their pampered pet alone with a sumptuous banquet of goodies — and an open window leading directly to the back alley. Through the open window now pour a half dozen of the alley's best, including, of course, the cat-who-will-soon-be-krazy.

The visitors receive a royal welcome from lonely Zoo Zoo, ending their visit by venting their long-stored wrath upon a portrait of a much-hated family dog, "Zipp," a regular neighborhood terror — particularly, it seems, so far as local trash can-can dancers are concerned.

These *Zoo Zoo* panels are of particular importance to Herriman scholars. Published in 1906, they antedate by three years Herriman's *Daniel and Pansy* strip (p. 21) — the cartoon adventure previously regarded as Herriman's first all-animal strip.

6

And Herriman would create still another "cat" strip in 1909 (p. 20).

This new strip was called *Alexander*, and it appeared — courtesy of the World Color Printing Company — on December 19th of that year.

In its formal interiors and scrupulously repeated decor, *Alexander* contrasted amusingly with the great Kat strip soon to follow.

The fall of 1909 proved to be major turning point for George Herriman, and his later career as America's most imaginative comic strip artist.

During the fall of that year, Herriman was devoting most of his creative energies to the adventures of a certain "Baron Mooch," another new daily comic strip which appeared on the pages of the *Los Angeles Examiner*.

In the December 11, 1909 episode of that strip (see above), we find the Baron applying for work at a boarding house run by a certain Mrs. Lillydale. Obviously having spent a few days between meals, the Baron is in the process of eating the kitchen parrot's bird food when something like magic takes place beneath his feet.

Our old friend the cat reappears, and so does a new duck-billed character known as "Gooseberry Sprigg."

"Oh sir," says the cat.

"Ah Kat," responds Gooseberry, "Were you not such a lowbrow, I would a tale unfold to you."

It is an altogether historic occasion.

A cat has been transformed into the kat right before our eyes.

A recurrent romper along the fringes of Herriman's fancy, a cat has become the kat at last.

Six months later — and a continent removed from Los Angeles — the kat will reappear in Herriman's first *New York Journal* daily strip, *The Dingbat Family*.

In the *Dingbat* episode for June 24, 1910, he can be found first in logo for that strip, sitting beside his beloved new master, E. Pluribus Dingbat.

He also makes a first appearance in the panels in the episode printed overleaf.

"You don't seem to know who you're shovin, kat. Do you?," a small dog says to him in the strip's last panel.

"Ehn?," the kat responds, confusedly.

Cat to Kat, the die has been cast for good.

Over the course of the next few months, the kat now known as Krazy — the mouse to be known as Ignatz will call him that, for the first time, on October 14,1910 (although a white cat had referred to him as "loony kat" a few weeks earlier) — can now be regularly found skittering around under the feet of the human principals who make up the Dingbat Family, battling, fleeing from, and being beaned regularly by an obstreperous mouse and an ebullient pup.

Pantomimic for a brief period, the kat and his new friends soon resort to acidic commentary, and then move on to more complex dialogue and action, ultimately receiving their own small daily panel structure running below the daily Dingbat Family adventures.

Indeed, by 1913, a regular *Krazy Kat* daily strip can be found on the pages of the *New York Journal*.

Readers are now able to turn from E. P. Dingbat's familial follies — or one of its many spin-off strips — to Krazy and Ignatz's daily bricknic on the very same *Journal* comic page.

The new "Krazy Kat" daily soon proved to be a great success with *Journal* readers. This early popularity seems to have resulted from the extreme simplicity of Herriman's art and gag structure.

The strip was virtually always just Krazy and Ignatz, with occasional walk-ons by the bull pup — still a few years from his badge and night stick — Joe Stork, and a number of one-time characters.

Each day the kat and mouse would run through a vaudeville turn, a Burns and Allen kind of skit, with Ignatz playing the part of the angry straight man reacting to Krazy's mad off-the-wall insights and remarks.

During this period the strip looked and read like a cross between *Mutt and Jeff* and *Peanuts*. The repetitive slapstick of the one and the easily grasped layout of the other proved enormously appealing to the reading public.

Anyone could follow the simple smart-stupid relationship of these two comic animals, enjoy the frequent punning punch lines, and quickly recognize the strip's passing references to politicians, writers, artists and actors then in the news.

Only at fleeting intervals — in occasional seizures of pure graphic and thematic inspiration — did the daily *Krazy Kat* of this period give more than a hint of the conceptual wonders of the strip it would become when it moved to the spaces allowed on Sunday's full and open page.

The sheer money-making appeal of Herriman's daily Kat adventures soon led the strip's publisher, William Randolph Hearst, to request a full page *Krazy Kat* for his Sunday papers.

It is unlikely, however, that Hearst had any inkling of the kind of work Herriman would now produce, his imagination sparked by the opportunity to return once again to work on a full-page newspaper canvas.

George Herriman's first Sunday *Krazy Kat* pages must have sent shockwaves through the entire network of Hearst's various local editors. These first Sunday pages simply stunned the Hearst bureaucracy, who quickly yearned for the relative simplicity of the earlier daily strip.

Certainly the changes in the strip were startling.

Suddenly the relatively barren, previous *Krazy* strip was populated with dozens of new characters.

Numerous new animals crowded the scene, tumbling out of odd corners everywhere.

The off-and-on bull pup visitor of the daily strip became overnight a police officer in some sort of complex, functioning society, while the unadorned stage world of the weekday gag now sprouted a bewildering array of foliage and landscape; a fantastic, shifting three-dimensionality of a kind never before seen on a comic page.

Those first *Krazy Kat* Sunday pages — as fresh and wondrous today as they were in 1916 — seemed to hit Mr. Hearst right where he lived.

William Randolph Hearst just adored his new Sunday *Krazy Kat* page.

However distorted he might seem at times by the exigencies of getting out a string of sensational dailies, Hearst's basic artistic instincts remained as sound as they had been back in 1889 when he corralled a visiting Thomas Nast to turn out new dozen cartoons for his first newspaper in San Francisco.

He remained the same sound judge of talent he had been when he paid the brilliant Winsor McCay a good deal of money to draw a weekly *Little Nemo* page that baffled his readers, and lost his paper circulation dollars for a time in 1911.

Would Herriman's explosion of creative energy be lost on his regular readers as well?

Hearst solved this problem much as he solved that of McCay, with editorial adroitness and financial largesse.

Just as he had previously evicted *Little Nemo* in a hurry from his national four-page color comic section to reassure readers that pure slapstick and tomfoolery would once again prevail in those limited pages, only to add the strip to the color back page of his weekly magazine section where its admirers could still find it; so Hearst now cancelled plans to release the Sunday Krazy as a syndicated color feature, and placed it instead on an inside black and white page of the paper's national drama and art section.

Here, Hearst reasoned, the intelligentsia could find and appreciate Herriman's new experiment, while regular readers could read their vastly more simplified daily Kat undisturbed by the possibility that their favorite cartoonist had suddenly gone bats!

Unfortunately Hearst reckoned without the reaction of his local editors. Although the color comics and magazine sections of the Hearst papers were pre-printed for inclusion in the Sunday editions of the Hearst chain around the country, the contents of the Sunday drama and arts, and political sections were sent out as boilerplate (paper mats ready for reproduction), and remained somewhat subject to local editorial decision.

It wasn't long before editors in Chicago, in Boston, in Los Angeles or San Francisco, rebelled against the inclusion of a sizable Sunday *Krazy Kat* page every week in the limited pages of a section where readers would presumably prefer to find more coverage on locally released movies and local and visiting dramatic productions.

Numerous letters backed up these editors in their feelings. Complaints about "this weird stuff nobody can understand" began to arrive regularly in the mail.

And slowly, but surely, local editors began to grow weary of the time and money required in writing explanatory and agreeable replies to such people, particularly when the letter-writer in question might be a local advertiser complaining that the readers who were now skipping over these various *Krazy Kat* pages, might also be skipping over their own paid-for ad.

Finally, the local editors rebelled.

The new *Krazy Kat* page was regularly pulled from local editions — only to be restored just as quickly when Mr. Hearst noted its absence and demanded that it be reinstated at once.

This internecine battle raged on into the 1920s, and then ebbed as Hearst's interests now began to take a more cinematic direction.

By 1925, *Krazy Kat* had received the full critical adulation Hearst had always felt it would finally draw. In 1925, a major John Alden Carpenter ballet production based on the strip hit Broadway. Later that year the leading arts journal of the time, *Vanity Fair*, added Herriman to its contemporary Hall of Fame.

While the average reader might still scratch his head from time to time, for people like Pablo Picasso and e. e. cummings, Charlie Chaplin and Gertrude Stein, Sunday with Krazy and Ignatz had become a real thrill in a decade George Herriman had more or less made into his own.

The present ongoing book series, now that it has finally looped back to Herriman's earliest Sundays *Krazy Kat* pages (see the explanation by our esteemed publisher in his introduction directly preceding this essay), offers the reader an altogether unprecedented opportunity. For the first time ever, he or she can now read Herriman's most masterful strip in a consecutive manner from the very beginning. Insights and associations merely hinted at in previous selections from this work take on full meaning as we witness the epic tale of Coconino County unfold week after week, year after year. The complete Sunday *Krazy Kat* is a visual record of extraordinary power, drama and delight.

The adventure, as they say, begins with this volume.

PLURIBUS DEAR, WE'RE ALL GOING OUT FOR THE DAY AND SO WOULD YOU MIND GETTING YOUR OWN DINNER WHEN YOU GET HOME TO-NIGHT.
ALL RIGHT WIFIE
HERE'S YER PAY ENVELOPE MR. DINGBAT.
TAP TAP
NOW, LET'S SEE, YOU GOT A PECK OF CHUTNEY, A ROAST GOOSE, SALAMI, CAMEMBERT CHEESE, A PICKLED HERRING, A QUART OF CAVIAR, NOW IS THERE ANY THING ELSE
DELICATESSEN
OH YES A PINT OF BRAZIL NUTS, NOW SEND THAT HOME RIGHT AWAY –
SURE, RIGHT AWAY SIR.
SEND ME A LARGE PORTER-HOUSE STEAK AND A YARD OF PORK SAUSAGES, QUICK.
MEAT MARKET
I HAVE TO LICK MY CHOPS WHEN I THINK OF THE SWELL FOOD I'M GOING TO HAVE, AND ALL BY MY SELF TOO
MERCY ME, WE CAN'T GO OUT NOW, LOOK AT THE GRAND VIANDS "DADDY'S" SENT US –
DINGBAT ?
COME IN YOU DEAR, SLY MAN, YOU SENT US THAT SWELL DINNER SO AS TO COAX US TO STAY HOME NEAR YOU, OH, I KNOW –
HYE DAD
EHN?
YOU DON'T SEEM TO KNOW WHO YOU'RE A SHOVIN KAT DO YOU?
GEO. HERRIMAN.

# BEFORE HE WENT "KRAZY":

## George Herriman's Aughts

### LARIAT PETE TAKES THE NEPHEW IN HAND

September 6th, 1903

### LARIAT PETE HELPS HIS NEPHEW CATCH THE CAT

September 20th, 1903

## LARIAT PETE MAKES TEN DOLLARS FOR HIS NEPHEW

September 27th, 1903

## LARIAT PETE AND HIS NEPHEW TAME A MAD DOG

October 18th, 1903

## LARIAT PETE DRAWS A FAT MAN FOR HIS NEPHEW

October 25th, 1903

## LARIAT PETE AND HIS NEPHEW CATCH THE THIEF



November 15th, 1903

# BUD SMITH, THE BOY WHO DOES STUNTS

I GOT SOME NEW TRICKS SIS.
DO TELL
THIS IS A TURNING POLE
YES
YOU GET UP LIKE THIS.
MY, AINT YOU STRONG
SSTPS
AND THEN LIKE —
LOVELY
SS PSTTS PSISP
OH MY.
G R R R R R OW R R
DO IT SOME MORE BUD.
GEO HERRIMAN 04

February 27th, 1905

BUD SMITH, THE BOY WHO DOES STUNTS
HELLO SIS! WOT IS IT? PINK TEA
YES, YOU ARE JUST IN TIME - HAVE SOME?
OH DE DIDDLE UM POW.
THERE'S PIPSY - GEE HE THINKS HE'S A WONDER
HOW MUCH SUGAR WILL YOU HAVE BUD?
B. SMITH COULD NT DO DIS.
SOCH EGOTISM - AS IF I COULDN'T.
OH BUD - HE'S ONLY TEMPTING YOU -
HUH?
MAY BE I CANT HEY - YOU - PIPSY.
MAY BE YOU C-A-N-T.
OH BUD
MISTER B. SMITH COULD NT DO DIS.
IS THE TEA TOO HOT BUD?
AND STILL THEY SAY LOVE YOUR NEIGHBOR
GEO HERRIMAN

November19th, 1905

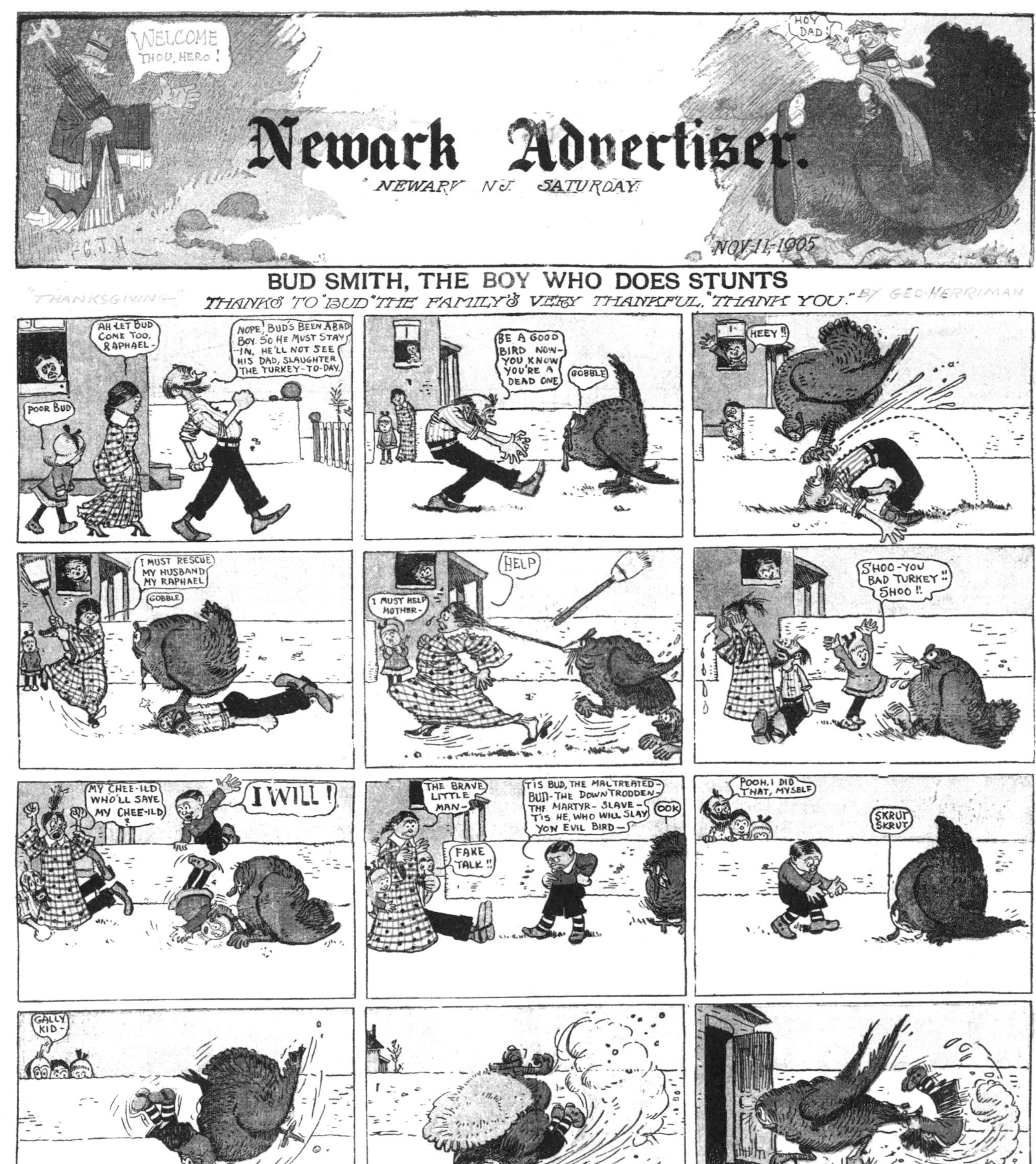
WELCOME THOU, HERO!
HOY DAD!
Newark Advertiser.
NEWARK N.J. SATURDAY
G.J.H
NOV-11-1905
BUD SMITH, THE BOY WHO DOES STUNTS
"THANKSGIVING"
THANKS TO "BUD" THE FAMILY'S VERY THANKFUL. "THANK YOU."
BY GEO. HERRIMAN
AH LET BUD COME TOO, RAPHAEL-
NOPE! BUD'S BEEN A BAD BOY. SO HE MUST STAY IN. HE'LL NOT SEE HIS DAD, SLAUGHTER THE TURKEY-TO-DAY.
POOR BUD
BE A GOOD BIRD NOW- YOU KNOW YOU'RE A DEAD ONE
GOBBLE
HEEY!!
I MUST RESCUE MY HUSBAND MY RAPHAEL
GOBBLE
HELP
I MUST HELP MOTHER-
SHOO-YOU BAD TURKEY!! SHOO!!
MY CHEE-ILD WHO'LL SAVE MY CHEE-ILD
I WILL!
THE BRAVE LITTLE MAN-
TIS BUD, THE MALTREATED- BUD- THE DOWNTRODDEN- THE MARTYR- SLAVE- TIS HE, WHO WILL SLAY YON EVIL BIRD-
OOK
FAKE TALK!!
POOH. I DID THAT, MYSELF
SKRUT SKRUT
GALLY KID-
BANG
GOBBLE GOBBLE
BING
ZIP
SKRUT
YOW
I DONT DARE LOOK OH-HO OOOH
GOBBLE
I GUESS I'M A GONER NOW
HE'S A TRIFLE DISFIGURED BUT JUST AS GOOD FOR ROASTING.
WILL YOU HAVE ICE CREAM OR SHERBET-? OR DO YOU WANT BOTH BUD DEAR?
HERE'S TWO DRUMSTICKS BUD, MY BOY. I WISH THERE WERE FOUR
WILL THE DARLINT HAVE, TAY, COFFEE OR COCOA? WOT?
HERE'S A NICE GIBLET BUD-

November11th, 1905

MY BUT MR TELL WAS A WONDERFUL MAN
THAT'S ALL MOON TALK
THE HISTORY OF WILLIAM TELL
YES, ROSY YOU CAN PLAY, WILLIAM TELL ALL YOU WANT TO. NOW RUN AWAY AND LET DADDY SLEEP
THANK YOU PAPA
I'M GLAD DADDY'S ASLEEP, HE WONT SHAKE THE APPLE OFF
CAT, I HAVE A PRESENTIMENT
PAPA 'LL BE SO SPRISED WHEN HE FINDS OUT WHAT A FINE WILLIAM TELL I AM—
OH OH OH
ME TOO, OH.
WHAT THE-- UH----
SPLUFF
HAVE YOU AND PAPA, BEEN HAVING A GOOD TIME, ROSY?
SCAT YOU MEASLY MUTT
PAPA AND I HAVE JUST HAD A FINE GAME OF WILLIAM TELL AND I HIT THE APPLE
AAH WOT DID I DO?

Rosy's Mama
September 3rd, 1906

DON'T I SEE
OH FRANK JUST LOOK
SOME OF ROSY'S CURIOSITY, I WONDER WHERE SHE GETS IT.
I WONDER
FOXY KID
AH FRANK SHE COULDN'T HAVE DONE IT, SEE HOW INNOCENT SHE LOOKS.
WOT DO YOU THINK OF THAT- HEY, CAT?

Rosy's Mama
Undated, 1906

ZOO ZOO GOES SHOPPING.
WOT AND TAKE ZOOZOO ALONG TOO ?
WHY YES, AND YOU'RE TO COME WITH ZOOZOO I MUST FINISH MY XMAS SHOPPING EMMETT.
DAY DAY
AAH WHO TOLD YOU IT WAS A CAT.
MEOW
TWO BITS FOR DE PUSSY BOSS
HAAY - PSST
PRRRUTTT PRRR CONTUCKITER VAIT.
YOU ARE TO STAND HERE UNTIL I COME OUT I WONT BE LONG
I'LL BUTTON UP MY COAT SO THEY WONT RECOGNIZE ME - YOU'LL FIND ME RIGHT HERE
GEE, BUT I HATE TO SEE PEOPLE MAKE SO MUCH MONEY.
I WONDER IF HE KNOWS ME ?
BLESS ME IF THAT PERSON HAS NOT THE FIGURE AND CONTOUR OF MY OLD PAL EMMETT POZNER JIMSON
SHHH
CAN'T YOU SNEAK AWAY FOR A MINUTE - I'LL BLOW TO THE SODIES, I'VE GOT TWO BITS TO SPEND
TWO SODIES
FFTTTT
OH LOOK AT ZOOZOO
WHICH IS ZOOZOO ?
YAS'M I JIS DONE SEEN 'IM GO IN DAT SODY STORE DOWN YONDER WIF A SMALL PARTY
DEPARTMENT STORE
OH PORTER DID YOU SEE A TALL MAN WITH A BASKET STANDING HERE ?
SODA
CANDIES
CONFECTI
FINE SODA
SIC 'IM ZOOZOO SCAT YOW
GEO HERRIMAN

December 14th, 1906

ZOO ZOO ENTERTAINS.
DON'T YOU WORRY— ZOOZOO IS AS SAFE AS IF WE WERE AT HOME - AND HE HAS LOTS TO EAT SPREAD OUT FOR HIM -
WE MUST HURRY BACK IT SEEMS SO SELFISH TO LOCK HIM UP THE HOUSE ALONE -
GOSH BOYS IT'S OPEN
OY YOI— THAT'S WOT A FELLER GETS FER BEING A SWELL ANGORA. I'D GIVE ANY THING TO BE JONE'S KILKENNY-
PAP
MILK
CREAM
MOUNTAIN TROUT
SWEET SHOWERS OF AQUA ZEMZEM WOT IS IT ?
PAP
MILK.
MOUNTAIN TROUT
THIS IS INDEED A MOST ELEGANT SURPRISE BOYS- LET ME SHOW YOU THE HOUSE.
ZOOZOO WE JUST KIND OF THOUGHT WE'D CALL ON YOU ——
YAAH, WE SAW THE FOLKS GO OUT-
AND THE WINDOW WAS OPEN-
SAY BIM- PULL THOSE FISH BONES OUT OF MY NECK ?
YOU LOOK LIKE A PORCUPINE
HERE, WE HAVE, ZIPP, MY MASTER'S FORMER HOUSE HOLD PET - WITH WHOM GROUND GLASS DID NOT AGREE - ALAS
DOME EYES DECEIVE MEH ?
HOW WELL I REMEMBER THE TIME HE BIT OFF MY TAIL
SPRINGER PUNX
"ZIPP, OUR DEPARTED PET.
REVENGE
HUH?
I'VE KNOWN HIM WELL
GEO. HERRIMAN
I GUESS WE DIDN'T ANDY COMSTOCK THAT POSE HEY ?
OUR PET

December 15th, 1906

ZOO ZOO AND THE CHRISTMAS PIE.
HASTE THEE YOUTH WITH THIS GOODLY GOODY TO THE ADDRESS HERE ON— RETURN, AND YOU SHALL RECEIVE BOUNTY TO THE EXTENT OF CINCO CENTAVOS —
MERRY XMAS THIS IS A PIE FOR THAT HAPPY OCCASION —FROM SWANSON
TCHOOR
DONG DONG DONG DONG DONG DONG DONG DONG DONG DONG DONG DONG
FROM THE OFFICE I'LL BET —
I WONDER WOT CAN IT BE,? OOHMMS— IT SMELLS LIKE PIE
WHO WAS IT WALDO THE OFFICE ?
SO IT WAS A PIE- DID YOU PUT IT AWAY ?
YEP IN THE PANTRY SAY WONT THAT MINCE PIE TASTE GOOD XMAS DAY ?
WE MUST INVITE A FEW FRIENDS, WE MUST SHARE WITH THEM— AND ZOOZOO —
SURE A BIG SLICE FOR ZOOZOO
DID YOU HEAR THAT NOISE —?
SOUNDED LIKE FROM THE PANTRY.
BE VERY, VERY PRUDENT NOW WALDO —
IT IS IN THE PANTRY —
PANTRY
AAAAH-HA!! ZOO-ZOO- HAAY ?
OH BUT I'M SO DISAPPOINTED AND ZOOZOO WAS SO BAD —
OH SORRY THE DAY.
SKIMMED MILK
ZOOZOO'S XMAS.
GEO HERRIMAN

December 20th, 1906

BOO - SAY YAH! HUH!!
THE SUNDAY REPOSITORY
CANTON, O., SUNDAY
NOV. 21, 1909

ALEXANDER FIRST, WHITE==THEN, BLACK==THEN, WHITE AGAIN!

I JUST WISH THAT CAT WOULD STOP THAT YOWLING, IT MAKES ME SO BLAMED NERVOUS -
UR-R-RYOW
THERE NOW I'LL BE BLAMED FOR THAT TOO -
YOWR
AND IT WASN'T MY FAULT EITHER -
ORWOWW
AL- AL- DON'T GO WAY ANGRY
YR-W-RWOW
YOWR-ROW
OOH - A STRANGE CAT - SHOO-OO-O
YR-ROO
SCAT !! - SHOO-OO
OH, MISTO POSSUM PLAYED, RANGITY BANG-BANG ON HIS OLE BA- A-A-AN —
JO- FO DUH LAN OB JUDY, WOT AM DAT ?
SWEET SHOWERS OB GRAVY - IF IT AIN'T, YAAS SUH - IF IT AIN'T - ALEXANDUH —
YUR-R
SH-H-H JINNY - NOT A WORD - SAVY - LET ME SEE, I THINK I'VE GOT A DOLLAR - SOME WHERE
MISTO VAN BONES, JES LOOK A WOT JUMPED IN MAH TUB OB WATER - AN- HE WAS JES AS BLACK - MY -
YOW
DIDN'T THAT STRANGE, BLACK CAT HAVE A NERVE THOUGH ? MY-MY -
HE DID
HM-M HE DID - FO A FAC
GEO. HERRIMAN.

November 21th, 1909

WOW! WOW! WUMP! 'SMATTER? "DANIEL AND PANSY" HAVE YOU GOT A PAIN?

OLD DOCTOR MUTTON
EVERY TIME YOU GET A PAIN TAKE A SWIG OF THAT MEDICINE -
ALL- RIGHT DOC. I WILL.
OH- CHEE- REE- BEANIE- BEANS- UMP TA RA RA YOO-
OOH-OOH- MY- I GOT A PAIN.
WHY- THE DECEFUL SWINE- HE TOLD ME HE'D SWORN OFF
AAA-HH- NASTY- BITTER STUFF- I'D RATHER HAVE THE PAIN- OOOOGH.
FINE NERVE, YOU GOT- JUST YOU SLIP YOUR UNCLE DAN THAT JUG. LEGGO.
BUT MY DEAR DAN
AR-R-R-R- WOT IS IT- WOT IS IT ANYHOW ?
I HOPE THERE'S ENOUGH LEFT TO CURE ME
WHAT'S THE TROUBLE DAN, SICK ? HERE HAVE A SWIG OF THIS.
AW- GET OUT.
GEO. HERRIMAN.

November 21th, 1909

WHO LIKES CRANBERRIES? "DANIEL AND PANSY" OH, ASK MRS. BEAR!

AH, SOON IT WILL BE ONE WILD SWEET SONG OF TOIKEY AND CRANBERRY SAUCE
CRANBERRIES
NIX NOW MR. COYOTE, YOU KNOW I'M STRONG FOR CRANBERRIES MY SELF.
NOW PANSY OLD BOY. YOU, AMBLE ONWARD. I WOULD NOT STAND BY AND SEE YOU RUIN YOUR STOMACH WITH CRANBERRIES FOR WORLDS - GO AND FALL OVER THE HORIZON LINE, - SLOPE - - -
UHM-HM- COME ON YOU CRANBERRIES
HONEST MA, I DID N'T KNOW THERE WAS A HOLE IN THE BAG-
WELL WE'LL GO BACK AND PICK THEM UP AGAIN -
CRAN
SO, DAN. COYOTE, 'TIS YOU, HEH ?
WHY DANIEL WELL WELL -
YOU SASSY LOW BROWED, IGNORANT RHUM-DHUM - FOR TWO CENTS I'D BIFF -
GEO. HERRIMAN

November 28th, 1909

# 1916.

Readers, please note: an Ignatz "dingbat" placed below a strip indicates a relevant or related footnote at the volume's end for that particular selection, all to be found in the "Ignatz Debaffler" section.

WOTSA MADDA ?
HUH !
WHAT AILS THAT 'KAT' ?
WHY ARE N'T YOU EATING YOUR 'ICE CREAM', 'KRAZY,' DON'T YOU THINK IT'S ANY GOOD, OR WHAT ?
COULD I TAKE MY 'ICE-CREAM' OVER THERE, BY THE OLD OAKEN TREE, PLEASE ?
ONE.
WEEY !! GATO MUCHO LOCO.
BASHFUL IDIOT-
FISH !!
BASHFUL ME FOOT !! THERE'S A SINISTER MOTIVE IN THAT 'KAT'S' ACTIONS, LET ME TELL YOU
I HOPE IT DON'T MELT.
TWO.
I CAN SEE NOW WE MADE AN AWFUL MISTAKE INVITING HIM TO OUR 'ICE-CREAM' PICNIC -
THAT 'KAT' IS N'T FOOLING ME ANY, I KNOW HIS LOW KUNNING NATURE, WE MUST FOLLOW HIM, AND FOIL HIS NEFARIOUS PLANS - COME ON -
OH, HOW I HOPE IT DON'T MELT.
TOFF MOG, DOZE 'KAT' NO-
THREE.
SHUH-H-H ADVANCE WITH CAUTION -
FOUR.
DID'N'T I TELL YOU ? UP LADS, AND AT HIM
IF IT ONLY DON'T MELT -
FIVE.
KEEP YOUR EYE ON HIM BOYS !!
YIZZA
MY MY, IF IT MELTS I'LL BE THE MOST UNHEPPY 'KET' WOT IS.
SIX.
IF IT DON'T MELT ALL WILL BE WELL, OTHERWISE ALL WON'T -
SEVEN.
DON'T MELT 'ICE-CREAM' DON'T MELT, I ESK YOU LIKE A BRUDDA -
EIGHT.
DON'T MELT 'ICE-CREAM' DAHLINK, NOT YET NOT YET -
NINE.
WHY, YOU MIZZABIL LOW-LIFE, NO 'KAT' CAN UPSET ME, AND LIVE TO TELL ABOUT IT -
DON'T MELT -
COAL CHUTE
TEN.
'KAT' YOUR DOOM IS AT HAND !!
COAL CHUTE
ELEVEN.
POOR LIL ORPHAN KITTIES DID'N'T OLE 'KRAZY' SAY HE'D HAVE 'ICE-CREAM' FOR YOU TO-DAY, HUH ?
TWELVE.
HUH-
COAL CHUTE
THIRTEEN.
FOURTEEN.
OFFICER, WE'RE LOOKING FOR THAT LOW KREATURE, 'KRAZY KAT,' WE WISH TO DESTROY HIM, HAVE YOU SEEN HIM AROUND ?
JUST KEEP RIGHT ON WALKING - MAY BE Y'LL FIND HIM - MARCH !!
FIFTEEN.
WHY HELLO 'KRAZY' HOW'S THINGS, HUH ?
OH, PUTTY NICE OFFICER 'PUPP' PUTTY NICE I MUST SAY FOR A FACK.
SIXTEEN.
HOW D' Y' LIKE TO GO TO THE 'PATROLMEN'S' ICE-CREAM SOCIAL TO-NIGHT, HEH 'KRAZY' ?
OH MY, Y'GOT NO IDA HOW HEPPY I'D BE TO GO, AND COULD YOU INVITE 'IGNATZ MICE' TOO, HE'S SUCH A DAHLINK -
SEVENTEEN -

April 23rd, 1916.

ONE

TWO.

THREE

FOUR

FIVE

SIX.

SEVEN.

EIGHT.

NINE

TEN.

ELEVEN.

TWELVE.

THIRTEEN.

FOURTEEN.

FIFTEEN.

SIXTEEN-

SEVENTEEN.

EIGHTEEN.

-I-

L'IL DAHLINK: I'M SO GLED IT WAS ONLY A DREAM-

SMACK.

-II-

I DREAMED AN ANGEL KISSED ME-

-III-

To Mrs Helen Dirks with best wishes from Geo Herriman May 1st 1916

-IV-

April 30th, 1916.

I MUST FIND THAT "KRAZY KAT". AND WHEN I DO, AH-H
ONE
KRAZ-EE-EE !!!
TWO
KRAZ-EE-EE--!!
THREE
?
FOUR
WHO DARES TO TELL ME, "GOOSEBERRY SPRIG" THE "DUCK DUKE" TO HALT !! HUH ?
GO NO FARTHER "DUKE", AT YOUR PERIL –
FIVE
JUST AS LOUD AS YOU CAN, "DUKE"
KWA-A-A KWA-A-A
SIX
HEAR THAT – HUH – HEAR THAT ?
KWA-A-A KWA-A-A
SEVEN
WHAT DO YOU MAKE OF IT, "DUKE" ?
HOW SHOULD I KNOW, FOOL, MOVE OVER A BIT, AND GIVE ME SOME ROOM –
EIGHT
WHAT'S THAT ?
JUST YOU CALL OUT LOUD, AND YOU'LL SEE –
YOU SURELY WILL, SIR.
NINE
BOW-WOW !!
TEN
SEE ?
SEE ?
I SEE
BOW WOW !
ELEVEN
?
?
?
TWELVE
I THINK I FORGOT SOMETHING, I-I-I'D BETTER GO BACK AND GET IT –
THIRTEEN
I THINK I DID TOO UH – IN FACT I'M SURE I DID –
FOURTEEN
AH-HAH – HERE COMES "KRAZY"
FIFTEEN
I WONDER WHERE IS IT "IGNATZ" ?
SIXTEEN
HE'LL BE SCARED TO DEATH –
OH "IGNATZ" OOH-HOO –
SEVENTEEN
MY GOODNESS, LISTEN TO THAT "ECHO"
OH "IGNATZ" OOH-HOO –
EIGHTEEN
WELL, I GUESS I'D BETTER BE FINDING "IGNATZ" LIL "AINJIL" –
NINETEEN
TWENTY
OLD SLOOTE
PLATO
ECHO
TWENTY-ONE
TWENTY-TWO
ZING
POW !
AH-H AT LEST, MY DAHLINK IS HERE
TWENTY-THREE
A-A-AH – SHUT UP !!
A-A-AH SHUT UP. !!
HERRIMAN
TWENTY-FOUR

May 7th, 1916.

HE COMES -

OY-YOY - AND A BOTTLES OF RUM.

SHOES

"ONE."

16 FELLAS ON A DEAD MAN'S BOOZUM, OY-YOY, AND A BOTTLES OF "SASPANILLA"

SPLASH !!

SHOES.

"TWO."

HARK !! I HEARD A SPLESH -

SHOES

"THREE."

BUT I GUESS IT WERE BUT A FISH JUMPINK HITHERLY, AND THITHERLY WITHIN THE RIVER.

"FOUR."

HIS DOOM IS NIGH -

SHOES

"FIVE."

?

SHOES

"SIX."

MY NOSE ITCHES, IT'S A SIGN THAT MY DAHLINK "IGNATZ" IS THINKING BY ME

REVENGE !!

SHOES

"SEVEN."

HE SHALL NOT ESCAPE ME THIS TIME

SHOES

"EIGHT"

MY, ANOTHER SPLESH - HOW EGITATED IS THE RIVER TODAY -

SHOES

"NINE."

THIS TIME - SURE.

"TEN."

JEE-WIZ !! YATCHING ON THE RIVER IS JUST ONE FOOL SPLESH AFTER ANOTHER -

SHOES

"ELEVEN."

AH-HAH-

AND IF THEY DONT STOP MY NERVE WILL BE ALL SHOT TO PIECES-

SHOES

"TWELVE."

"THIRTEEN" AND AS USUAL, VERY UNLUCKY -

HOO-ROOR !! HE'S WRECKED !! HE'S GONE, HOO-RAY !!

SHOES

"FOURTEEN."

WELL-WELL SO YOU ARE "KRAZY-KAT-FISH" HUH ?

YES, I AM - LET ME INTRODUCE YOU TO MR - "MANNIE MUSH-RAT"

"FIFTEEN."

"MANNIE" THIS IS MR "KRAZY KAT," A LAND RELATIVE OF MINE, WHO IS GOOD FRIENDS TO A LAND RELATIVE OF YOUR'S, BY THE NAME OF "IGNATZ MOUSE"

WELCOME - ANY FRIEND OF COUSIN "IGNATZ" IS ALWAYS A FRIEND OF MINE - COME IN -

SIXTEEN

"KRAZY," MEET MY WIFE "MINNIE," AND ALL MY CHILDREN -

PLEASED TO MEETCHA -

HOW D'DO ?

SEVENTEEN.

THAT'S OUR BACK-DOOR, IT TAKES YOU OUT ON LAND THROUGH THE OLD HOLLOW TREE - GOOD-BYE. GIVE OUR LOVE TO COUSIN "IGNATZ"

ADIOS -

DA-A-GUNNIT -

OJEE-OJEE, HE'S GONE GONE FOREVER - OOH-HOOOOO -

EIGHTEEN.

OH, WHY DID I EVER TREAT HIM SO CRUEL - OH WHY OH - -

WHY, L'IL AINJIL - WHY WEEPS THOU ?

"NINETEEN."

IT'S ONLY ME DAHLINK -

"TWENTY."

POW !!

ZIZ

"TWENTY-ONE."

"KRAZY KAT"

L'IL LOLLY-POPS HOW HE LOVES ME

HERRIMAN - AND - TWENTY-TWO.

May 14th, 1916.

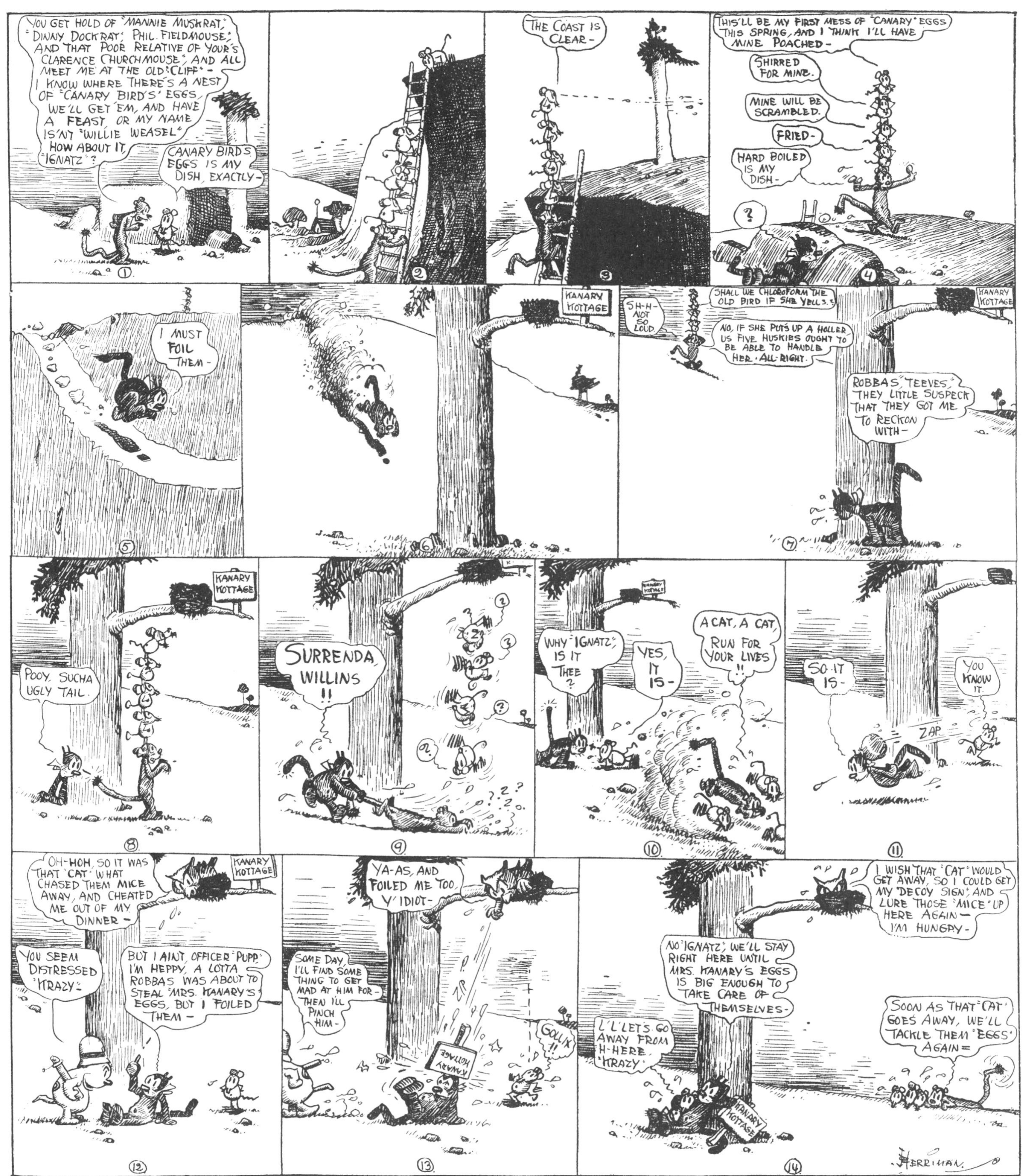

YOU GET HOLD OF "MANNIE MUSKRAT," "DINNY DOCKRAT," "PHIL. FIELDMOUSE," AND THAT POOR RELATIVE OF YOUR'S "CLARENCE CHURCHMOUSE," AND ALL MEET ME AT THE OLD "CLIFF" - I KNOW WHERE THERE'S A NEST OF "CANARY BIRD'S" EGGS, WE'LL GET 'EM, AND HAVE A FEAST, OR MY NAME IS'NT "WILLIE WEASEL" HOW ABOUT IT, "IGNATZ"?
CANARY BIRDS EGGS IS MY DISH, EXACTLY-
1
2
THE COAST IS CLEAR-
3
THIS'LL BE MY FIRST MESS OF "CANARY" EGGS THIS SPRING, AND I THINK I'LL HAVE MINE POACHED-
SHIRRED FOR MINE.
MINE WILL BE SCRAMBLED.
FRIED-
HARD BOILED IS MY DISH-
?
4
I MUST FOIL THEM-
5
KANARY KOTTAGE
6
SH-H- NOT SO LOUD.
SHALL WE CHLOROFORM THE OLD BIRD IF SHE YELLS?
NO, IF SHE PUTS UP A HOLLER US FIVE HUSKIES OUGHT TO BE ABLE TO HANDLE HER. ALL RIGHT.
KANARY KOTTAGE
ROBBAS, "TEEVES," THEY LITTLE SUSPECK THAT THEY GOT ME TO RECKON WITH-
7
KANARY KOTTAGE
POOY, SUCHA UGLY TAIL.
8
SURRENDA, WILLINS !!
9
WHY "IGNATZ" IS IT THEE?
YES, IT IS-
A CAT, A CAT, RUN FOR YOUR LIVES !!
10
SO IT IS-
YOU KNOW IT.
ZAP
11
OH-HOH, SO IT WAS THAT "CAT" WHAT CHASED THEM MICE AWAY, AND CHEATED ME OUT OF MY DINNER-
KANARY KOTTAGE
YOU SEEM DISTRESSED "KRAZY"
BUT I AINT, OFFICER "PUPP" I'M HEPPY, A LOTTA ROBBAS WAS ABOUT TO STEAL "MRS. KANARY'S" EGGS, BUT I FOILED THEM-
12
YA-AS, AND FOILED ME TOO, Y' IDIOT-
SOME DAY, I'LL FIND SOME THING TO GET MAD AT HIM FOR - THEN I'LL PINCH HIM-
GOLLY !!
KANARY KOTTAGE
13
I WISH THAT "CAT" WOULD GET AWAY, SO I COULD GET MY "DECOY SIGN" AND LURE THOSE "MICE" UP HERE AGAIN - I'M HUNGRY-
NO "IGNATZ," WE'LL STAY RIGHT HERE UNTIL MRS. KANARY'S EGGS IS BIG ENOUGH TO TAKE CARE OF THEMSELVES-
L'L'LETS GO AWAY FROM H-HERE "KRAZY"
SOON AS THAT "CAT" GOES AWAY, WE'LL TACKLE THEM "EGGS" AGAIN=
KANARY KOTTAGE
14
HERRIMAN.

May 21st, 1916.

AH, "IGNATZ," YOU'VE GOT NO IDA, HOW MUCH I LONG TO BE A "HERO"-
POO-POODLE: POO-POODLE: WHO EVER HEARD OF A "KAT" BEING A "HERO" ?
ONE.
WHY TO BE A "HERO," YOU'VE GOT TO BE LIKE "NAPOLEON," AND "ROMEO, AND JULIET," AND JOHN. L. SULLIVAN," AND VILLA," AND OLE CAPT. KIDD" - FULL OF FIGHT AND GINGER"-
TWO.
AND, AIN'T I LIKE THAT, "IGNATZ" ?
NO
ZIZ
THREE.
PAP !!
ZEP
FOUR.
SO- MR. "KAT," S'YOU- HUH ?
FIVE.
POW !!
ZEEP
SIX.
SEVEN.
EIGHT.
PAM !!
ZOP
NINE.
DAG NABYA !! NO "KAT" CAN TRIFLE WITH ME LIKE THAT !!!
ZAP
TEN.
POW !!
JOWY
ELEVEN.
??
TWELVE.
AND THE NEXT TIME MR. "KRAZY KAT," YOU SHY A DORNICK AT ME - WA-AL YOUR WHOLE NINE LIVES WONT BE WORT THAT- SAVVY ?
SNAP
THIRTEEN.
B-B-BUT OFFICER "PUPP" I-I-I- -
FOOL-
FOURTEEN.
I'M LETTING YOU OFF EASY THIS TIME "KRAZY" BECAUSE IT'S YOUR FIRST OFFENSE, BUT DON'T DO IT AGAIN- I'M A BA-A-AD BEAR" WHEN I'M INFURIATED, A BA-A-A-AD, BA-AAD BEAR"- - YASSA !!
PLOOP
FIFTEEN.
SOFT SHELL-
SIXTEEN.
I-I-I DID'NT ACT EXACKLY LIKE THEM NAPOLEONS," AND THEM OTHER FELLAS WOULD'A ACTED, DID I, "IGNATZ" ?
I SHOULD SAY YOU DID NOT !!
SEVENTEEN.
ODEER, ODEER, THEN I GUESS I AIN'T NO "HERO"-
EIGHTEEN
HEY !! "HERO" !!!!
HUH- I WONDER- I WONDER-
ME TOO-
HERRIMAN
NINETEEN.

May 28th, 1916.

NOW "KRAZY" YOU TAKE LITTLE "KATRINA" OUT FOR AN AIRING – BUT REMEMBER, NO LALLYGAGGING, NOR KOODAFOODLING AROUND WITH THAT BAD "MOUSE" "IGNATZ" D'YOU HEAR ?
YES, ENT TEBBY VERRA WELL-
THE HOUR I SPEND BY YOU DEAR HEARTS, IS LIKE A STRING OF POILS TO ME-EEE –
HELLOA "KRAZY" LET'S PLAY "SPANIOLA"
OOH, I COULD'NT DO IT TODAY, "KETTAPILLA", 'CAUSE I GOTTA GIVE L'IL "KETRINA" HIS ERRING IN THE GO-BUGGY, AND EVEN WITH "IGNATZ", I CAN'T PLAY – SO ADIOSES.
AH HAH.
I CAH-HOUNT THEM EVER ONE A-PART – MY ROSY-REE MY-HY ROSY-REE –
A-AH SHUXLES !! WHAT'S THE USE OF HOMINY, MY HEART AIN'T MUSICAL WHEN "IGNATZ" AIN'T NIGH-
?
ZIP
NOW I KNOW WHY THEY CALL EM GO-BUGGIES
MARY-ANN MC CARTHY SHE WENT OUT TO DIG A CLAM –
WHA-A HOOOOOOU
!
AH GOO-
AH GOO ? I'LL AH-GOO YOU, Y' BAT-FACED CAT – I'LL AH-GOO YOU IN JAIL-
HOLD ! OFFISSA "PUPP" RESTRAIN YOUR-SELF !!
OH-HOH.
THERE "OFFISSA" IS ALL I GOT, SIX CENTS, AND A COLLA BUTTONS WHAT I WAS SAVING TO BUY FOR "IGNATZ", A BIRTHS-DAY PRESENT.
HAND IT OVER, THAT "MOUSE" CAN BUY HIS OWN PRESENTS
LOOK !! S'GONE A-GAIN !!
DOIND, IF IT AIN'T- !!
?
HERE'S YOUR INFANT "MRS. TABBY" WHAT I FOUND.
I DO HOPE YOU WILL FORGIVE ME FOR THINKING YOU WERE A BAD "MOUSE" WON'T YOU ? – AND, OH, WON'T I PUNISH THAT "KRAZY" NEPHEW OF MINE WHEN HE GETS BACK –
YES, AND JUST GET ME A "BRICK" AND I'LL HELP YOU DO HIM UP –
SH-H- HERE HE COMES.
OH, WHAT'LL "ENT TEBBY" SAY – – ODEER, IF "IGNATZ" WAS ONLY HERE NOW TO COMFIT ME IN MY HOUR OF TEARS. BOO-HOOOOOO
HERRIMAN

June 4th, 1916.

-"JOE" STORK, WHO LIVES ON THE "ENCHANTED MESA" GOES OUT, EARLY THIS MORNING -
- THE LUMP OF COAL IN THE CORNER IS "KRAZY-KAT" WHO WAS OUT LATE LAST NIGHT. -
KO-VADIS ?
- AND "KRAZY" IS AS FULL OF "KURIOSITY" AS ANY OF HIS TRIBE. -
AND.
IGNATZ MOUSE
NOW THAT HIS "KURIOSITY" IS SATISFIED, LET'S GO ON WITH THE "TALE"
FURNITURE
FURNITURE
A PERFECT "BRICK" - A PERFECT "DAY" - AND THAT "KAT" NO WHERE IN SIGHT -
ZIZ
ZIP
AND OH, YOU THOUGHTFUL MAN, YOU'VE BROUGHT THE LITTLE "DEARS" A LOVELY "GO-CART" -
SO THAT'S WHAT HIT ME - GOSH, I THOUGHT IT WAS A AUTO MO BILE.
HE'S AN IDEAL FATHER
WELL, I GUESS I MIGHT AS WELL INTRODUCE 'EM TO "KELLY'S BRICK-YARD" - NOTHING LIKE STARTING THEIR EDUCATION, YOUNG -
I WONDER WOULD HE LET ME BE A "NEAR-UNCLE" TO THEM - "LIL DAHLINKS" -
HERRIMAN

June 11th, 1916.

GRAFT
PFOO, NOW I'LL COVER IT UP, AND ADD ONE MORE "BONE" TO MY SAVINGS ACCOUNT.
STOP THIEF !! STOP THIEF !!
"DON" KIYOTE, THE MEXICAN BANDIT, OR DO MY EYE DECEIVE ME -
STOP THIEF !! PO-LICE POLICE !!
DUTY CALLS
STOP THIEF
OH, UNCLE "KRAZY" HOW KLEVER YOU ARE
YES L'IL KETRINA, I'M A PRETTY SMART "KET" - LISKEN, ONCE A LONG TIME A-GO THERE WAS LIVINK ON THIS "WOIL" ENIMALS BIG LIKE A HOUSE - THERE WAS "DINNY-SORRISES", "NEEGA-NODONS", "MEGA-PHONIUMS", "MEMMOTHS" -
AND GREAT BIG "LIZZIES", UH, I MEAN "LIZZIDS" WHAT WAS CALLED "ITCH-THYOSORRISES" BECAUSE THEY WAS GREAT SCRATCHERS OF GARDENS, AND THINGS, THEN THEY WAS BIG KANARY BIRDS WHAT WAS CALLED "PETER-DECKTILS" BUT A-LAS "KETRINA" ALL THEY IS LEFT OF THEM NOWADAYS IS THEIR "BONES" - JUST "BONES" - AIN'T THAT AWFIL ?
ODEER ODEER ODEER
AND LOOK, "BLESS ME ON MY SOUL", IF THERE AINT ONE THEM WERRA-WERRA "BONES" OF WHOM I WAS SPEAKING -
GAZE WELL UPON IT "KETRINA", BECAUSE FROM IT A GREAT-OLD AGE LOOKS AT YOU, ONCE IT WAS PART OF A "SABER-TOOTH" TIGA, NOW IT IS BUT A MERE "BONE" - AH, HOW SUCH IS THE "WOIL" - A-LAS -
DONT GET EXCITE, "KETRINA", S'ONLY "IGNATZ", HE'LL BRING THE "BONE" BECK THE L'IL "AINJIL"
GIVE ME THAT "BONE"
GOOD HUNTING !!
YOU'RE GOING TO LEAVE THE WORLD BEHIND FOR A WHILE, "DON", ABOUT THREE MONTHS I SHOULD SAY.
SILENCE.
MORE THAN THAT, IF I CAN FIX IT WITH THE "JUDGE"
WELL, I MIGHT AS WELL SLOW UP A BIT, I'VE OUT-DISTANCED THAT FOOL "KAT"
MY "SOUPER" !!
DA-AH-GUNYA !! I GOTCH YA !! HUH ? WITH THE "GOODS" ON, TOO - Y' GAYCAT !!
ONE SIDE, ONE SIDE I'M GOING A-WAY FROM HERE !!
HE'S GONE HE'S GONE !!
STOP THIEF, STOP THIEF !!
AH-HAH -
SEE, "KETRINA", I SAID HE WOULD
AS GOOD AS A "BRICK"
KA-PLOP
ZAP
NOW, AS I WAS SAYINK, "KETRINA", ABOUT THIS OLD "BONE" — MILLYINS OF YEARS AGO, BEFORE "CRISTOFUS COLUMBIA" DISCOVERED THE WORLD - ...
ETC.
YES-YES, "UNCLE", YES YES
HERRIMAN

June 18th, 1916.

AH-H- T'IS THE "HOUR OF THE BALCONY"
DONG - BONG DONG
GLONG DONG
DONG - LONG DONG
AND WHEN ALL THE WOIL MAKES LOVE, I SHOULD HAVE TO BE BAKING "TORTILLAS"
A MENDOLEEN
PLINKITY PLINKA PLINKA TLING
ODEER, ODEER WERE ONLY IT "IGNATZ" WERE IT ONLY HE
OH
OH-H THAT FACE, OH THAT FACE
S'ONLY OLE "DON KIYOTE" PRETENDING TO MY MAIDEN "ENT TEBBY" - WHEN IT SHOULD HAVE BEEN MY DAHLINK "IGNATZ"
I QUIT, DA-A-GONNIT, I QUIT - THAT FACE HAS TAKEN ALL THE SONG OUT OF MY SOUL - THERE SHOULD BE A LAW AGIN SUCH FACES
NOW, LET'S CUT BACK TO WHERE "KRAZY" LEFT THE "TORTILLA" SIMMERING INSIPIDLY UPON THE STOVE
OH-HOH "TORTILLA" - T'IS WELL !!
SNIFF
DANG DONG GLONG
NOT A "TORTILLA" ON THE STOVE, AND "KRAZY" NO WHERE IN SIGHT - OH THE LAZY, WORTHLESS, SCOUNDREL
HE'S PROBABLY OUT IN THE YARD MOONING ABOUT AS USUAL, THE WAGABONE !!
AGAIN WE CUT BACK TO WHERE WE LEFT "KRAZY" IN A STATE OF GLOOM UPON THE "BALCONY"
OH "KUPID" I AM THY WILLINK WICTIM - A-LAS
OH-HOH EVIDENCE OF AN INTERRUPTED SERENADE
T'IS HIM T'IS HIM
I WONDER HOW ONE OF THESE THINGS IS PLAYED ?
FLINK !!
"IGNATZ" !! AINJIL !!
PLAP !!
OH - S'YOU - HUH ?
ZAP
OJEE, HOW HE LOVES ME - L'IL ADONIUS
I'M SO HEPPY I'M MIZZABIL - AH - WHAT A WONDERFUL THING IS "LOVE"
OH, SO THERE YOU ARE HUH ?
YES "ENT TEBBY" - HERE I ARE AND THAT'S A FACK
SOON AS HE GETS A LITTLE DEEPER IN THAT TRANCE, THAT "TORTILLA" IS MINE AGAIN
OH, FOR WHY MUST SUCHA PERFICK DAY END SO SOON ?
HERRIMAN

June 25th, 1916.

1. AND THE WIND RAISED UP IN THE SOU-SOU-WEST
AND TOSSED "JIM" AND "JOE" KOKOKNUTT OUT OF THEIR NEST.
—YEZZA.
THEY LOOK LIKE A COUPLE OF MOTHERLESS ORPHANS WITHOUT ANY DAD-
2. AND THE VERY FIRST THING DID "UNCLE SUN" SEE
WHEN HE CAME UP FOR A BIT OF A "LOOK AROUND"
WAS IT "JIM" AND "JOE" ROOSTING UP IN THE TREE?
NO, NO THE L'IL KOKOKNUTT KIDS WERE DOWN ON THE GROUND.
—"BYRON"—
KELLY'S BRICK-YARD.
DON'T MISS HIM.
I NEVER DO.
3. MISTER "KOLIN KELLY" RUNS A SWELL BRICK YARD
AND THE GOODS HE SELLS ARE TOUGH, AND HARD.
=YOOBETT
THAT "KAT" IS THE WORRY OF MY LIFE.
4. IGNATZ MOUSE, A YOUNG RODENT, CALM, AND SERENE,
WICKED, AND SINFUL, AND VICIOUS, AND MEAN,
ON HIS JOURNEY OF MISCHIEF HERE CAN BE SEEN,
FOR TO BEND A BIG BRICK OVER KRAZY KAT'S BEAN.
KWITE SO
KO-VADIS? PHOES, OR ENEMIES?
FT FT FT FT
5. A KWEER KAT IS "KRAZY KAT"
A SIMPLE SOUL IS HE.
HE'S GOT THE BRAINS OF A GNAT
TUCKED UNDER HIS HAT,
AND HIS MIDDLE NAME'S "KURIOSITY".
—SEGURAMENTE—
HEE-EE- ONLY "KOKOKNUTTS"
6. HAVING PEERED, HAVING PRIED
HAVING QUITE SATISFIED
HIS AMAZING AMOUNT OF "KURIOSITY"
HE STARTS PURRING WITH PLEASURE,
EXULTS BEYOND MEASURE
WITH A TUNEFUL OUTBURST OF VERBOSITY.
—VERILY—..
FEAR.
FATE
7. OH "FATE", MYSTERIOUS MISTRESS OF OUR LIVES
A "KAT" HERE ON THY BOUNTY THRIVES
AND A "MOUSE'S" VILLAINY BECOMES THE BUTT
OF JAMES, AND JOSEPH KOKOKNUTT"—
SIN DUDA
KELLY'S BRICK-YARD.
?
ONE SIDE, ONE SIDE!!
8. THAT VILLAIN'S SPEED IS IN THE HIGHEST GEAR
WHOSE HEART IS THROWN INTO THE CLUTCH OF FEAR.
= Y'DERNTOOTTIN.
MY DAY-DREAM WAS OF "IGNATZ" L'IL AINJIL — AND I'M A HEPPY, HEPPY KET.
9. YES, IT WAS
—THE WIND THAT BLEW FROM THE SOU-SOU-WEST
THAT TOSSED JIM, AND JOE. KOKOKNUTT OUT OF THEIR NEST.
= BUT = HIS DAUGHTER —— MISS "ZEPHYR" WITH HER SONG FROM THE WEST
LULLS "JIMMY," AND "JOEY," GENTLY TO REST.
= ADIOS =
10
HERRIMAN

July 2nd, 1916.

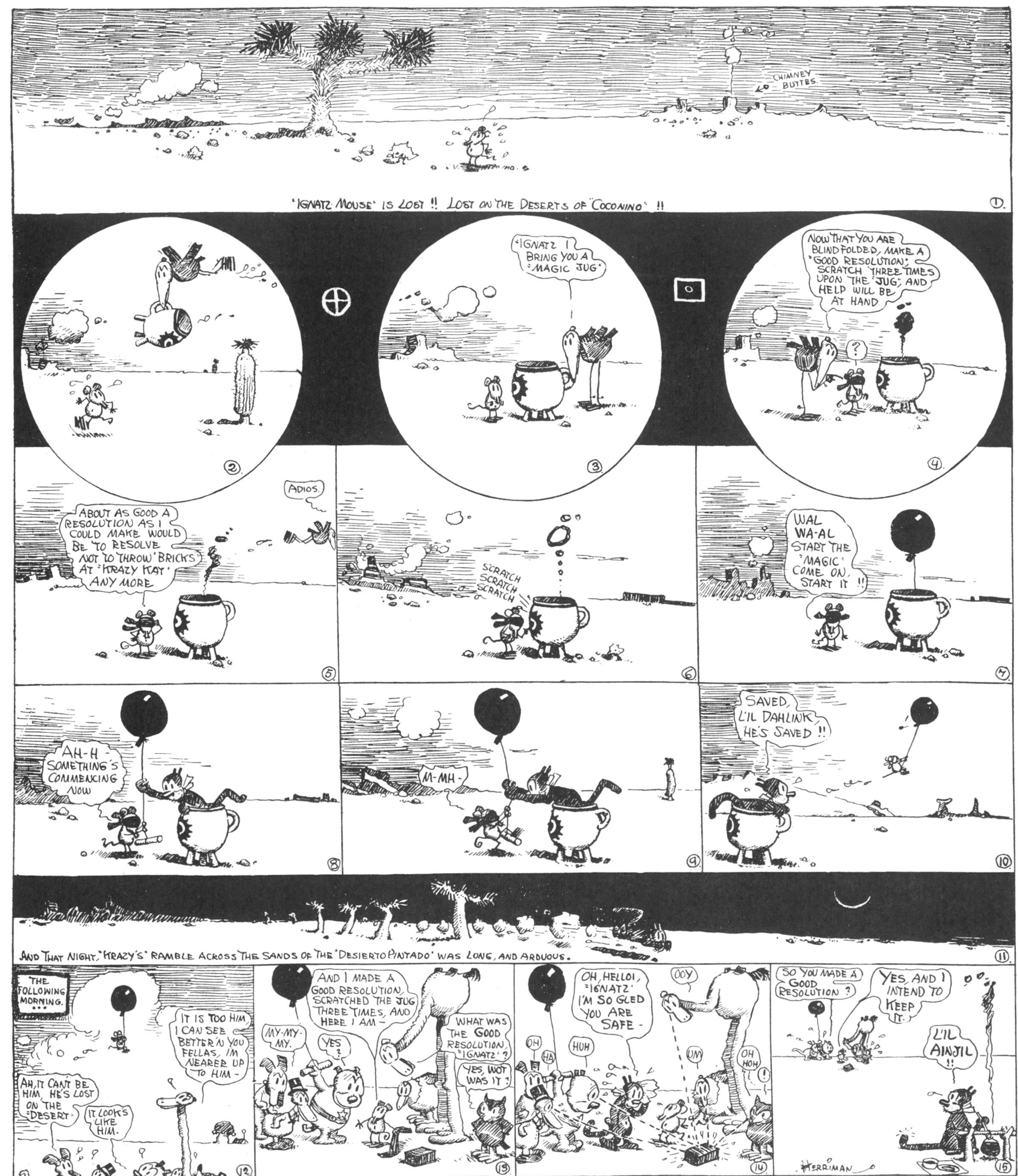
CHIMNEY BUTTES.
"IGNATZ MOUSE" IS LOST !! LOST ON THE DESERTS OF "COCONINO" !!
"IGNATZ I BRING YOU A "MAGIC JUG"
NOW THAT YOU ARE BLIND FOLDED, MAKE A "GOOD RESOLUTION", SCRATCH THREE TIMES UPON THE "JUG", AND HELP WILL BE AT HAND
?
ABOUT AS GOOD A RESOLUTION AS I COULD MAKE WOULD BE TO RESOLVE NOT TO THROW "BRICKS" AT "KRAZY KAT" ANY MORE
ADIOS.
SCRATCH SCRATCH SCRATCH
WAL WA-AL START THE "MAGIC" COME ON, START IT !!
AH-H SOMETHING'S COMMENCING NOW
M-MH-
SAVED, L'IL DAHLINK HE'S SAVED !!
AND THAT NIGHT, "KRAZY'S" RAMBLE ACROSS THE SANDS OF THE "DESIERTO PINTADO" WAS LONG, AND ARDUOUS.
THE FOLLOWING MORNING.
IT IS TOO HIM. I CAN SEE BETTER'N YOU FELLAS, I'M NEARER UP TO HIM-
AH, IT CAN'T BE HIM, HE'S LOST ON THE "DESERT"
IT LOOKS LIKE HIM.
AND I MADE A GOOD RESOLUTION, SCRATCHED THE JUG THREE TIMES, AND HERE I AM-
MY-MY-MY.
YES ?
WHAT WAS THE GOOD RESOLUTION, "IGNATZ" ?
YES, WOT WAS IT ?
OH, HELLO! "IGNATZ" I'M SO GLED YOU ARE SAFE-
OOY
OH
HA
HUH
UM
OH HOH
!
SO YOU MADE A GOOD RESOLUTION ?
YES, AND I INTEND TO KEEP IT.
L'IL AINJIL !!
HERRIMAN

July 9th, 1916.

AS I LOOK ABOUT ME TO-NIGHT, AND GAZE UPON THIS VAST, AND INTELLIGENT AUDIENCE, I CAN READ IN IT'S EYE THE MESSAGE OF IT'S MIND, THE ONE BIG IDEA, THE ONE SOLID CONCEPTION, THE ONE CONCRETE BELIEF - "PRE-PAREDNESS" BURSTING INTO LIFE —— -ETC-
HEAR HEAR.
I WILL NOW TAKE THE "AUDIENCE" INTO MY INNERMOST CONFIDENCE - - AUDIENCE LOOK WELL UPON THIS -
YIZZA.
I WILL ALSO ASK THE AUDIENCE, HAS IT A "ENEMY"?
YIZZA, I HAVE, BUT, OH HE'S SUCH A SWEET LI'L "ENEMY" - HE'S SO NICE -
BEWARE OF SUCH A "ENEMY" !! HE STRIKES IN THE DARK !!! BUT, WITH MY "LITTLE GEM VANISHER" YOU NEED FEAR NO ENEMY - ONE THRUST OF THE HEAD, THUS, AND BEHOLD YOU ARE INVISIBLE TO THE WORLD, AND YOUR ENEMY !!
OOY-
THE "LITTLE GEM VANISHER" IS NOT A STATIONARY ARTICLE IT MOVES, IT TRAVELS, IT TAKES YOU ABOUT, FROM PLACE TO PLACE UNSEEN, AND INVISIBLE !
I WONDER IF REALLY I DON'T SEE HIM, OR NOT ?
AND FOR 60 CENTS THIS LITTLE ARTICLE OF SAFETY IS YOURS -
"SIXTY CENTS" AH-HAH, I THOUGHT THEY WAS A "JOKA" IN THE DECK, SOMEWHERES !!
60¢
HUH - 60¢
60¢ - ROBBA, !! BECK ELLIES IS FULL OF "VANISHERS," AND HERE I AM INVISIBLE FREE FOR NOTHING -
OH-HOH
BA-AM!
ZIP
DON'T EVER KEEP ME WAITING TWO HOURS FOR YOU AGAIN !! KRAZY KAT !!
NOT ONLY A ROBBA, BUT ALSO A "FIBBA" !!
ZIP
NEVER A-GAIN WILL I BE A "INTELLIGENT AUDIENCE" !!
HERRIMAN

July 16th, 1916.

"WILLIAM BEE" ALIAS "BUM" BILL" — A. LABORER, A DRONE, A VAGABOND, WITHOUT A HOME, WITHOUT A WIFE, HE HAS NO ENEMY, HE HAS NO FRIEND —
CONTINUED IN LOWER RIGHT HAND CORNER.
HELP, HELP !!
HELP, HELP !!
I'M CAMINK, I'M CAMINK !!
HELP !!
GRAB A-HOLD ATTA BEE —
I GOT IT —
YOU'VE GOT NO IDEA HOW THANKFUL I AM TO YOU, "KRAZY," I WAS DOWN FOR THE THIRD TIME TOO —
OH, DUNT MENTION IT MR. BEE, BY ME IT ALSO WAS A PLEASURE I INSURE YOU —
RIGHT OVER THE PLATE —
ZIP
I GOT HIM —
AH-H-H — IGNATZ IS NIGH.
ZIZZ
BUZZ-ZZ
ZUZZ
ZZZ
BZEE
ZUMM
BZAA
PSMM
ZMM
BUMM
BZMM
"AINJIL MICE."
— HE IS A CHILD OF DESTINY WITHOUT A DESTINATION, A PILGRIM ON THE ROAD TO "NOWHERE."
— "SAY TOO"
HERRIMAN

July 23rd, 1916.

HURRY HOME WITH THAT 'SOAP' 'KRAZY' YOUR 'AUNT TABBY' NEEDS IT RIGHT AWAY.
GROCER
YIZZA.
?
TA DA DA-DAAA
OD-ZIGGETY-
I CALL THIS RATHA KLEEVA, I DO-
GOSH !!
OOY-
LOOKOW, LOOOO-KOW !!
HIS DOOM IS AT HAND. !!
NO 'MOUSE' CAN WALK ON MY FACE, AND LIVE.
HALT.
ZZZ-FEE GZEE
OH, I'LL GETCHA-
GEEVIM, GEEVIM.
AH- MY 'SOAP.' FOR ONCE IN HIS LIFE, 'KRAZY' GOT A MOVE ON HIMSELF.
ZIPS
GOODY, GOODY.
PHLEBOTOMY HAS BEEN PERFORMED UPON HIS NOSE.
OMY OMY.
?
SPARE HIM, 'ENTIE'; OH SPARE THE LITTLE DAHLINK.
MIZZABIL MOUSE-
WHAT DANGEROUS EYES YOU'VE GOT, MISS 'TABBY'.
OH, OFFISSA 'PUPP,' QUIT YOUR KOODAFOODLIN-
POOR L'IL AINJIL.

July 30th, 1916.

HAH, A PERSON OF MYSTERY -
HIS FAMILY WOULD BE BETTER OFF WITHOUT HIM.
FOR MY PART I DONT CARE HOW LONG HE'S LOST FOR -
HE CANT BE LOST TOO LONG TO SUIT ME, HE CANT -
S' NOT SO MUCH OF A LOSS, S'FAR AS I CAN SEE.
BANGA BLANG- BLANG
HOYEZ, HOYEZ, HOYEZ !! BEHOLD A SORROWING FAMILY !! MRS. MATILDA MOUSE, AND HER THREE STALWART SONS, MILTON, IRVING, AND MARSHALL MOUSE. THEY GRIEVE THE LOSS OF A GOOD HUSBAND, AND A FOND FATHER, "IGNATZ MOUSE" WHO IS THIS DAY LOST !! SO SEARCH YE, SEARCH YE, SEARCH YE. A "REWARD" OF ONE POUND OF BEST "CHEESE" GOES TO WHOEVER LOCATES THE MISSING ONE
WEE - WEE - WEE
SKWEEK KWEEK WEE -
1.
ALDERMAN "TSHEEZ" ANNOUNCES A SAD EVENT TO HIS CONSTITUENTS
HE'S UP TO NO GOOD -
2
AH-HAH, SO HE HOBNOBS WITH THAT MEXICAN BANDIT "DON KIOTY," HUH? NOW I KNOW HE'S A CROOK.
HE WENT OVER THERE, PAST THE MESA "DEDO DEL PIE GRANDE" ON TOWARDS THE TOWN, SO I GUESS IT'S A DATE HE'S GOT, OR ELSE WHY SHOULD HE GO TO TOWN, HUH, WHY? ANSWER ME THAT -
3
HE SURE DOES KNOW ALL THE "GOOFERS"
HOUND, AND PUP, I'VE LIVED IN THIS "PUEBLO" NIGH ONTO SIXTEEN YEARS, AND THERE'S NOTHING IN THE WAY OF NEWS, OR COMMENT I'VE MISSED, NOZZA, - ALL THE NEWS WHAT'S FIT TO PEDDLE I KNOW FROM BACK IN 1900 WHEN "LEMUEL OWL" RUN FOR SHERIFF UP TO TEN MINUTES AGO WHEN I SEEN "JOE. BEAMISH" IN "HEN. BISKIT'S" GROCERY STORE BUYING A NICKEL'S WORTH OF CHEESE, AND A MOUSE TRAP; NOW STRANGER WHAT MORE CAN I INFORM TO ? HUH -
4.
AH, SO ITS A "BURGLAR" HE IS, UH-HUH
BEAMISH
5
HE'S GONNA PLAY THE KITCHEN WINDOW -
6
I'LL NAIL HIM WHEN HE COMES OUT, WITH THE "GOODS" ON HIM - I'LL BE MADE A "CAPTAIN" FOR THIS NIGHT'S WORK, SURE.
7
STOP !! "IGNATZ MICE" !! GO NO FURDA, AT YOUR PEERIL !!!
?
8.
WHO DARES TO DEPRIVE ME OF YON CHEESE ?
ME, "KRAZY KAT," !! DAHLINK, NOT YOUR "DEPRIVER," BUT YOUR "PRESERVER" FROM YON MICE-TREP !!
ZIP
SNAP
9.
AND WHEN I GET THE "REWARD" I'LL GIVE IT ALL TO YOU -
WELL, YOU'D BETTER.
DAH-GUNNIT !! EVERY TIME I GET NEAR TO BEING A "CAPTAIN" - SOMETHING HAPPENS.
10.
HERRIMAN

August 6th, 1916.

12 OH-KLOCK, AND ALL SEEM'S WELL !!!
MEXIKO
EL RIO GRANDE.
U.S.
THE "LONE SENTINEL" ON THE RIO GRANDE.
BEHOLD, UPON THE HOSTILE SHORE AN ENEMY IS VIGILANT—
Z-ZZ-Z ZP-ZP-
WHO GOES HERE ???
PEP
OH-HOH !! SO'S YOU L'IL "MEXICAN JUMPINK BEAN", HUH ?
I GOT A GOOD AIM AT YOU, RESKIL, SO YOU BETTA GO BECK OVER THE BORDA WHERE YOU BLONG OR ELSE—
BIPP
BOOM
HA-A-ALP- NAVY- ARMY, MILLISHA- HALP !!!
AH, A BONNIE BRICK TO BOUNCE OFF THAT "KRAZY KAT'S" BEAN—
LOOK-OW, LOOK-OW !!!
THE DAY IS AT HAND, FOOL, WHEN THE BELLS OF DOOM WILL RING FOR YOU, AND I SHALL TOLL THEM—
Y'MEAN TO TELL ME THAT ONE OF THEM MEXICAN BEANS HAD THE NERVE TO JUMP OVER THE BORDER DO YOU ?
OYESS, "OFFISSA PUPP" OYESS INDEED.
MAKE WAY MAKE WAY-
ATTACK A OFFICER WILL YA- !!
OOY- GOODY GOODY-
BAPP
HALT !! WILLAINOUS BEAN, "KORPORAL KRAZY KET" OF THE U. KNIGHTED STATES MILLISHA", KOMMANDS YOU !!
HERRIMAN.
AND SO, NEXT SUNDAY, WE HOPE TO COMPLETE OUR TALE WITH THE AID OF THAT VERY CAPABLE AND POTENTIAL BIRD "MR. W. CEPHUS AUSTRIDGE"— TRUSTING YOUR PATIENCE WILL ABIDE UNTIL THEN, AT WHICH TIME WE PROMISE THAT THE HONOR OF THE "LONE SENTINEL" WILL BE VINDICATED— UNTIL THEN— "DEAR FRIENDS" = ADIOS.

August 13th, 1916.

THE 'SITUATION' AS WE LEFT IT LAST WEEK.
TRUCE!
GEEVEM GEEVEM -
1.
'IGNATZ MOUSE', OFFICER B. PUPP, AND KRAZY KAT, AT BAY — AND 'WILLI MENDOZA', THE MEXICAN JUMPING BANDIT BEAN 'FROM OVER THE BORDER' WHO IS HOLDING THEM 'AT BAY', AND FOR WHOSE CAPTURE A REWARD OF $5. IS OFFERED — AND 'WALTER CEPHUS AUSTRIDGE' AT LARGE.
GWELL GWELL -
2
GOTCHA -
SNAP
3
HOOROOR !! MR AUSTRIDGE HAS CAPTURED THE BANDIT - HOOROOR !!
AND HE SHOULD GET THE REWARD -
DIVVY ON THAT REWARD 'WALTER' - DIVVY -
4.
WILF-F-F ???
5.
6.
HOW DAST YOU, 'FOOL FOWL' INVADE THE ELEMENT OF THE KING OF BIRDS HUH ?
7
BACK TO THE 'MOLE HILLS' FOR YOUR'S — AND REMEMBER, THE 'EAGLE'S AERIE' IS NOT FOR SUCH AS YOU -
8
WHAT HOH !! APPROACH VARLETS AND REMOVE THE DEBRIS !!
9.
WHO GETS THE REWARD, MR AUSTRIDGE, MR EAGLE, OR US ?
ME.
GOSH, BY ME IT'S ALL A METTER OF MYSTERY -
10
EL CARCEL
$5 REWARD FOR THE CAPTURE OF WILLI MENDOZA THE MEXICAN BANDIT BEAN.
VERDE
HOWEVER - BE IT KNOWN, THAT THE END IS NOT YET - NEXT WEEK WE PROMISE THE MOST STARTLING, AND SENSATIONAL DEVELOPMENTS IN THE FANTASTIC CAREER OF 'WILLI MENDOZA' THE 'BANDIT BEAN' — AND SO, ADIOS =
11
HERRIMAN!

August 20th, 1916.

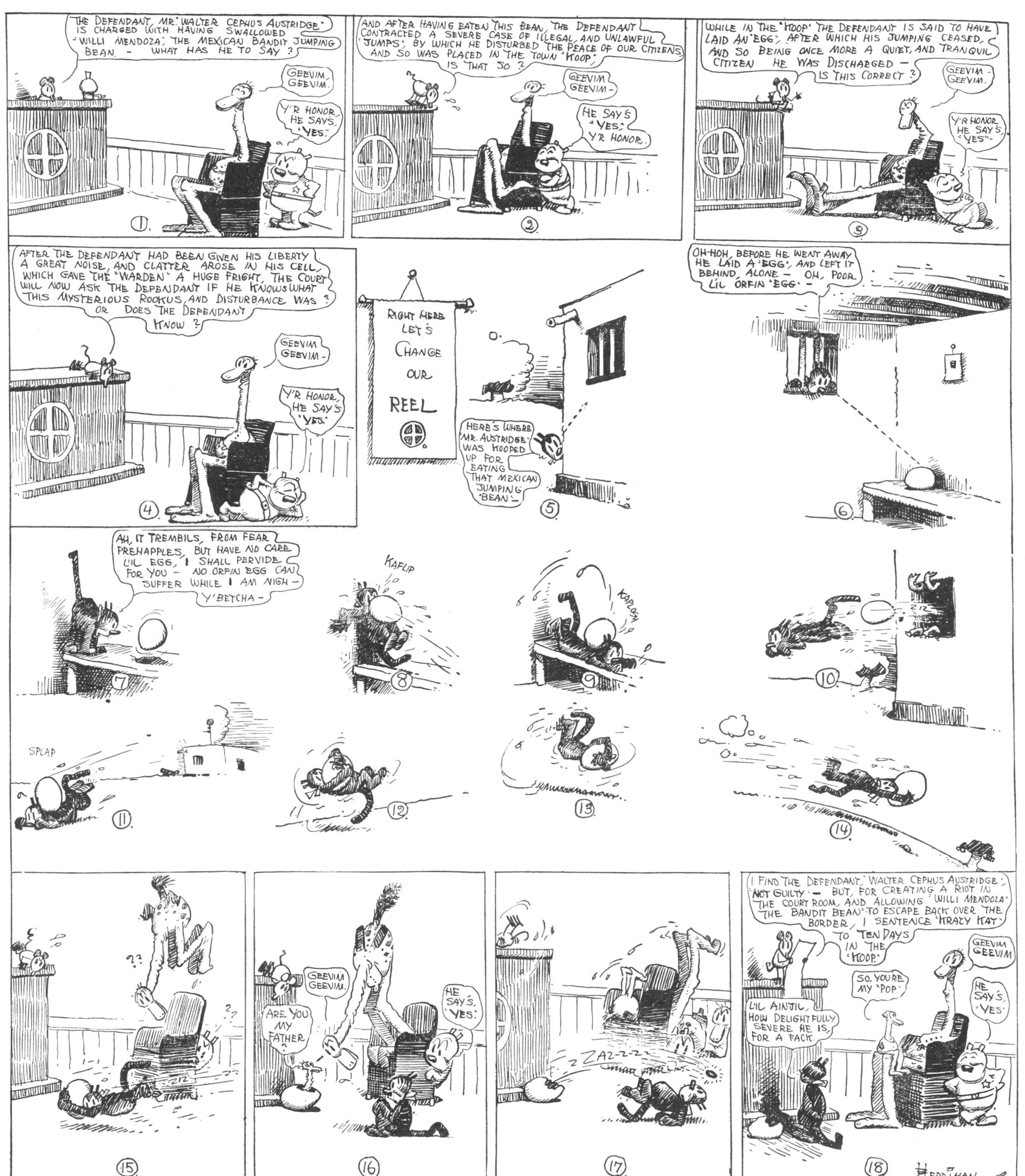
THE DEFENDANT, MR. WALTER CEPHUS AUSTRIDGE, IS CHARGED WITH HAVING SWALLOWED 'WILLI MENDOZA' THE MEXICAN BANDIT JUMPING BEAN. - WHAT HAS HE TO SAY ?
GEEVIM, GEEVIM.
Y'R HONOR, HE SAYS, 'YES.'
AND AFTER HAVING EATEN THIS BEAN, THE DEFENDANT CONTRACTED A SEVERE CASE OF ILLEGAL, AND UNLAWFUL 'JUMPS', BY WHICH HE DISTURBED THE PEACE OF OUR CITIZENS, AND SO WAS PLACED IN THE TOWN 'KOOP', IS THAT SO ?
GEEVIM GEEVIM -
HE SAYS 'YES,' Y'R HONOR.
WHILE IN THE 'KOOP' THE DEFENDANT IS SAID TO HAVE LAID AN 'EGG', AFTER WHICH HIS JUMPING CEASED, AND SO BEING ONCE MORE A QUIET, AND TRANQUIL CITIZEN HE WAS DISCHARGED - IS THIS CORRECT ?
GEEVIM - GEEVIM.
Y'R HONOR, HE SAYS, 'YES' -
AFTER THE DEFENDANT HAD BEEN GIVEN HIS LIBERTY A GREAT NOISE, AND CLATTER AROSE IN HIS CELL, WHICH GAVE THE 'WARDEN' A HUGE FRIGHT, THE COURT WILL NOW ASK THE DEFENDANT IF HE KNOWS WHAT THIS MYSTERIOUS ROOKUS, AND DISTURBANCE WAS ? OR DOES THE DEFENDANT KNOW ?
GEEVIM GEEVIM -
Y'R HONOR, HE SAYS 'YES.'
RIGHT HERE LET'S CHANGE OUR REEL
HERE'S WHERE 'MR. AUSTRIDGE' WAS KOOPED UP FOR EATING THAT MEXICAN 'JUMPING BEAN.' -
OH-HOH, BEFORE HE WENT AWAY HE LAID A 'EGG', AND LEFT IT BEHIND, ALONE - OH, POOR LIL ORFIN 'EGG' -
AH, IT TREMBILS, FROM FEAR PREHAPPLES, BUT HAVE NO CARE LIL EGG, I SHALL PERVIDE FOR YOU - NO ORFIN EGG CAN SUFFER WHILE I AM NIGH - Y'BETCHA -
KAFLIP
KAPLOSH
SPLAP
GEEVIM GEEVIM.
ARE YOU MY FATHER ?
HE SAYS 'YES.'
ZAZ-Z-Z
I FIND THE DEFENDANT, WALTER CEPHUS AUSTRIDGE, NOT GUILTY - BUT, FOR CREATING A RIOT IN THE COURT ROOM, AND ALLOWING 'WILLI MENDOZA' 'THE BANDIT BEAN' TO ESCAPE BACK OVER THE BORDER, I SENTENCE 'KRAZY KAT' TO TEN DAYS IN THE 'KOOP.'
GEEVIM GEEVIM
SO, YOU'RE MY 'POP'
HE SAYS, 'YES'
LIL AINJIL, HOW DELIGHTFULLY SEVERE HE IS, FOR A FACT.
HERRIMAN

August 27th, 1916.

ONE.
TWO
THREE
FOUR.
FIVE.
SEVEN.
EIGHT.
NINE.
GZZZ GZZZ GZZ
AGZAZ ZAZ-GZ BOPZ
TEN.
HERRIMAN

September 3rd, 1916.

"IGNATZ MOUSE," THE FEARLESS, THE UNDAUNTED, IS ABOUT TO PASS AMONG THE ABODES OF THOSE DEPARTED — =YEZZA=
BONG BONG BONG BONG BONG BONG BONG BONG BONG BONG
HARK !! THE BELLS TOLL TWELVE — THE HOUR OF THE "WRAITH" —
HOH-HOH-H-H —
AA-A-A-AH — THERE AINT NO SUCH THINGS AS "GHOSTS" —
BUT HE NEITHER WAVERS, NOR FALTERS —
MEANS GOODNESS, IS IT A FIRE ?
GEEVIM ? GEEVIM ?
BURGLARS ??
INVASION ?
HOY !! HOY !!! HOY !!!
MEANS WHERE ?
GEEVIM ? GEEVIM ?
WHERE ?
NO — GHOSTS !!!
W-W-W WHERE ?
GEEVIM - GEEVIM -
MEANS, GOODY GOODY
OH -
FEAR NOT, I HAVE DISPOSED OF THEM
AH-H -
L'IL AINJIL, HOW BRAVE HIS MIND IS
GEEVIM - GEEVIM -
MEANS YES-YES GO ON
BUT JUST AS MY STRENGTH WAS ABOUT TO GIVE OUT, WITH ONE GREAT SUPER-MOUSE EFFORT I STRETCHED THE LAST OF THOSE 16 WILD "GHOSTS" LIFELESS UPON THE GROUND — YEZZA —
GOSH, WOT A GRAND ORNAMENT YOU'D BE ON THE FORCE.
HE SHOULD BE MADE A DUKE OR SOMETHING FOR THIS.
AND SO, THROUGH THE NIGHT A TERRIBLE TALE OF DARING DEEDS WAS TOLD — WHICH ENDS HERE, AS A NEW DAY BEGINS —
— TOOBEE SHOOR - TOOBEE - SHOOR —
HERRIMAN

September 10th, 1916.

BUT "IGNATZ" DAHLINK ALL WILL BE SO LONESOME AND USELESS WITH OUT YOU - PLEASE, CAN'T I GO WITH YOU ?
NEVER !! YOU GO AS FAR AS THE FORK IN THE ROAD, UNDER THE "ENCHANTED MESA" WHERE "JOE STORK" LIVES - AND THERE YOU STOP - SAVVY ?
MOHI BUTTES
PARA LA CASA DE JOSE CIGUENO
"IT SEEMS LIKE "IGNATZ MOUSE" IS GOING SOMEWHERE -"
I'LL TAKE THIS ROAD - GOOD-BY, AND DON'T YOU DARE FOLLOW ME -
ADIOSES, AINJIL - ADIOSES
GONE - ALASSES - GONE
DAH-GUNYA !! DID'NT I TELL YOU NOT TO FOLLOW ME, HUH, DID'NT I ???
YOU FOLLOW ME THIS TIME, "KAT", AND YOUR DOOM WILL BE AT HAND -
MY, AIN'T HE ECTINK UP PEE-COOL-YA -
SA-A-AY !! WHAT DID I TELL YOU - HUH ?
WHAT'S ALL THIS "ROOKUS" HERE ANY HOW ?
IT'S HIM, "OFFICER", I WISH YOU WOULD RESTRAIN HIM, HE INSISTS UPON FOLLOWING ME, HE'S A PEST !!
OOH, OFFISSA' PUPP, I HAVE N'T NEEDA, BY ME IT'S ALL A MYSTERIOUS MISTAKE.
GOOD IDEA -
"IGNATZ" YOU GO THAT-A-WAY !! "KRAZY" YOU GO THAT-A-WAY !! MARCH !!!
GOSH, I DON'T WISH TO TREVEL.
"SOLOMON" WITH ALL HIS WISDOM, COULD N'T HAVE SETTLED IT BETTER -
S'PUNNY, IF I WAS N'T SURE I WAS GOING OPPOSITELY I'D SWEAR I WAS MEETING HIM -
GAH-SHAANGIT !! IF HE WAS N'T GOING THE OTHER WAY I'D BE ALMOST SURE HE WAS FOLLOWING ME, AGAIN -
?
GWAHN !!! STRAIGHT AHEAD !! KEEP MOVING !!
ROAD CLOSED !!
HERRIMAN

September 17th, 1916.

FROM OCEAN, TO OCEAN I HAVE SAILED, AND NOT A SIGN OF HIM — OH "IGNATZ", WHEREFORE IS YOU, "IGNATZ" ?
AWAY FROM THAT PEST OF A "KAT" AT LAST — IN MY LITTLE "AERO-SUBMARINE" AH, THIS IS THE EXISTENCE —
SO IT IS FOR "IGNATZ MOUSE" YOU GRIEVE HEH, "KRAZY" ?
YES, KOUSIN "KETFISH" IT IS FOR HE I SORROW, HIM WHOM I HAVE SEEKED THIS MANY DAY UPON THE OCEAN'S BUZZUM WITHOUT A SUCCESS —
OGOSH — OGOSH —
POOR "KRAZY"
THIS IS THE QUIET LIFE IN THE DEPTHS OF THE SEA, IN MY LITTLE "FLYING-DIVING-BELLE"
YES SIR —
HEY !! FELLAS, COME QUICK !!
WE MUST INFORM OUR "KOUSIN KRAZY" HE'S LOOKING ALL OVER FOR HIM —
DAH-GUNNIT !! I AM DISCOVERED !! BUT I'LL FOIL THEM YET —
HOH, FOOLS !! YOU LITTLE RECKONED ON THE WISDOM OF "IGNATZ MOUSE" —
FOR GOODNESS SAKE "KRAZY" WHAT AILS YOU ?
OH KOUSIN "KET-BIRD", I AM GRIEVING ALONE ON THE DEEP, FOR "IGNATZ" — HIM WHOM IS LOST — ODEER-ODEER, MY SOUL IS SPLITTING —
POOR "KRAZY"
OGOSH-OGOSH —
?
THEY'LL NEVER TRAIL ME UP HERE THE LOW UPSTARTS —
WE MUST INFORM OUR KOUSIN "KRAZY" HE'S LOOKING ALL OVER FOR HIM —
S'NO USE, THE WHOLE UNIVERSE IS FULL OF "KATS"
SPLOP !!
HERRIMAN

September 24th, 1916.

THIS HAS GONE FAR ENOUGH - HE MUST EITHER 'PAY UP' OR GO TO THE DEBTOR'S PRISON -
LEDGER
KLICK KLIK.
MR. KOLIN KELLY, THE WELL KNOWN 'BRICK MERCHANT' FINDS A DELINQUENT ACCOUNT ON HIS LEDGER ——
JUST SAY — 'IGNATZ MOUSE'
DEAR SIR — UNLESS YOU COME ACROSS WITH FULL PAYMENT OF YOUR 'BRICK BILL' WHICH IS NOW LONG OVERDUE IT SHALL BECOME MY PAINFUL DUTY NOT ONLY TO SEND YOU TO THE TOWN JAIL, BUT TO FURTHER DEPRIVE YOU OF ANY 'CREDIT' WHATSOEVER WITH THIS INSTITUTION — YOUR'S SOULFULLY KOLIN KELLY
KLIK-KLIK-KLIK-
WHERE UPON HE PUTS THE WHEELS OF 'BUSINESS' IN MOTION WITH MAJESTIC, AND MERCURIAL ECLAT —
AND IN DUE TIME THE GOVERNMENT'S MOST FAITHFUL, AND NEGLECTED SERVANT ENTERS, IN A ROLE OF MAGNIFICENT UNIMPORTANCE —
A LETTER FOR YOUR HUSBAND, MRS. MOUSE.
MAIL
A LETTER FOR YOU, DEAR -
GIVE IT HERE.
I AM LOST, LOST, LOST !!! ALL IS AT AN END -
IF IT WAS'NT THAT I'D BE DOING THE 'WORLD' A GREAT INJUSTICE, I'D COMMIT SUICIDE — GOSH !! I NEVER THOUGHT 'KELLY' WOULD DO SUCH A THING.
BRICK BILL
HE SLUMBS, L'IL 'ANJIL' — HE SLUMBS —
BRICK BILL
OH- HOH - A DEBT - !!
TO 'KELLY'S' BRICK-YARD
THERE, MR. KELLY - THAT MAKES $632 - THAT PAY'S UP THE BILL IN FULL - DON'T IT ?
IT DOES, AND NOW YOU CAN INFORM 'MR. MOUSE' THAT THIS PAYMENT NOT ONLY SAVED HIM FROM JAIL, BUT IT ALSO RE-ESTABLISHES HIS 'CREDIT' WITH OUR FIRM -
HOW ANNOYFUL THIS MUST HAVE BEEN TO A NATURE SO DELICATE LIKE HIS'N -
PAID IN FULL
THERE NOW
PAID IN FULL K. KELLY
I KNEW HE'D BE SURPRISED - HE THINKS MR. KELLY DONE IT - L'IL INNISINT -
OH-HOH! SO 'KELLY' RECEIPTED MY BILL, HEH? THE LOW 'TRADE PERSON' I GUESS HE GOT SCARED WHEN HE REALIZED WHO HE WAS TRIFLING WITH -
ONCE MORE HIS SPIRIT IS HEPPY -
NOW THAT MY CREDIT IS GOOD AGAIN, I'LL STROLL DOWN TO 'KELLY'S' FOR A NICE NEW 'BRICK' TO ADORN THAT 'KRAZY KAT'S' BEAN WITH —
HERRIMAN

October 1st, 1916.

WE'LL GET HIM TO-NIGHT BOYS, JUST AS HE LEAVES HIS OFFICE - THE REST WILL BE EASY-
ATSA STUFF, "CAP" ATSA STUFF.
"ROGER ROQUEFORT" THE "ROBBER RAT," AND HIS BAND OF RECKLESS RODENTS, FOR WHOSE CAPTURE THERE IS A STANDING REWARD OF $15.
"KRAZY KAT," OFFICE-BOY, AND AMANUENSIS TO MR. "IGNATZ MOUSE," PRESIDENT OF THE I. MOUSE CHEESE SYNDICATE. LIMITED - DECIDES TO TAKE A BIT OF A "KAT-NAP" =
MR. I. MOUSE, SAID PRESIDENT OF THE "I.M.C.S. LIMITED" CONCLUDES TO KNOCK OFF, AND CALL IT A DAY'S WORK
I. MOUSE & CO.
SLAM !!
AND AS IS THE CUSTOM OF ALL PROFOUND MEN OF BUSINESS HE CLOSES THE "SAFE"
AND IS ABOUT TO PASS OUT =
WE GOT HIM -
KA BOMP !!
BUT FATE, AND "ROGER ROQUEFORT" AND HIS BAND OF RECKLESS RODENTS HAVE OTHERWISE ORDAINED HIS COURSE =
FOLLOW ME MEN, ON TO THE TREASURE VAULT.
LEAD ON, "CAP"
WE FOLLOW -
ONWIDS -
THERE LIES THE PLUNDER ME LADS -
EYE-EYE "CAP"
EAR EAR -
ALL TOGETHER NOW BOYS - HAIV-A-O
HAIV-A-O -
EEY-YO -
SKWEE -!!
KWEE-KWEE
WEEX-WEEX !!!
KWEEK KWEE !!!
KWEEX
MY GOODNESS, AND TO THINK I WAS UNCONSCIOUS WHEN I DID ALL THIS -
LI'L AINJIL, WHAT A GRAND MIND FOR BUSINESS HE'S GOT -
WAL, THEY ALMOST GOT ME AT FIRST, BUT I FINALLY CONQUERED THEM - SEND UP THE "PATROL WAGON" AND THE "REWARD" QUICK !!!
HERRIMAN

October 8th, 1916.

THE HOURS I SPEND WITH YOU DEAR HAH-HA-HART -
KELLY'S EXCLUSIVE BRICK YARD
IS LIKE A STRING OF PUH-HUH-HEARLS T'MEEE -
I COUNT THEM O-VA, EVEREEE ONE UH-PART -
MONDI, TOOZDI, WENSDI, THURSDI, FRIDI, SATIDI
MY ROSIE REE MY-HY ROSIE REE -
EACH HOUR, A BRICK -
EACH BRICK A PUH-RAYER -
HERRIMAN

October 15th, 1916.

WAIT— HEY— WAIT FOR ME !!
POOR LI'L FELLA, LOOK'S LIKE HE'S DUE TO SPEND THE WINTER WITH US—
BOREAS.
TICKETS
1
BE IT KNOWN THAT MR. ROBIN REDBREAST HAS MISSED HIS TRAIN — THE LAST "LIMITED" OF THE SEASON, BOUND FOR THE "SOUTH" —— AND FROST IN THE AIR =
K.
WHAT ARE YOU BLATTING ABOUT ANY-WAY ? GEE-WIZ, IF THE SPARROWS, AND CHICKADEES CAN STAND IT, I SHOULD THINK YOU "ROBINS" COULD—
OH, MR. MOUSE THERE WAS A TIME WHEN WE COULD — BUT NOW WE CANT—
2
WHAT'S THE REASON YOU CANT ?
I SHALL TELL YOU ALL, SIR— SO HARK TO THE TALE OF A DOLEFUL "ROBIN"—
3
IN THE OLD DAYS, US "ROBINS" FEARED NEITHER ICE, NOR ICE-BERGS, NEITHER RIME, NOR SNOW—
4
BRING ON YOUR ARCTIC BLASTS — I SCORN THEM—
ICE FLOE
FOR UPON OUR PROUD BOSOMS REPOSED A GREAT GIFT OF NATURE — A "RED WOOLEN CHEST PROTECTOR" — WHICH ENABLED US TO DEFY THE ICIEST OF ICY BLASTS ——
5
COME IN SWEETIE, Y'GOT NO IDA HOW ELEGANT IS THE WATER—
TEASE ME NOT FAIR ONE— TEASE ME NOT—
BUT ONE SAD DAY, HE WHOM WE CALLED "CHIEF" FELL FOR THE COAXINGS OF A LORELEI "DUCK"—
6
HA-HA- HE SWIMS LIKE A GRAND-PIANO, FOOL !!
HELP !!
BLINDED BY THE BLANDISHMENTS OF THIS "VAMPIRE" HE PLUNGED INTO THE WATER, HEEDLESS OF HIS PRECIOUS "RED WOOLEN CHEST-PROTECTOR" =
7
HE'S A SIMP—
SURE—
REDUCED TO THE STATUS OF A "BOOB"— HE PULLED HIMSELF OUT — THE FIRES OF HIS ARDOR, NOW NAUGHT BUT ASHES ——
8
OH, FOOL WHAT I AM—
BUT WORST OF ALL, HIS "RED WOOLEN CHEST-PROTECTOR" HAD SHRUNK TO A MERE NOTHING — LEAVING ONLY A RED MARK UPON HIS CHEST WHERE IT HAD FADED =
9
AND SO TODAY, ALL OF US "ROBINS" ARE PAYING THE PENALTY OF A RASH FOLLY OF ONE OF OUR ANCESTORS—
OH-HOH, NOW I KNOW WHY YOUR CHEST IS "RED"— GOSH, I ALWAYS HAD AN IDEA YOU "ROBINS" WAS AFFLICTED WITH A "CHRONIC RASH" OR SOMETHING—
10
WHAT ARE YOU KNITTING, "KRAZY" ?
A "CHEST-PROTECTOR" ENT "TEBBY" — A "RED WOOLEN CHEST-PROTECTOR" — WINTA IS COMING AND MAYBE THERE IS SOMEBODY WHAT WILL NEED IT—
11
NOK NOK NOK
?
?
12
HE MISSED HIS TRAIN FOR THE "SOUTH"
IS NT THAT TOO BAD
OH, POOR LI'L BIRD—
13
WHY IT'S A PERFECT FIT—
THERE, LI'L ROBIN BIRD PUT ON THIS "CHEST-PROTECTOR", AND DONT SHIVVA NO MORE—
14
WAS'NT IT SWEET OF MR. MOUSE TO BRING ME HERE ?
OH, "IGNATZ" IS ALL WAYS SWEET, HE'S A LI'L DAHLINK—
SWEET ME EYE, HE'S A LITTLE HYPOCRITE
15
HERRIMAN
A NICE NEW "BRICK", "KELLY"
WE'VE GOT SOME FRESH ONES, JUST MADE. STEP IN, AND HELP YOURSELF.
KELLY'S BRICK YARD.
16
NOW, LET'S BACK TO "BUSINESS"—

October 22nd, 1916.

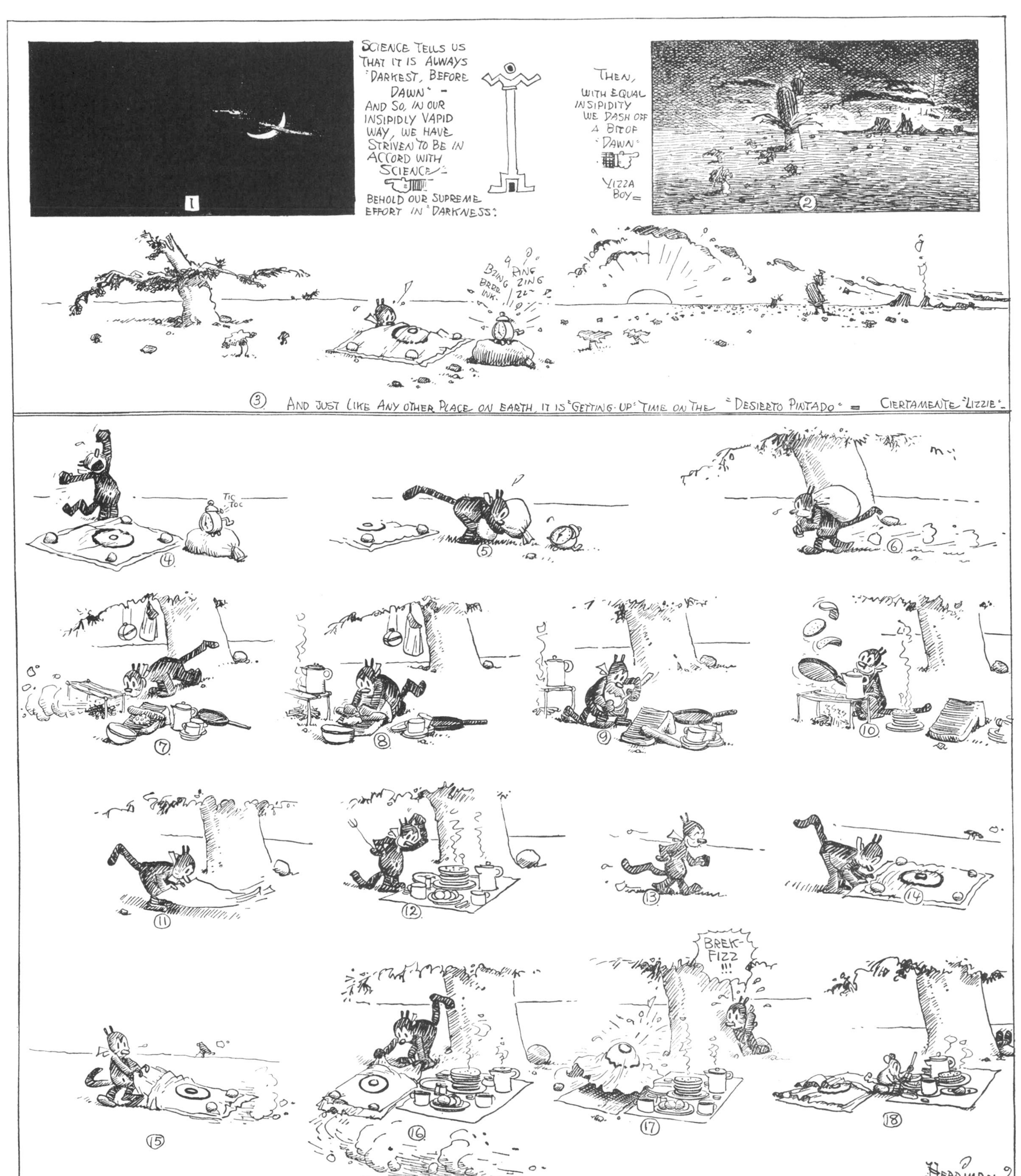

SCIENCE TELLS US THAT IT IS ALWAYS "DARKEST, BEFORE DAWN" - AND SO, IN OUR INSIPIDLY VAPID WAY, WE HAVE STRIVEN TO BE IN ACCORD WITH SCIENCE -
BEHOLD OUR SUPREME EFFORT IN "DARKNESS"
THEN, WITH EQUAL INSIPIDITY WE DASH OFF A BIT OF "DAWN"
YIZZA BOY
BZING BRRR INK
PING ZING ZZ
AND JUST LIKE ANY OTHER PLACE ON EARTH, IT IS "GETTING-UP" TIME ON THE "DESIERTO PINTADO" - CIERTAMENTE "LIZZIE".
TIC TOC
BREK-FIZZ !!!
HERRIMAN

October 29th, 1916.

OH-HOH !! THE 'CHESTNUTS' ARE FALLING — MY FAVORITE FRUIT TOO.
'CHESTNUTS' ARE NOTHING FOR A CULTURED PERSON LIKE ME TO TRIFLE WITH — I'LL SIC 'KRAZY' ON THEM — IT'S A 'KAT'S' JOB ANYWAY =
THE WIND IS IN THE 'CHESTNUT TREE' 'KRAZY,' AND THEY ARE FALLING DOWN BY THE HUNDRED, YOU GO, AND GATHER THEM UP, AND I'LL GIVE YOU HALF OF WHAT YOU GET —
YOU JENERIS L'IL MICE, I WILL DO SO WITH PLEASURE.
GOSH-DINNY-IT !! THERE AINT A SELFISH BONE IN 'IGNATZES' WHOLE SOUL — 'AINJIL' —
HALF IS TOO MUCH FOR HIM, WHEN HE GETS BACK I'LL CHANGE MY MIND, AND NOT GIVE HIM ANY =
KWEE — KWEE — KWEE —
KWEE — KWEE — KWEE
IT'S BECK OF THAT OLD JUNIPA TREE, AND IT SOUNDS A HEAP LIKE A DISTRESS =
KWEE KWEE KWEE
SHIVEREE MY TIMBILS !! IF IT AINT A MESS OF CHILD 'HEDGE-PIGS' — OH, POOR L'IL FELLAS — POOR L'IL FELLAS —
NOW TELL ME — WHERE IS THE 'MAMA,' AND WHERE IS THE 'PAPA' ? DUNT FIB NOW —
WE LOST THEM —
KWEE KWEE
HUSHA-BYE DUNTCHA-CRY — WE WILL FIND THE 'MUMMA' WE WILL FIND THE 'PUPPA' — BYE-YIN + BYE.
HE'S GOT THEM !! A BIG ARM FULL — TOO —
GIVE ME THOSE 'CHESTNUTS' FOOL !!
KEEP KOOL, KEEP KOOL !! S'ONLY 'IGNATZ,' ALL IS AS WELL AS CAN BE —
BLOMP !
ZIB
SO, MONSTER !! YOU ATTACK OUR CHILDREN HUH ?
UH-UH-H — I-I-I-I — THOUGHT THEY WERE 'CHESTNUTS'
YOU RILLY MUST NOT MIND 'IGNATZ,' HE'S ONLY GOT A GREAT SENSE OF 'FIZZIKILL HUMOR' — THAT'S ALL —
AND DONT NEVER SHOW THAT CHEAP MUSH OF YOUR'S AROUND HERE NO MORE — SAVVY ?
MY CHILDREN !!!
MA-A-A-MA !!!
ODEER, EVERY THING IS SO HEPPY IT MAKES ME WEEP BY JOY — OOHOOOOO —
GOSH — THEY LOOK LIKE A LOTTA 'CHESK-NUTS' —
JEE-EEE WIZ, THAT REMINDS ME !!
HERRIMAN

November 5th, 1916.

POO-POOH!! SILLY TWADDLE.
I AINT NEVER SEEN IT MYSELF BUT I GOT AN IDA IT'S LIKE LIGHTNING AINT IT ?
I'D SAY THEIR WHOLE HEADS WERE LIGHT, VERY LIGHT-
HEAR HEAR
GAS LIGHT-
I KNOW THERE'S A LIGHT IN MY WIFE'S EYES, SHE CAN SEE IN THE DARK-
LORELEIGHTS YEH-
1
"MID-NIGHT IN THE ALISO GROVE, CHATTING OF THIS, AND THAT, — WHEN THE TALK TURNS TO THE "LIGHT" THAT LIES IN WOMAN'S EYES—
AND SO IT HAS COME ABOUT THAT THE GLORIOUS ILLUMINATION THAT LURKS IN WOMAN'S EYES MUST BE BANDIED ABOUT BY THE RABBLE — WHAT DO YOU FEEBS KNOW OF THE LUMINIFEROUS LAMPS OF WOMAN-KIND, I ASK YOU WHAT ?
WE DONT KNOW, WE WAS JUST ARGUING - AT'S ALL-
FIRE IS A LIGHT, AINT IT ?
THE LADIES DONT LIKE ME MUCH FOR SOME REASON-
WHAT IF THE DAME HAS A GLASS EYE ?
2
3
4
HE LOVES OUR EYE— L'IL AMOROUS AINJIL— HE LOVES OUR EYE—
5
HERRIMAN

November 12th, 1916.

1
2
3
BUT, I'M THE 'EARLY BIRD' I'M AFTER A 'WORM', I TELL YOU -
YOU AIN'T FOOLING ME MUCH - YOU IS EFTA MY EPPIL, I KNOW - GO !!
4
HE SAVED MY LIFE -
5
DAH-GUNNIT" I THOUGHT SURE I HAD A SWELL BREAKFAST -
OH- HOH- HOH ! A APPLE - THE KING OF VEGETABLES -
6
AND THE PROPRIETOR IS FAST ASLEEP. ODEER ODEER - I AM IN GRAND GOOD FORTUNE - LETS EAT -
S'NO PLACE FOR A 'WORM' RIGHT NOW -
8
OOHMM - YIM-MM - YIM-MM -
9
10
GRAND FOOD IS APPLES, GRAND FOOD - YIZZA-BOY -
GOSH DINGIT !! THIS IS NO 'WORM' HOTEL !! GIT OUT !!
11
AH- HAH ! MR. GOPHER !! YOU ALSO IS EFTA MY EPPIL, HUH ?
12
I WAS AFTER A 'WORM'
THAT'S WHAT THE 'EARLY-BIRD' SAID, BUT I KNOW BETTA, MIZZABIL INSECK - I KNOW BETTA -
13
I MUST SQUARE MYSELF
AH-
AH, THAT'S THE ONE -
14
THE BEST IS NONE TOO GOOD FOR HIM -
15.
16
WHY 'IGNATZ', 'IGNATZES' AINJIL !!
IT MUSTA BEEN ONE OF THEM TEEVES WHAT WAS EFTA MY EPPIL WHAT DONE IT -
17
IF I KNEW WHO IT WAS, I'D SETTLE HIM -
18 O'CLOCK, AND ALL IS WELL -
18
HERRIMAN

November 19th, 1916.

THERE, MR. MOUSE, IT IS FINISHED, AND I MUST ADMIT I HAVE LIMNED A PERPETUATION OF THE MOST CLASSIC FEATURES EVER ENDOWED A LIVING BEING =
MY FEE IS ONE DOLLAR, AND SIX BITS, INCLUDING THE FRAME - IT SHALL BE DELIVERED TO YOU BY SPEEDY MESSENGER, WITHIN THE HOUR ——
ANOTHER "GEM" IS LOOSED UPON THE WORLD OF ART — ISSUING FROM THE STUDIO OF MR. MICHAEL O'KOBALT, ARTIST, PAINTER OF PORTRAITS, SIGNS, FENCES, AND INTERIORS, MENDER OF SINKS, KEYS, AND SHOT-RIFLES, BUYER OF 2ND HAND FALSE TEETH, AND POPULAR PURVEYOR OF KATNIP, AND LAVENDER TO THE ROYAL FAMILY ==
1
STUDIO
DELIVER IT SAFELY, AND SPEEDILY, "KRAZY"
IT SHELL BE DID.
2
THERE IS A HEPPY LEND
AH, SO, THAT'S THE SPEEDY MESSENGER HUH ?
3
FUR-FUR A-WA-A-AY-
WELL, HE CAN DELIVER ME - ALSO-
4
WHERE THEY HAS HEM-IN-NEGGS-
HOME, JAMES !!
5
SEV-RI-I-I-IL TIMES A DAY-
6
LI'L AINJIL, HOW NETURAL HE LOOKS, ALMOST I COULD OBSERVE A QUIVA IN HIS WHISKA-
7
O. HOW THE BORDAS YELL—
8
PLOB !!
ZIP
9
NETURAL, OH SO NETURAL = EVEN UNTO HIS HEBITS - SWEETNISS —
FOOL-
10
IT'S SURE IS A GOOD "TAKE OFF" OF HIS UGLY MUG, "KRAZY," I MUST SAY-
OH, "GOOD" IS NO WORD FOR IT OFFISSA PUPP, IT'S SO POSITIVELY NETURAL HE THREW A DORNICK AT ME - AIN'T THAT WUNDAFIL ?
11
WELL S'LONG, "KRAZY," LOOK OUT THAT PICTURE ISN'T "NATURAL" ENOUGH TO BITE YOU —
ADIOS, OFFISSA, "IGNATZ" IS IN A HURRY TO GET THIS -
12
GOL-DINGIT, ONLY MIDNIGHT !! THESE LONG WINTER NIGHTS SURE GET MY GOAT —
HERRIMAN

November 26th, 1916.

GALLEON HO !! THREE POINTS ON THE PORT BOW, CAP'N -
HOOROO !! GOLD !! LOOT !! PLUNDER !!
JITNEY PIECES OF FIVES !!
WOOY
HEAVE A 'BRICK' OVER HIS BOWS MATE, AND BRING HIM TO. THEN RUN UP THE 'BONNY BLACK JACK' -
LOVE IN A KESTLE, OR LOVE IN A HUT IS ALL THE SAME BY ME, LOVE ON A HILL OR LOVE ON A PLAIN OR I DUN'T CARE IF IT'S LOVE ON THE SEA AS LONG AS IT'S LOVE WITH HE" —
— O-HOH — LOVE ANY WHERE LOVE EVERY WHERE AS LONG AS IT'S LOVE WODDA I CARE -
1
2
PWOP !!
3
OH-HOH, A 'BRICK' - THAT MEANS, 'IGNATZ' IS NIGH UPON THE LOFTY SEA — BLESS HIS L'IL NEPTUNIC NAUGHTICAL HEART -
4
SURRENDER, FOOL !!
'IGNATZ', TO SURRENDA TO YOU IS POSITIVELY A JOY -
5
WOT'LL WE DO WITH HIM BOYS ?
THE YARD ARM -
THE PLANK
AYE - THE PLANK -
THE PLANK
THE PLANK
6
THE 'PLANKS' HAVE IT -
HOO-ROAR !!
7
WEEY - GIVE HIM THE DRINK -
THE DRINK -
THE DRINK -
THE DRINK -
SOME BODY'S GONNA TREAT -
8
WOOY -
9
10
OH, MR. 'PLATYPUS', WILL YOU TAKE MY COUSIN 'KRAZY KAT' BACK ON LAND THROUGH YOUR LAND ENTRANCE — I FEAR AN ACCIDENT HAS HAPPENED TO HIM -
WHY, SURE MR. 'KAT FISH', I WILL GLADLY DO SO.
11
HUH, ACCIDENT ME FOOT - FOUL PLAY I CALL'S IT - PIRATES WORK, OR I'M NO DUCK-BILL -
12
I'LL UNTIE HIS ARMS THEN DUCK BACK IN MY HOLE BEFORE SOME ZOOLOGICAL NUT KIDNAPS ME -
13
HE'S ALRIGHT NOW -
AH - FREE - ET LEST
14
'IGNATZ'S VOICE =
WHAT DID WE DO WITH HIM, MATES ?
OH, WE GIVE HIM THE PLANK -
THE PLANK -
HOO ROO
15
SURE IT'S HIM, L'IL ROYSTERA
OH, A BELLERING BAND OF SEA-GOOPERS ARE WE - NOTHING CAN SCARE US ON LAND, OR ON SEA — FO-O-OR WE -
YO HOH - YO-HOH - YO-HOH - HOH - HOH - YO !!
16
OH, 'IGNATZ' YOO-HOO - HELLO! -
A GHOST !!!
17
18
FOR TO-NIGHT I AM A WIDOW - IN A KOT- TUDGE BY THE SEA -
19
HERRIMAN

December 3rd, 1916.

December 10th, 1916.

"IGNOSH MOUSE" WUFFAW YOU CATCHEM BIG KNIFE, HUH? WUFFAW?
IF IT'LL DO YOU ANY GOOD TO KNOW, "MOCK DUCK," I'LL TELL YOU = I'M GONNA CUT OFF A "KAT-TAIL" WITH IT - THEN I'M GONNA SOAK THAT "KAT-TAIL" IN KEROSENE AND LIGHT IT - NOW YOU KNOW -
OH-HOH, IS DASH SO? YOU CUT OFF KAT'S TAIL HUH? WELL, I BET "FO-DOLLA- SICK-BIT" YOU NO DO - "LITTY HIGH BINDA"
PO-LEESHI - PO-LEESHI- MAN!!
PO-LEESHI-MAN!! OH- PO LEESHI-MAN!
PO-LEESHI-MAN -
HAY- PO-LEESHI-MAN HA-A-AY!!
"IGNOSH MOUSE," HE GOT BIG KNIFE, HE SAY, HE GONNA CUT OFF "KRAZY-KAT'S TAIL," AND PUT LOTSA KALLA-SEEN ON IT, DEN MAKE BIG FYAH WIT IT - COME QUICK PO-LEESHI-MAN, COME QUICK -
LEAD ME TO THE SCENE OF THE MAYHEM I'M WITYA
HE GO DISHY WAY -
NOW, YOU POUR THE "KEROSENE" ON IT "KRAZY" - THEN WE'LL LIGHT IT AND HAVE A SWELL TORCH -
MY WHAT WONDAFIL IDAS YOU GOT, "IGNATZ"
AA-HAA-A-A THE "CHINK" WAS SPOOFING ME, HUH -
JEE KLISMIS -
YOU MONGOLIANS COME OVER HERE, AND RIGHT AWAY Y'THINK Y'CAN CHUM UP WITH US "AMERICANS" - BUT I'LL LEARN YOU DIFFERENT YOU SLOPE EYED TUB HOUND -
WASHA-MALLA YOU, HUH, WASHA MALLA, ALLA TIME GIVE PO LIL CHINA DUCK SPANISHY LUN -?
HERRIMAN
ALL OF WHICH EXPLAINS THE MYSTERIOUS LIGHT BY THE "TULE SWAMP" THAT NIGHT.

December 17th, 1916.

WINTER ANNOUNCEMENT !!
KOLIN KELLY THE BRICK MERCHANT WILL CHANGE HIS LINE FOR THE SEASON FROM "KLAY BRICKS" TO "KARBON BRIQUETS" THE WORLD'S CHEAPEST FUEL - BUILD A HOUSE OR A FIRE
RASCAL,!! HE TOLD ME NAUGHT OF THIS -
WHAT'S THIS I HEAR ABOUT YOU HANDLING "BRIQUETS" INSTEAD OF "BRICKS" "KOLIN"
T'IS A BIT OF BUSINESS, "IGNATZ" - FOR THE WINTER ONLY -
YOU'LL FIND THEM AS SWEET A MORSEL TO DEAL OFF THAT "KAT'S" BEAN AS EVER A KLAY BRICK WAS, BESIDES KEEPING AWAY THE CHILL - THESE COLD DAYS -
I SEE -
AND SO, SOON FROM THE HOUSE OF IGNATZ MOUSE ISSUED A GREAT VOLUME OF SMOKE, AND FUME DENOTING GREAT CHEER AND WARMTH WITHIN =
PARA EL MESA ENCANTADA LA CASA DE JOSE CIGUEÑO
WHILE FROM THE MEAGRE KENNEL OF THE "SENORA PELONA CHIWAWA" A MEXICAN WAR-BRIDE, AND HER THREE FATHERLESS PUPS, ALL WAS DRAB, AND DREAR, AND GAVE NO TOKEN OF CHEER -
GOLLY! IT'S A "KAROL", A "KRISMIS KAROL" - THAT REMINDS ME -
XMAS MORNING = AND "KRAZY" IS AROUSED BY A GREAT CHIRPING IN THE OLD "SMOKE TREE"
BRIQUETS
I'LL STOP THAT 'KAT' AND HIS FOOL CAROLS -
COME ALL YE WEARY WANDERERS BENEATH THE WINTRY SKY -
"KELLY" WAS RIGHT, THESE "BRIQUETS" ARE GOOD FOR OTHER THINGS BESIDES BUILDING FIRES -
BRIQUETS
SKAT -
OH-HOH "BRICKWETS" HUH?
WELL HE KNOWS NOW MY INTENSHINS WAS GOOD, ANYHOW - LI'L KRISMIS GIFF
AH, SENOR "GATO LOCO" MY THREE PELONITOS, AND MYSELF SUFFER GREATLY FROM THE COLD. WE BE WITHOUT FUEL, AND FAR FROM OUR DEAR "MEXICO" AND IT'S WARMTH -
THERE, MRS CHIWAWA - THIS 'LL KEEP YOU WARM -
GRATIAS SENOR GRATIAS -
MISTLETOE
"MERRY KRISMIS", AND A HEPPY NEW YEAR" !!
HERRIMAN

December 24th, 1916.

JUST A 'KRAZY KWILT' ----- KWY-TSO — KWITE SO — QUITE SO !!
YIZZA-BOY-
AND AS WE SAID BEFORE JUST A 'KRAZY KWILT' — YEZZIN-DEED —
HERRIMAN

December 31st, 1916.

# 1917.

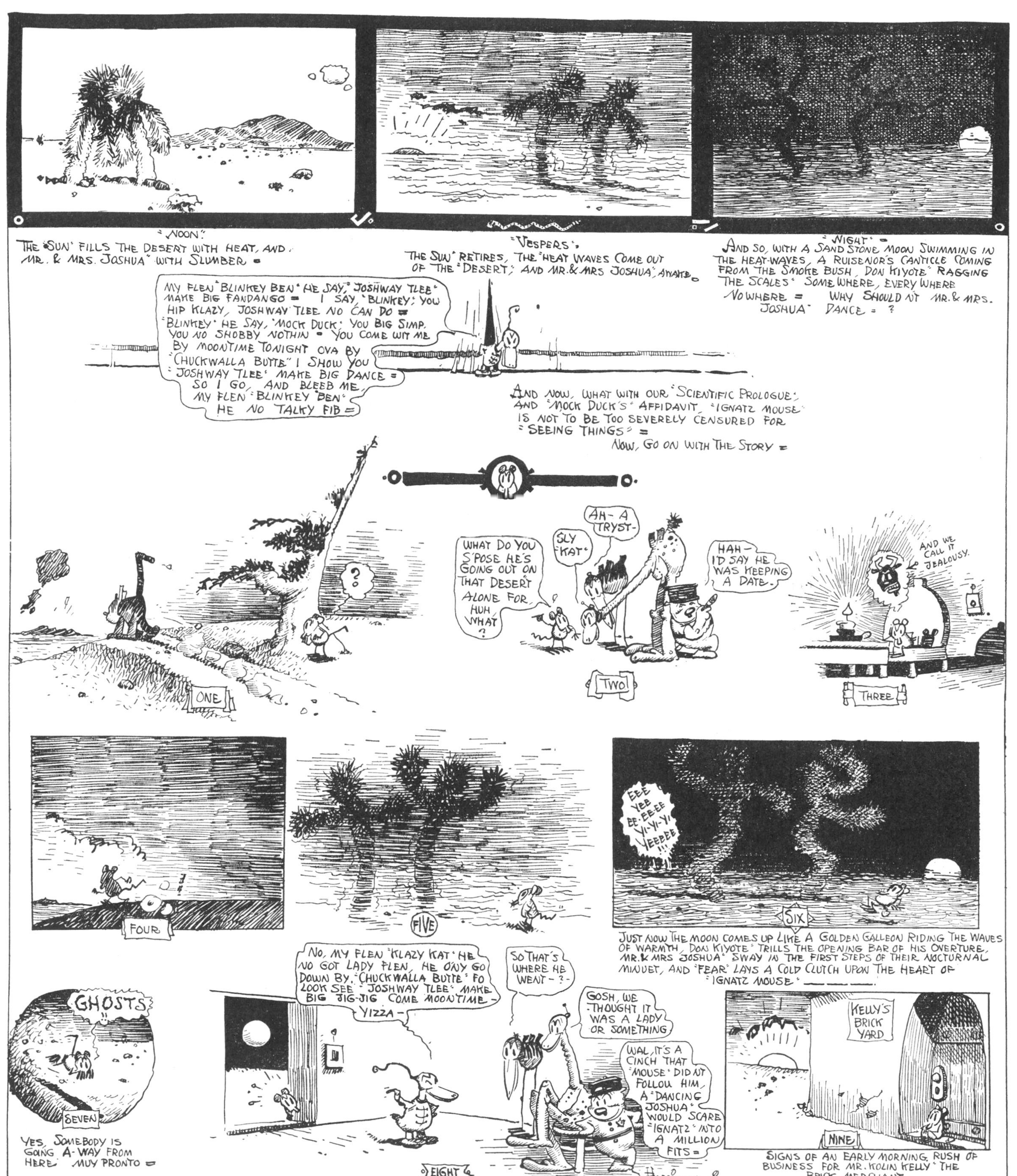
"NOON"
THE "SUN" FILLS THE DESERT WITH HEAT, AND MR. & MRS. JOSHUA" WITH SLUMBER =
"VESPERS"
THE "SUN" RETIRES, THE "HEAT WAVES COME OUT OF THE "DESERT," AND MR. & MRS JOSHUA" AWAKE.
"NIGHT" =
AND SO, WITH A SAND STONE MOON SWIMMING IN THE HEAT-WAVES, A RUISENOR'S CANTICLE COMING FROM THE SMOKE BUSH, DON KIYOTE" RAGGING THE SCALES" SOME WHERE, EVERY WHERE NOWHERE = WHY SHOULD NT MR. & MRS. JOSHUA" DANCE = ?
MY FLEN "BLINKEY BEN" HE SAY, "JOSHWAY TLEE" MAKE BIG FANDANGO = I SAY, "BLINKEY," YOU HIP KLAZY, JOSHWAY TLEE NO CAN DO = "BLINKEY" HE SAY, "MOCK DUCK," YOU BIG SIMP, YOU NO SHOBBY NOTHIN = YOU COME WIT ME BY MOONTIME TONIGHT OVA BY "CHUCKWALLA BUTTE" I SHOW YOU "JOSHWAY TLEE" MAKE BIG DANCE = SO I GO, AND BLEEB ME, MY FLEN "BLINKEY BEN" HE NO TALKY FIB =
AND NOW, WHAT WITH OUR "SCIENTIFIC PROLOGUE," AND "MOCK DUCK'S" AFFIDAVIT, "IGNATZ MOUSE" IS NOT TO BE TOO SEVERELY CENSURED FOR "SEEING THINGS" =
NOW, GO ON WITH THE STORY =
?
ONE
WHAT DO YOU S'POSE HE'S GOING OUT ON THAT DESERT ALONE FOR, HUH, WHAT ?
SLY "KAT"
AH- A TRYST-
HAH- I'D SAY HE WAS KEEPING A DATE.
TWO
AND WE CALL IT JEALOUSY.
THREE
FOUR
FIVE
EEE YEB EE-EEEE YI-YI-YI YEEBBE !!!
SIX
JUST NOW THE MOON COMES UP LIKE A GOLDEN GALLEON RIDING THE WAVES OF WARMTH, DON KIYOTE" TRILLS THE OPENING BAR OF HIS OVERTURE, MR. & MRS JOSHUA" SWAY IN THE FIRST STEPS OF THEIR NOCTURNAL MINUET, AND "FEAR" LAYS A COLD CLUTCH UPON THE HEART OF "IGNATZ MOUSE" ———
GHOSTS
SEVEN
YES, SOMEBODY IS GOING A-WAY FROM HERE MUY PRONTO =
NO, MY FLEN "KLAZY KAT" HE NO GOT LADY FLEN, HE O'NY GO DOWN BY "CHUCKWALLA BUTTE" FO LOOK SEE "JOSHWAY TLEE" MAKE BIG JIG-JIG COME MOONTIME - YIZZA -
SO THAT'S WHERE HE WENT - ? -
GOSH, WE THOUGHT IT WAS A LADY OR SOMETHING
WAL, IT'S A CINCH THAT "MOUSE" DID NT FOLLOW HIM, A "DANCING JOSHUA" WOULD SCARE "IGNATZ" INTO A MILLION FITS =
EIGHT
HERRIMAN
KELLY'S BRICK YARD
NINE
SIGNS OF AN EARLY MORNING RUSH OF BUSINESS FOR MR. KOLIN KELLY" THE BRICK MERCHANT.

January 7th, 1917.

LOOK, "KRAZY," ANOTHER ONE -
DON'T BE AFRAID, "IGNATZ," THIS ONE WON'T HURT YOU, EVEN IF HE IS A TWIN BROTHER TO "MR. RATTLER," HE'S A NICE L'IL FELLA
GOOD MORNING.
GOOD MORNING
GOOD MORNING MR. GARTER SNAKE.
HOW CAN HE BE A TWIN TO MR. RATTLER IF HE'S A GARTER SNAKE
JUST THE SAME "IGNATZ" IT'S SO -
GOOD BYE
PAUSE, "IGNATZ," PAUSE!! WHAT "KRAZY" SAYS IS TRUE, THEY ARE TWINS -
HARK TO THE TALE I WILL TELL YOU -
OH, I'M SO GLED "MR. STORK," Y'SEE "IGNATZ" IS SUCH A SKEPTICKLE L'IL CHEP
HE DOUBTS ME.
THEY MUST BE "TWINS" AND WE MUST HAVE THEM RIGHT AWAY -
WELL, ON SEPTOBER THE TWICE, NINETEEN HUNDRED AND TRETTY-TRET, IN MY HOUSE ON THE "ENCHANTED MESA", I RECEIVED A HURRY CALL FROM MR AND MRS. JIMUEL SNAKE =
AND WITH GREAT PROMPTNESS I SET OUT TO DELIVER THE "GOODS" =
NEVER MIND MY DEAR, THEY'RE TWINS ANY WAY -
STILL I'D MUCH RATHER THEY'D EACH HAVE THEIR OWN SKIN -
NEVER DREAMING, THAT IN MY HASTE I HAD NEGLIGENTLY GIVEN THESE DEAR INFANTS BUT ONE SKIN = ALAS -
THEY WERE NAMED "RIGLIUS," AND "SKWIRMIUS" - AND THEY GREW INTO "SNAKE HOOD" ENDOWED WITH MUCH HEALTH, WEALTH, AND REPTILIAN BEAUTY = NAUGHT COULD BE MORE FAIR =
GRA-A-A WAF-F-F
"RIGLIUS" DEVELOPED A GROUCH, AND BECAME CHARGED WITH RANCOR AND VENOM, WHILE "SKWIRMIUS" WAS EVER BINIGN, AND FULL OF THAT SWEET HUMILITY WHICH CHARACTERIZES A DOVE'S EGG =
NOW CHILDREN, TODAY IS OCTEMBER THE TOOT-TOO THE DAY WHEN ALL OF US SNAKES CHANGE OUR "SKINS" -
THEN CAME THAT DAY OF DAYS SO FULL OF MEANING IN A SNAKE'S LIFE --
"RIGLIUS" WOULD NOT LET ME GET INTO OUR NEW SKIN WITH HIM, AND HE HAS GONE AWAY -
THE NEXT MORNING IN THE CHILL OF DAWN, I FOUND THAT, THE "WICKED ONE" HAD FLED WITH THE NEW "COMMUNITY PELT", AND LEFT THE "GENTLE ONE" BARE, AND NUDE TO THE INHOSPITABLE RIGORS OF THE WEATHER -
IT'S ALL MY FAULT TOO, GOSH, I'VE GOTTA DO SOMETHING, AND DO IT QUICKLY -
I THOUGHT OF THE APPROACHING WINTER, AND MY HEART ACHED - SOMETHING HAD TO BE DONE -
AH -
SO I WENT ABOUT TO DO IT -
AND DID IT = WITH A STOCKING -
HOW KIND OF YOU MR. STORK
DON'T MENTION IT -
AND GARTER -
THERE NOW, GO FORTH, AND BE HAPPY.
ADIOS -
WHICH IS WHY THIS GENTLE "KNIGHT OF THE GARTER" NOW WINDS HIS SERPENTINE WAY THROUGH LIFE, A SYMBOL OF GRATITUDE =
AND WHAT BECAME OF THE "WICKED ONE" MR. STORK?
OH, HIM = WELL -
YES, WHAT DID?
I RAN ACROSS HIM ONE DAY ON THE "DESIERTO PINTADO", ASLEEP ON A HOT ROCK - SO I TIED A "RATTLE" ON HIS TAIL =
KOISES !!
AND SO TODAY, THE SINFUL VILLAIN MUST EVER ANNOUNCE HIS BALEFUL PRESENCE =.
IF I ONLY DAST GET MY HAT -
IF I ONLY DARED TO GET MY "BRICK"
HERRIMAN

January 14th, 1917.

TEN CENTS IS A LOT OF MONEY TO PAY FOR A "BRICK"
KOLIN KELLY DEALER IN "BRICKS"
"KRAZY" IS OVER BY THE LAKE, WATCHING THE "SUNSET"
I THANK YOU
AH, HOW KUTE IS THE "SUN" WHEN IT IS ALL OF A SET, MYMYMY
OH-HOH-!!
OOH- LOOKLOOK - NARKIKKUS
ONE DIME
DA-A-AH-GUNNIT!! I MISSED !!
KA PLUNK!
A EEL CHILD AT PLAY, PREHEPS
THANK GOODNESS THE POOR FOOL DID NT NOTICE IT - I'LL BEAT IT BEFORE HE FINDS OUT - THE DISGRACE WOULD BE UNBEARABLE
A "DIME" FOR THAT "BRICK" ROBS ME OF MY PURSE, THAT MISS ROBS ME OF MY GOOD NAME, "O WOTTA WOIL, WOTTA WOIL
" AND SO, "DESPONDENCY" SPREADS ITS SOMBRE WINGS OVER THE HOUSE OF "IGNATZ MOUSE."
NOW !!
LET US TRAIL THAT "BRICK" ON ITS SUB-AQUEOUS JOURNEY. GOING DOON !!
OH IF ONLY I HAD "BRICKS" TO TOSS AT THAT "KRAZY KATFISH," LIKE MY LAND RELATIVE "IGNATZ" HAS TO TOSS AT THAT "KRAZY KAT" - OH IF ONLY I HAD, I'D BE THE HAPPIEST "MUSKRAT" WHAT EVER WAS
FORTUNE SMILES - T'IS INDEED A BRICK.
"MANUEL", AH MANNIE" WILL YOU NEVER SMILE UPON ME ?
I COULD LINGER AT HIS DOOR, FOREVER, AND FOREVER LITTLE SPRITE
THE CHANCE OF MY LIFE IS AT HAND !!
SUFFERING WHALE FISHES!! I MISSED !!!
TZVIP
BUT, S'NO USE A-LAS - S'NO USE, HE LOVES NOT ME
ELECTRIC EEL.
MY ONE OPPORTUNITY AND I MISS, GOSH, "IGNATZ" MUST NEVER HEAR OF THIS - SUCH A BLOW TO OUR FAMILY PRIDE HE'D NEVER SURVIVE
WO WO
AND "WOE" ABIDES IN THE HOME OF MANUEL MUSKRAT; YEA, WOE, DIRE, AND DOUR.
WOE
OH, "IGNATZ" WHERE FORE IS YOU, IGNATZ" - LONG HAS I WAITED FOR YOU, AND YET YOU COMEST NOT - A-LESS
ZWAZ
YES, "KRAZY," ALL OF MY DAYS HAVE I WAITED FOR ONE WHO NEVER COMES - I FEAR "MANUEL" HATH ANOTHER LOVE
HAH, S'JUST LIKE ME, AND "IGNATZ," ALWAYS I KEEP A TRYST WITH HIM, A-LONE - BUT, MAYBE TO-MORROW COMES HE, HUH, ? TO-MORROW
AH-H-H- TOMORROW
UH-HUH- TOMORROW-
HERRIMAN.

January 21st, 1917.

THIS IS "IGNATZ MOUSE'S" BIRTH-DAY MR. KELLY SO I WANT TO BUY A LOAD OF "BRICKS" FOR HIM = I WANT THE BEST YOU HAVE, MONEY BY ME AINT A OBJECT.
GOSH, A "KASH KUSTOMBR", AND NOT A "BRICK" IN THE SHOP, "IGNATZ" HAVING JUST BOUGHT THE LAST LOAD =
ANYTHINK FOR "IGNATZ" MR. KELLY I'D WAIT FOR EVVA, AND EVVA =
FINE, YOU WAIT RIGHT HERE, AND I'LL GET YOU A LOAD OF NICE, NEW FRESH ONES.
THERE, THAT LOOKS ENOUGH LIKE HIM TO BE HIS TWIN =
HERE I AM WITH A QUANTITY OF THE FINEST ASSORTMENT OF BRICKS I'VE EVER HAD, AND THAT FOOL "KAT" NO WHERE AROUND
AH-H-HAH !!
THE LAST SHOT IN THE LOCKER = AND MAY IT BE THE LAST OF THIS TOUGH "KAT" =
BZIZZ
ZIP
ZIP
HE'S ABOUT OUT OF BRICKS NOW - SO I'LL HAUL DOWN THE DUMMY -
WOOY !! I GOTTIM !!
ZABZZ
POPF !!
THAT WAS A GLORIOUS VICTORY
OOH, NICE, NEW ONES WHAT AINT NEVER BEEN USED = MY, BUT WONT "IGNATZ" HAVE A DELIGHTFUL BIRTH-DAY =
OUTSIDE OF THE 50% INCREASE IN PRICE, "KRAZY" I'M SURE YOU'LL BE WELL PLEASED WITH THESE "BRICKS" =
AH, LIL TOOTSA-WOOTSA, HE SLUMBAS = WHAT A HEPPY BIRTH-DAY HE'LL HAVE WHEN HE A-WAKES UP =
MENNY HEPPY COME BECKS OF THE DAY - K.K.
AND I REPEAT = IT WAS A GLORIOUS VICTORY =
HERRIMAN

January 28th, 1917.

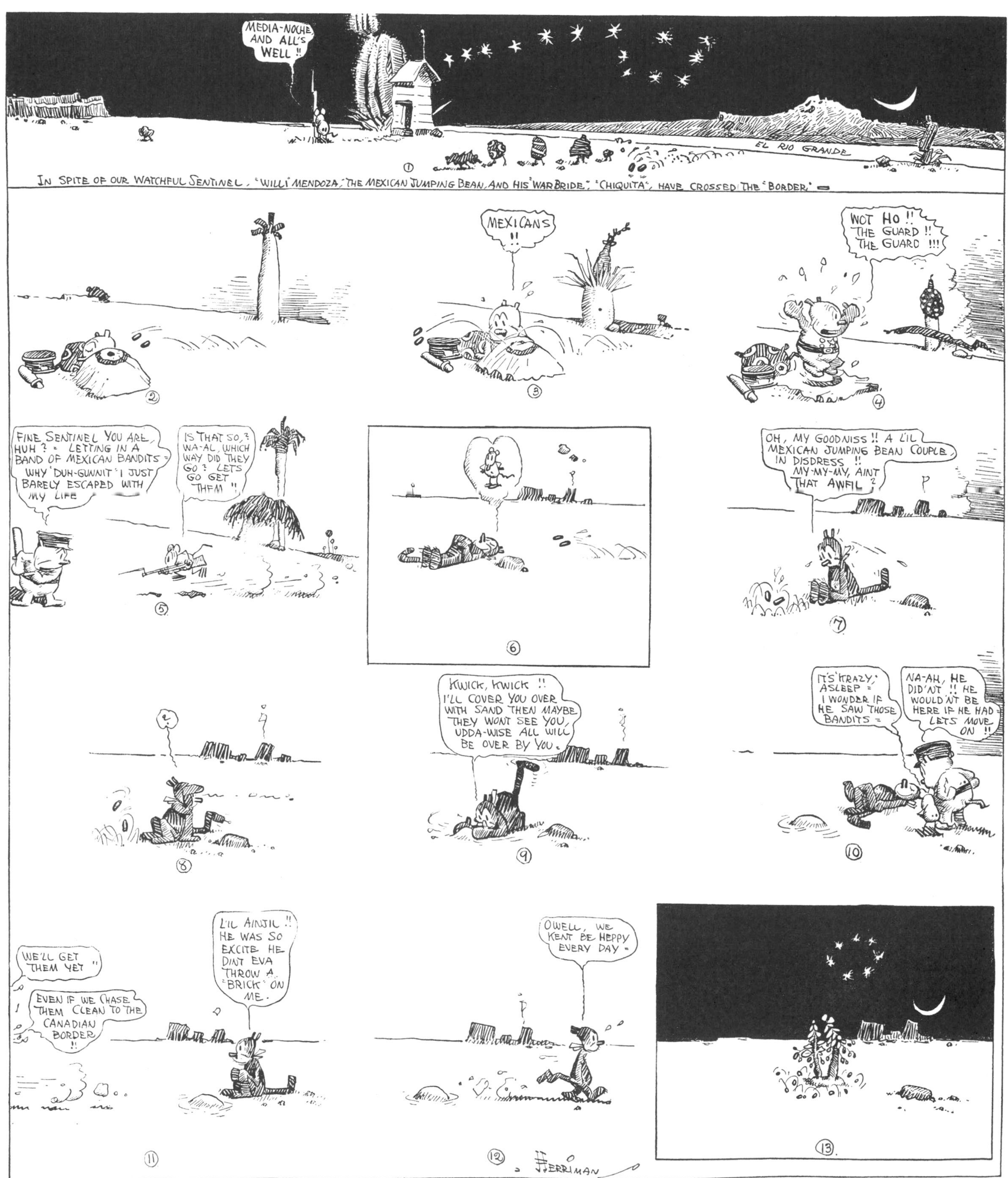
MEDIA-NOCHE AND ALL'S WELL !!
EL RIO GRANDE
IN SPITE OF OUR WATCHFUL SENTINEL, "WILLI MENDOZA", THE MEXICAN JUMPING BEAN, AND HIS "WAR BRIDE", "CHIQUITA", HAVE CROSSED THE "BORDER" —
MEXICANS !!
WOT HO !! THE GUARD !! THE GUARD !!!
FINE SENTINEL YOU ARE, HUH ? = LETTING IN A BAND OF MEXICAN BANDITS - WHY "DUH-GUNNIT" I JUST BARELY ESCAPED WITH MY LIFE
IS THAT SO, ? WA-AL, WHICH WAY DID THEY GO ? LETS GO GET THEM !!
OH, MY GOODNISS !! A L'IL MEXICAN JUMPING BEAN COUPLE, IN DISDRESS !! MY-MY-MY, AINT THAT AWFIL ?
KWICK, KWICK !! I'LL COVER YOU OVER WITH SAND THEN MAYBE THEY WONT SEE YOU, UDDA-WISE ALL WILL BE OVER BY YOU.
IT'S "KRAZY", ASLEEP = I WONDER IF HE SAW THOSE BANDITS =
NA-AH, HE DID'NT !! HE WOULD'NT BE HERE IF HE HAD LETS MOVE ON !!
WE'LL GET THEM YET "
EVEN IF WE CHASE THEM CLEAN TO THE CANADIAN BORDER !!
L'IL AINJIL !! HE WAS SO EXCITE HE DINT EVA THROW A "BRICK" ON ME.
OWELL, WE KENT BE HEPPY EVERY DAY.
HERRIMAN

February 4th, 1917.

YES "KRAZY," YOU WERE ALL BROUGHT HERE BY ME = "WALTER CEPHUS AUSTRIDGE" I HID AS A MERE EGG BACK OF A HOT ROCK IN THE "KALAHARI" WHERE HIS MOTHER FOUND HIM = "TERRY TURTLE, HE TOO WAS AN EGG, ONE OF A DOZEN I HAD BURIED IN THE SAND ON THE EDGE OF THE ARROYO SECO" = "GOOSEBERRY SPRIG," ANOTHER EGG, HIM I PLACED IN A DISCARDED HIGH HAT = "IGNATZ MOUSE," I BROUGHT SIGHTLESS, SQUEALING, AND SQUIRMING, AND DROPPED HIM INTO AN EMPTY CRACKER BOX = "KOLIN KELLY," WAS ONE OF SIX FOR WHOM I FOUND SANCTUARY IN A SUGAR BARREL UP A BACK ALLEY = AND YOU, "KRAZY" WITH FOUR OF YOUR KIND, I MADE COMFORTABLE IN A WASH-BOILER IN THE CELLAR OF THE HAUNTED HOUSE = AND SO IT GOES = AND SO IT GOES.
WUNDAFIL MR. STORK JUST SIMPFULLY WUNDAFIL.
THERE WASN'T A GRANDER CASTLE IN ALL THE "KALAHARI" THAN THE ONE IN WHICH I WAS BORN = THAT WAS ME, STARTING LIFE AS A INFANT, SWATHED IN THE PURPLE OF ROYALTY, AND A GOLDEN SPOON IN MY MOUTH = YIZZA-BOY.
HAH, YOU PRATE OF CASTLES, AND GOLDEN SPOONS, AND YOU BOAST OF THE PURPLE, BUT KNOW YOU MY FRIENDS THAT I, "TERRAPIN TURTLE" HAD ALL THAT STUFF AT MY BIRTH, AND MORE, MY SWADDLING CLOTHES WERE DIAMONDS, = SEGURA MIGUEL.
I'M A DUKE, A DUCK DUKE; THAT'S ALL ONE ROYAL GENT. HAS GOTTA SAY TO ANOTHER ROYAL GENT. = YE-E-EH.
FAIR WOMEN, AND BRAVE MEN GATHERED ABOUT MY CRADLE, AND CROWNED HEADS PAID ME HOMAGE = I WAS MIGHTY EVEN AS AN INFANT =
WHILE I AM, SO TO SPEAK, "IN TRADE," YET MY ADVENT INTO THE WORLD WAS ONE OF MIGHTY MONARCHICAL MOMENT = BUT GAH-SHANGIT I BECAME A DEMMYCRAT = A ROYAL DEMMYCRAT, DON'T FERGIT THAT
WHEN KINDRED SOULS GATHER AT THE KLUB.
KLUB
IT'S "KRAZY."
SURE IT IS.
HOW DEAR TO MY HEART IS THE SCENE OF MY INFINT-HOOD, WHERE FOND RECHILLECTION PREEE-E-E-ZENTS THAM-M-M TO VIEW
2
THE CLOCKS OF THE UNIVERSE ARE CHIMING THE HOUR OF "NOW" = AND JOE. STORK, WHO DWELLS ON THE TOPSIDE OF THE "ENCHANTED MESA" IN THE "DESIERTO PINTADO" = AND WHO PILOTS PRINCES, AND PAUPERS, POETS, AND PEASANTS, PUPPIES, AND PUSSY-CATS ACROSS THE RIVER WITHOUT ANY OTHER-SIDE TO THE SHORE OF HERE = IS TELLING "KRAZY KAT" A TALE WHICH MUST NEVER BE TOLD, AND YET WHICH EVERY ONE KNOWS =
THE OLD "HAUNTED-HOUSE" AND THE CELLAR UNDA-NEET IT, AND THE DEAR OLD "WASH-BOILA" EE-E-EN WHICH I WAS "BORN" =
3
OH, THAT US ARISTOCRATS HAS GOTTA BREATHE THE SAME AIR AS A "WASH-BOILER" BRED BOOR = S'AWFUL =
LOW CHURL
THEM BUMPKINS SHOULD BE KEPT DOWN =
OH WOTTA WOIL, WOTTA WOIL
BASE VARLET.
4
AND EVERY LOVED SPOT WHOM MY INFINT-HOOD KNEW =
5
OH-HO-HMMM = MIDNIGHT = TIME TO HUSTLE UP A BIT OF LUNCH.
"DON KIYOTY" WHO SLUMBERS AT NOON, AND DINES AT MIDNIGHT.
PARA LA CASA DE JOSÉ CIGUENO
HERRIMAN

February 11th, 1917.

A MYSTERIOUS SPOTTED VISITOR LEFT THE HOUSE OF "MOUSE" LAST NIGHT = YES = THE STARS SAW HIM =
OH, MY POOR CHILDREN, OH, MY POOR BEAUTIFUL CHILDREN !!
WHICH MAY, OR MAY NOT HAVE HAD SOMETHING TO DO WITH THE FACT, THAT "MILTON," "IRVING," AND "MARSHAL MOUSE," CHILDREN OF MR. & MRS. IGNATZ MOUSE" HAD THE "MEASLES" NEXT MORNING.
1.
MA-A- MA-A-
OH, "IGNATZ", WHAT WILL WE DO - WHAT WILL WE DO ?
JUST CALL IN A "DOCTOR", AND WHEN THEY'RE WELL, LET ME KNOW = I'M GOING AWAY = NO MEASLES FOR MINE IF I CAN HELP IT = Y'BET.
2.
IT'S SURE TOUGH WHEN ONE'S CHILDREN GET THE "MEASLES" = ONE IS SO APT TO CATCH THEM ONE'S SELF =
3
OH "KRAZY" I'M SO GLAD YOU CALLED, THE CHILDREN ARE DOWN WITH THE "MEASLES" "IGNATZ" HAS GONE AWAY, I CAN'T GET A DOCTOR, AND I JUST DON'T KNOW WHAT TO DO =
OH-HO-HO, THEY GOT MIZZLES, HEH ? SHUX !! MRS MICE" WE'LL CURE THEM, WE DUNT NEED NO "DOCTA"
4
THE IDA IS TO KEEP 'EM WARM, AND AS I GOT A LOTTA FURS I CAN DO SO = SEE THE MIZZLE SPOTS IS ALREADY DROPPING OFF
YOU DEAR SOUL, YOU HAVE RENDERED ME A MOST WONDERFUL SERVICE
5
THANKS EVER SO MUCH "KRAZY", AND IF YOU SEE "IGNATZ" TELL HIM THAT ALL IS WELL, AND THAT HE CAN COME HOME NOW =
I'LL DO THAT, MRS MICE, WITH CONSIDABLE PLEASURE.
6
BLESS MY EYE, IT'S "IGNATZ" !! MY !! WUNT HE BE A HEPPY L'IL MICE WHEN HE FINDS OUT HIS CHILDS AINT GOT NO MORE MIZZLES = BUT I WUNT WAKE HIM UP, I'LL TELL IT TO HIM IN THE MORNING = L'IL SLIPPING BEAUTIFIL
IT SEEMS, AS WE HERE SEE, THAT "IGNATZ" HAD SOUGHT SANCTUARY FROM THE "MEASLES" IN "KRAZY'S" HOME =
-BUT-
7
THE NEXT MORNING = AH-H-H- RELENTLESS FATE =
8.
YES, MRS. MOUSE, THEY BOTH HAVE THE "MEASLES" AND IT WILL BE BEST TO LEAVE THEM JUST AS THEY ARE = THEY'LL BE WELL IN A FEW DAYS.
WHEN'S PA COMING HOME, MA ?
VERY WELL DOCTOR.
9.
HERRIMAN

February 18th, 1917.

KOLIN KELLY'S BRICK YARD
YES IGNATZ, THAT'S THE FINEST THING IN THE BRICK LINE I'VE EVER BUILT, IN FACT IT IS A "BRICK DE LUXE" AS IT WERE, - BUT YOU'D BETTER TAKE IT OVER THE LEVEL ROAD, I'M AFRAID IT'S TOO HEAVY TO HANDLE ON THE HILL ROAD.
THE HILL ROAD IS THE SHORTEST, MR. KELLY, AND AS I AM VERY ANXIOUS TO FLATTEN THAT "KRAZY KAT" OUT WITH THIS GORGEOUS BRICK, THAT'S THE ONE I SHALL TAKE
WON
"KELLY" MUST THINK I'M A WEAKLING
TOO:
BUT I'LL SHOW HIM
THREEY
OH-HOH, SOMEBODY NEEDS HELP
THE SHORTEST ROAD TO THAT "KAT" IS THE EASIEST NO MATTER HOW STEEP
PHO.
AH-H, NOW I'M GETTING MY SECOND WIND
PHYVE.
HUH - WITH ONE HAND -
SICKS.
HELLO "KRAZY"
LOOKA - LOOKA - WITH THE TAIL EVEN
7.
HELLO!, L'IL KETTAPILLA HAVE YOU SEEN "IGNATZ" TODAY?
WHOA!!
AYTE.
NEIN.
TEHNN.
I SAID, DID YOU SEEN "IGNATZ" TO DAY?
SURE, HE JUST THIS MINUTE WENT DOWN THE HILL
EELEV-N
I THENK YOU.
OH, DONT MENTION IT
12.
HERRIMAN.
AS FAR AS WE ARE CONCERNED, THIS ENDS THE TALE OF THE BIGGEST, HEAVIEST, AND SINKIEST "BRICK" THAT WAS EVER BUILT.
THIR TEEN.

February 25th, 1917.

MY, LOOK HOW DEMP MR. & MRS. MEXICAN JUMPING BEAN' - IT'S DEW AINT IT MR. STORK !!
DEW, ME NECK, THEM'S TEARS Y'SEE, SOMEBODY HAS KIDNAPPED THEIR CHILDREN, AND THEY ARE VERY, VERY SAD =
ONE.
ODEER, I WUNDA WHO KIDNEPPLED THEM LIL JUMPING BEANS, WHO COULD'A BEEN SO CRUEL LIKE THAT ?
TWO.
THREE.
OH-HOH-
FOUR.
LOOK FELLAS, S'ONLY A OLD STOCKING WITH A COUPLE OF HOLES IN THE HEEL.
"KRAZY KAT" IS NOT THE ONLY ONE WHO'S KURIOSITY HAS LED TO GREAT DISCOVERIES, HOW ABOUT "KRIS: KOLUMBUS" ?
FIVE
I GOT A PURR-FICK 36 TAIL. IT JUST FIT.
SIX.
MY GOODNISS, BUT I FEEL SO DRESSED UP =
SEVEN.
HI-HI-HI = H-YUP !!! GET-UP YOU JUMPING BEANS', IM GONNA START A CIRCUS WITH YOU - GIDDY YAP !! HI-YUP !!!
EIGHT.
!
NINE.
TEN.
WHY IT'S THEM LIL LOST JUMPING BEANS !!
ELEVEN.
I'M GONNA TAKE YOU ALL HOME TO THE MOMMA', & THE POPPA', Y'GOT NO IDA HOW UNHEPPY THEY ARE, YOU NUTTY, NUTTY CHILDS =
TWELVE.
NOW DUNT NEVER RUN AWAY NO MORE, Y'HEAR !!
THIRTEEN.
NOW, I WILL FIND 'IGNATZ', AND SHOW HIM MY NEW TAIL STOCKING, HE'LL BE SO JOYFIL TO SEE IT = LIL AINJIL
FOURTEEN.
HERRIMAN

March 4th, 1917.

March 11th, 1917.

I'VE LOST MY BEARINGS, AND I KNOW THERE ARE ROCKS AND BREAKERS AHEAD, I FEAR THE WORST IS AT HAND.
THERE IS A STORM TOSSED MARINER MOUSE ON THE BLUSTERING BRINE THIS DARK AND MOONLESS NIGHT.
BUT, "KRAZY-KATFISH", KRAZY KAT'S AKWATTIC KOUSIN REALIZES THAT ALL IS NOT WELL =
ONE.
KRAZY !! OH-H-H KRA-A-A-AZY !!!
TO YOU, AND TO US, IT WOULD MEAN THE TREBLE TUMULT OF THE "TRITONS" "TEMPEST SERANADE" =
TWO.
IT'S MY KOUSIN "KRAZY KETFISH" AND IT MEANS THAT DAINJA IS AT HEND = OMY OMY.
KRAZY !! OH-H-H-H KRA-A-AZY.
NOT SO TO "K.K."
THREE.
THE LIGHT IN THE LIGHT HOUSE IS OUT, AND "IGNATZ" OUT IN THE STORM.
ODEER - ODEER.
FOUR.
ODEER - ODEER
FIVE.
WHAT'S THE IDA OF A DARK LIGHT HOUSE WHEN THE NICEST LIL SAILA IN THE WORLD IS OUT IN YUN STORMFIL SEA, HUH ?
CAN'T HELP IT, KRAZY; I AIN'T GOT A DROP OF OIL ON THE PLACE = NO OIL, NO LIGHT Y'KNOW.
SIX.
ODEER, ODEER.
SEVEN.
MR. & MRS GLIMMERING GLOWERM.
EIGHT.
THEY SLEEP -
NINE.
IT'S JUST GOTTA BE DONE.
TEN.
THAT'S IT, GLOW, GLOW, GLOW LIKE EVER THINGS, AND FOR-EVVA, AND EVVA WILL I KEEP ALL THE BAD BUTCHA-BIRDS, AND SPERROWS AWAY FROM YOUR HOUSE SO THEY WON'T EAT YOU UP =
AND SO, IN THEIR JOY, MR. & MRS GLIMMERING GLOWERM GLOWED THEIR GLOWIEST, AND THERE'S NO GLOW QUITE SO GLOWY AS THE GLOW OF JOY
ELEVEN.
HERRIMAN
WELL, AT LAST !! THAT IDIOT "LIGHT HOUSE KEEPER" HAS MADE A "LIGHT"; IT WAS NO JOKE TRYING TO MAKE SHORE WITH A BOAT LOAD OF "BRICKS" ON A NIGHT LIKE THIS.
TWELVE.
AND REMEMBA, I'LL KEEP MY PROMISE.
THIRTEEN.

March 18th, 1917.

AH, THE DAY DAWNS MOST BEAUTIFUL, IT BEHOOVES ME TO DO A GREAT DEED, AND SO SHALL I GIRD MY LOINS, AND PROCEED FORTH TO MAKE THIS A DAY OF GREAT MEMORY
"IGNATZ" PRATES OF "GIRDING HIS LOINS" (YOU GRIN, SO DO WE) AND IT NO DOUBT STRIKES YOU, AS WELL AS US, TO BE BUT THE VAPID VAUNT OF A VAIN MOUSE, AH, TRUE, BUT "IGNATZ" IS A SELF SUFFICIENT RODENT, AND SO MUST YOU, AND US BUT SMILE AT THIS LITTLE VAURIEN'S VAPORINGS.
ONE.
T'WAS EVER ON SUCH A DAY AS THIS THAT IT WAS DECREED I DO A MOST MAGNIFICENT DEED-
TWO.
KOLIN KELLY DEALER IN BRICKS
"KELLY," I WISH TO PERPETUATE THIS DAY BY PURCHASING YOUR GRANDEST BRICK, I SHALL HAVE BIG NEED OF IT.
AH, AND STRANGE TO SAY, I HAVE THIS VERY DAY, MADE THE BRICK I CONSIDER MY MASTER PIECE THAT ONE YOU SHALL HAVE.
THREE
"KRAZY KAT" THY DOOM IMPENDS
FOUR
A CHILD STORM-CLOUD.
FIVE.
THE MAMA STORM-CLOUD
THE PAPA STORM-CLOUD
A CLOUD'S SHADOW.
SIX.
SEVEN
EIGHT.
NINE.
HE GOT CAUGHT IN THE STORM MRS. MICE, AND HE'S FAINTED.
SERVES HIM RIGHT, CHUCK HIM ON THE BED HE'LL COME AROUND PRETTY SOON.
TEN.
L'IL AINJIL, S'NO KIND'A WEATHA FOR HIM, HE'S TOO DELIKIT-
LOAFER=
WHAT'S A LOAFER, "MA" ?
ELEVEN.
AH, THE DAY DAWN'S MOST BEAUTIFUL IT BEHOOVES ME TO DO A GREAT DEED AND SO SHALL I GIRD MY LOINS, AND PROCEED FORTH TO MAKE THIS A DAY OF GREAT MEMORY.
TWELVE
T'WAS EVER ON SUCH A DAY AS THIS, THAT IT WAS DECREED I DO A MOST MAGNIFICENT DEED.
THIRTEEN.
"KELLY," I WISH TO PERPETUATE THIS DAY BY PUCHASING YOUR GRANDEST "BRICK," I SHALL HAVE BIG NEED OF IT =
AH, L'IL SOOPEERYA BEAN.
AH, AND STRANGE TO SAY, I HAVE THIS VERY DAY MADE THE "BRICK" I CONSIDER MY MASTER-PIECE, THAT ONE YOU SHALL HAVE.
FOURTEEN
HERRIMAN

March 25th, 1917.

FELLOW CITIZENS, IT IS WITH A SAD HEART THAT I TELL YOU THAT LAST NIGHT SOME BURGLAR ENTERED OUR MINT, AND STOLE THE "BRICK" OF GOLD WHICH FORMED THE WEALTH, AND TREASURE OF OUR COMMUNITY = AS YOUR "MAYOR" I NOW ANNOUNCE THAT A REWARD OF ONE DOLLAR IS OFFERED FOR THE RETURN OF THE "BRICK", AND NO QUESTIONS ASKED.
MINT
$1.
AH-H-
"DON KIYOTE", COUNT OF COCONINO, WHO LABORS NOT, AND LOVES A LIFE OF EASE.
ONE.
$1
TWO.
AH, SENOR "KELLY", YOU ARE POSSESSED OF MANY, MANY OF THOSE "BRICK" ARE YOU NOT ?
KOLIN KELLY DEALER IN BRICKS
I'M ALL OUT OF "BRICKS" RIGHT NOW, "DON" = I DID'NT EVEN HAVE ONE TO SELL "IGNATZ MOUSE" YESTERDAY.
THREE.
AND THAT AMIABLE HUSBAND OF THINE "SENORA MOUSE", IS HE ABOUT, MAY I ASK ?
I AIN'T GOT THE LEAST IDEA WHERE HE IS, "DON" THE LOAFER DID'NT COME HOME AT ALL LAST NIGHT.
FOUR.
$1
FIVE
A MOST HAPPY DAY TO YOU SENORA "TABBY", "GATA HERMOSA", AND WHERE IS LOCATE THY NEPHEW, "KRAZY KAT", I ASK MOST HUMBLY.
"KRAZY" WENT OVER BY THE OLD SMOKE TREE "DON" HE IS PROBABLY THERE NOW.
SIX.
TO THE OLD SMOKE TREE
SEVEN.
AND TAKE IT FROM US, WHEN THERE IS SOMETHING TO MOVE FOR, "THE DON" CAN SURE TWIDDLE A HASTY HOOF, HE'S LOPING AN EASY 80 RIGHT NOW.
AH-H-
MY, MY, MY, BUT "IGNATZ" IS GETTING FENCY, AND STYLISH, BEANING ME WITH SUCH A SWELL YELLA "BRICK" ALL POLISHED, AND SHINY LIKE A BRESS DOOR'S KNOB.
EIGHT.
"TEN CENTS" IS A LOTTA MONEY TO GIVE FOR A BRASS BRICK "KRAZY", A LOTTA MONEY = HOWEVER, FAR BE IT FROM ME NOT TO BE GENEROUS TO SUCH A CLEVER "KAT" LIKE YOU.
OH, I KNOW IT IS, MR. DONS KIYOTE, I KNOW IT IS. AND YOU GOT NO IDA HOW MUCH I EPPRECIATE YOUR JENNY ROSSITY.
90¢ CLEAR PROFIT
NINE.
I WANT FIVE CENTS WORTH LOLLY-POPS AND FIVE CENTS WORTH OF YOUR BEST CHOCALITS, AND BUN-BUNS = THEY MUST BE THE BEST BECAUSE THEY IS A PRESENT TO "IGNATZ MICE"
TEN.
HERRIMAN

April 1st, 1917.

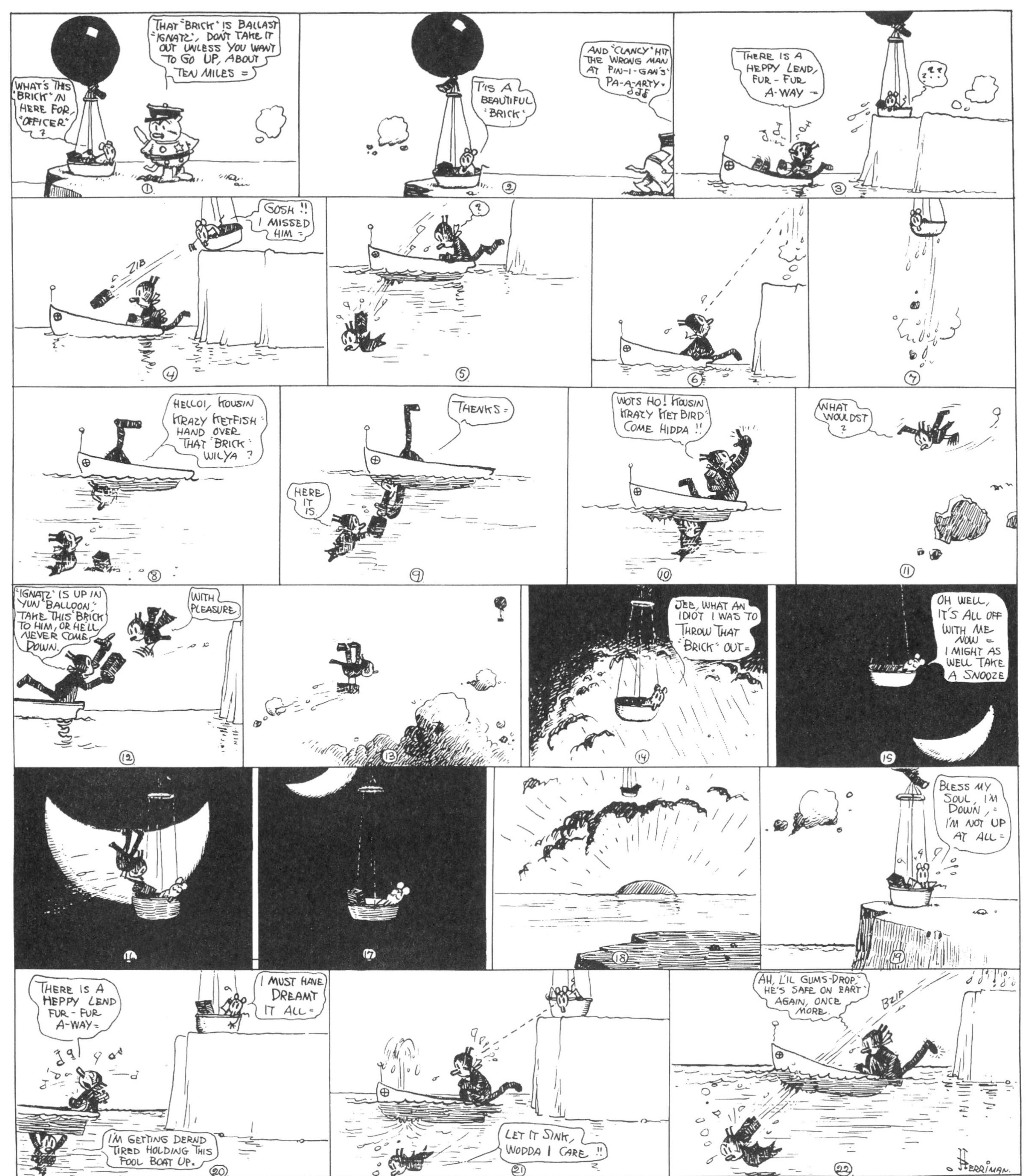
WHAT'S THIS "BRICK" IN HERE FOR, "OFFICER" ?
THAT "BRICK" IS BALLAST "IGNATZ", DON'T TAKE IT OUT UNLESS YOU WANT TO GO UP, ABOUT TEN MILES =
T'IS A BEAUTIFUL "BRICK"
AND "CLANCY" HIT THE WRONG MAN AT PIN-I-GAN'S PA-A-ARTY =
THERE IS A HEPPY LEND, FUR - FUR A-WAY =
GOSH !! I MISSED HIM =
ZIB
HELLO!, KOUSIN KRAZY KETFISH HAND OVER THAT "BRICK" WILYA ?
THENKS =
HERE IT IS.
WOTS HO! KOUSIN KRAZY KET BIRD COME HIDDA !!
WHAT WOULDST ?
"IGNATZ" IS UP IN YUN "BALLOON" TAKE THIS "BRICK" TO HIM, OR HE'LL NEVER COME DOWN.
WITH PLEASURE.
JEE, WHAT AN IDIOT I WAS TO THROW THAT "BRICK" OUT =
OH WELL, IT'S ALL OFF WITH ME NOW = I MIGHT AS WELL TAKE A SNOOZE
BLESS MY SOUL, I'M DOWN, = I'M NOT UP AT ALL =
THERE IS A HEPPY LEND FUR - FUR A-WAY =
I MUST HAVE DREAMT IT ALL =
I'M GETTING DERND TIRED HOLDING THIS FOOL BOAT UP.
LET IT SINK, WODDA I CARE !!
AH, L'IL GUMS-DROP, HE'S SAFE ON EART AGAIN, ONCE MORE.
BZIP
HERRIMAN.

April 8th, 1917.

STOLEN !! A HOD OF BRICKS FROM MR. PERCIVAL POODIL THE EMINENT MASON. A REWARD OF TWO BITS CASH IS OFFERED FOR THE APPREHENSION OF THE ROBBER
"DON KIYOTY," COUNT OF COCONINO IS GREATLY IMPRESSED BY THE POTENTIALITIES OF A CERTAIN BIT OF LITERATURE.
— ONE. —
• WHICH SETS HIM WONDERING, AND WANDERING OVER THE EARTH IN A STATE OF GREAT MENTAL DISQUIET.
— TWO —
SKWASBO!! THE THREE TOED EEL.
ZULIEKA, THE SUL-TAN'S FA-VO-RITE
POW !!
JUST MISSED HIM.
WEEY !! ATSA BOY 'IGNATZ' GIVE 'IM ANOTHER ONE.
GOOD KID
BIG FAIR 10¢ ADMISSION
— THREE —
AH-H-H
25
ATTA BOY.
THE SPORT OF THE AGE, MEN, THE PASTIME OF KINGS, AND DUKES
EVERY TIME YOU KREASE THE KAT'S KOKO, YOU GET A GOOD CIGAR 3 THROWS FOR 5
GOOD
THAT'S WINGING THEM OVER.
GREAT DELIVERY.
- FOUR -
FUR-R-R-RD MURTCH !!
EXHIBIT A.
THAT WAS A NICE BIT OF DETECTIVE WORK, "DON" HERE'S THE "TWO BITS" REWARD.
THANKS OFFICER "PUPP" THANKS.
FAIR
- FIVE. -
AND IN DUE TIME THE GREAT RIGHT ARM OF THE LAW FELL UPON "IGNATZ MOUSE," PILFERER OF BRICKS, AND A MATTER OF SOME "TWENTY FIVE CENTS" PASSED INTO THE POSSESSION OF "DON KIYOTY."
WELL "KRAZY" WE'VE HAD A BIG DAY TODAY, - HERE'S YOUR PAY -
BE ON THE JOB EARLY TOMORROW -
OVEZZA
1$
- SIX. -
"TWO DOLLAS," MY, BUT THATSA LOTTA MONEY TO GET FOR THE PLEASURE OF HEVING "IGNATZ" THROW BRICKS AT YOU.
SEVEN.
WELL, I'LL GO HOME, AND GET A GOOD NIGHT'S SLEEP, I NEED IT.
EIGHT.
IGNATZ !!
YES, THEM BRICKS HE USED ON YOU WAS STOLEN BY HIM - AND AS NOBODY WILL GO HIS BAIL FOR A "DOLLAR," HE'S GOTTA STAY IN THE KOOP.
JAIL.
- NINE. -
HERE'S THE "DOLLA" OFFISSA, RELEASE HIM IMMEDIATELY !!!
HOORAY !!!
TEN.
ELEVEN.
HERE'S A "DOLLA" KESH MONEY MISTA KELLY SEND "IGNATZ" UP A HOD OF YOUR BEST BRICKS QUICK !!
KOLIN KELLY - DEALER IN BRICKS
OH, IS HE OUT AGAIN ?
TWELVE
WELL BOSS, HERE I ARE AGAIN, AND I GOT A 'IDA WE IS GONNA HAVE ANOTHER BUSY DAY.
GOOD !! GET THE HEAD IN THE HOLE AND WE'LL START TO WORK.
THIRTEEN.
HERRIMAN.

April 15th, 1917.

"KRAZY KAT," PROWLER OF THE NIGHT, AND FULL OF KURIOSITY HEARS WHAT HE HEARS AT THE DOOR OF JOE STORK'S HOUSE, ON THE CREST OF THE "ENCHANTED MESA."
DON
A LARGE ORDA, A OFFIL LARGE ORDA.
PARA LA CASA DE JOSÉ CIGUENO
FURNITURE
NOW REMEMBA, A "AIR" ONE, A "SEA" ONE AND A "LAND" ONE, ALSO DELIVVA THEM PROMPLY.
THEY SHALL BE THERE "ON TIME" MR. KAT.
ONCE MORE, I AM MANY TIMES A "UNKIL", OH, WOTTA WOII OF JOY THIS IS
HUH - THINK THEY'RE SOME BODY.
AND SO, IN THE HOME OF MR. AND MRS. "KRAZY KATBIRD," MUCH HAPPINESS ABOUNDS.
AS WELL AS IN THAT OF MR. AND MRS. "KRAZY KATFISH."
ALL SWELLED UP.
POO POO.
ALSO, AS MUCH AS CAN BE REASONABLY EXPECTED IN THE DOMICILE OF MR. AND MRS. "IGNATZ MOUSE."

April 22nd, 1917.

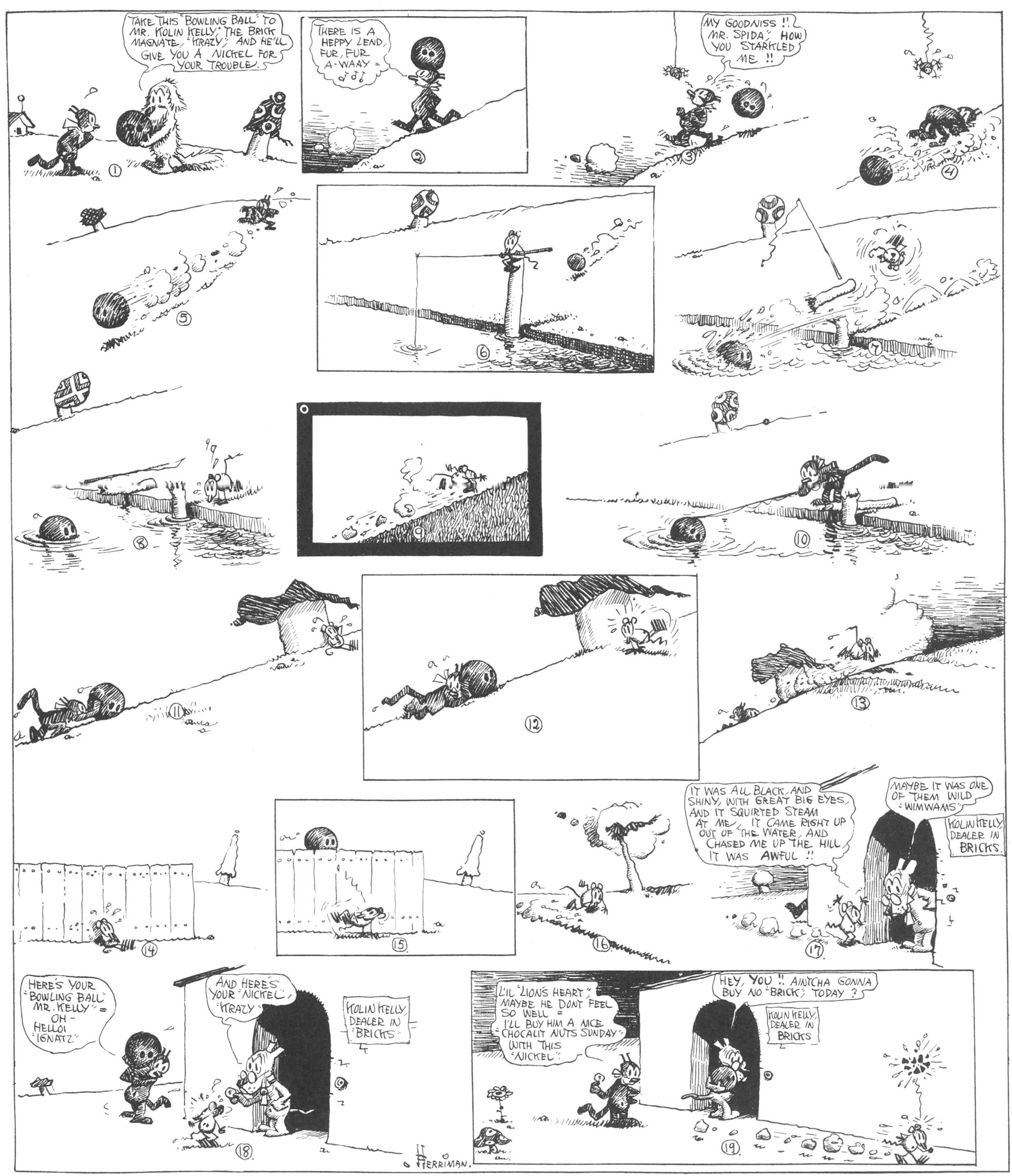
TAKE THIS "BOWLING BALL" TO MR. KOLIN KELLY, THE BRICK MAGNATE, "KRAZY," AND HE'LL GIVE YOU A NICKEL FOR YOUR TROUBLE.
THERE IS A HEPPY LEND, FUR, FUR A-WAAY =
MY GOODNISS !! MR. SPIDA, HOW YOU STARTLED ME !!
IT WAS ALL BLACK, AND SHINY, WITH GREAT BIG EYES, AND IT SQUIRTED STEAM AT ME, IT CAME RIGHT UP OUT OF THE WATER, AND CHASED ME UP THE HILL IT WAS AWFUL !!
MAYBE IT WAS ONE OF THEM WILD "WIMWAMS"
KOLIN KELLY, DEALER IN BRICKS.
HERE'S YOUR "BOWLING BALL" MR. KELLY = OH - HELLO! "IGNATZ"
AND HERE'S YOUR "NICKEL" "KRAZY"
KOLIN KELLY, DEALER IN "BRICKS"
L'IL "LIONS HEART" MAYBE HE DONT FEEL SO WELL = I'LL BUY HIM A NICE "CHOCALIT NUTS SUNDAY" WITH THIS "NICKEL"
HEY, YOU !! AINTCHA GONNA BUY NO "BRICK" TODAY ?
KOLIN KELLY, DEALER IN BRICKS
HERRIMAN.

April 29th, 1917.

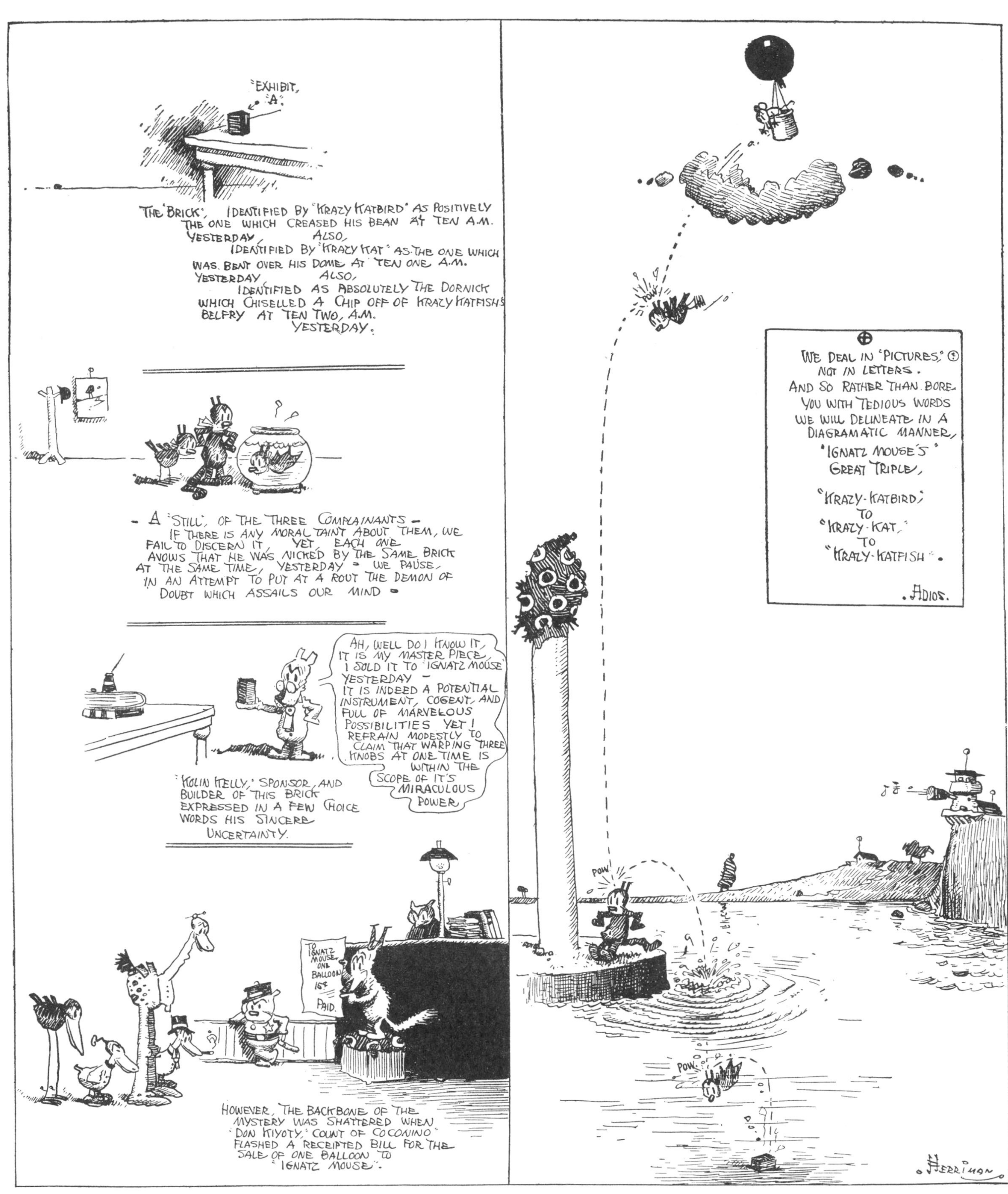
"EXHIBIT, 'A'"
THE 'BRICK', IDENTIFIED BY 'KRAZY KATBIRD' AS POSITIVELY THE ONE WHICH CREASED HIS BEAN AT TEN A.M. YESTERDAY, ALSO, IDENTIFIED BY 'KRAZY KAT' AS THE ONE WHICH WAS BENT OVER HIS DOME AT TEN ONE A.M. YESTERDAY, ALSO, IDENTIFIED AS ABSOLUTELY THE DORNICK WHICH CHISELLED A CHIP OFF OF KRAZY KATFISH'S BELFRY AT TEN TWO, A.M. YESTERDAY.
- A 'STILL' OF THE THREE COMPLAINANTS - IF THERE IS ANY MORAL TAINT ABOUT THEM, WE FAIL TO DISCERN IT, YET, EACH ONE AVOWS THAT HE WAS NICKED BY THE SAME BRICK AT THE SAME TIME, YESTERDAY - WE PAUSE, IN AN ATTEMPT TO PUT AT A ROUT THE DEMON OF DOUBT WHICH ASSAILS OUR MIND -
AH, WELL DO I KNOW IT, IT IS MY MASTER PIECE, I SOLD IT TO 'IGNATZ MOUSE' YESTERDAY - IT IS INDEED A POTENTIAL INSTRUMENT, COGENT, AND FULL OF MARVELOUS POSSIBILITIES YET I REFRAIN MODESTLY TO CLAIM THAT WARPING THREE KNOBS AT ONE TIME IS WITHIN THE SCOPE OF IT'S MIRACULOUS POWER
'KOLIN KELLY,' SPONSOR, AND BUILDER OF THIS BRICK EXPRESSED IN A FEW CHOICE WORDS HIS SINCERE UNCERTAINTY.
TO IGNATZ MOUSE ONE BALLOON 15¢ PAID
HOWEVER, THE BACKBONE OF THE MYSTERY WAS SHATTERED WHEN 'DON KIYOTY,' COUNT OF COCONINO' FLASHED A RECEIPTED BILL FOR THE SALE OF ONE BALLOON TO 'IGNATZ MOUSE'.
POW
WE DEAL IN 'PICTURES,' NOT IN LETTERS. AND SO RATHER THAN BORE YOU WITH TEDIOUS WORDS WE WILL DELINEATE IN A DIAGRAMATIC MANNER, 'IGNATZ MOUSE'S' GREAT TRIPLE, 'KRAZY-KATBIRD,' TO 'KRAZY-KAT,' TO 'KRAZY-KATFISH'.
. ADIOS.
POW
POW
HERRIMAN

May 6th, 1917.

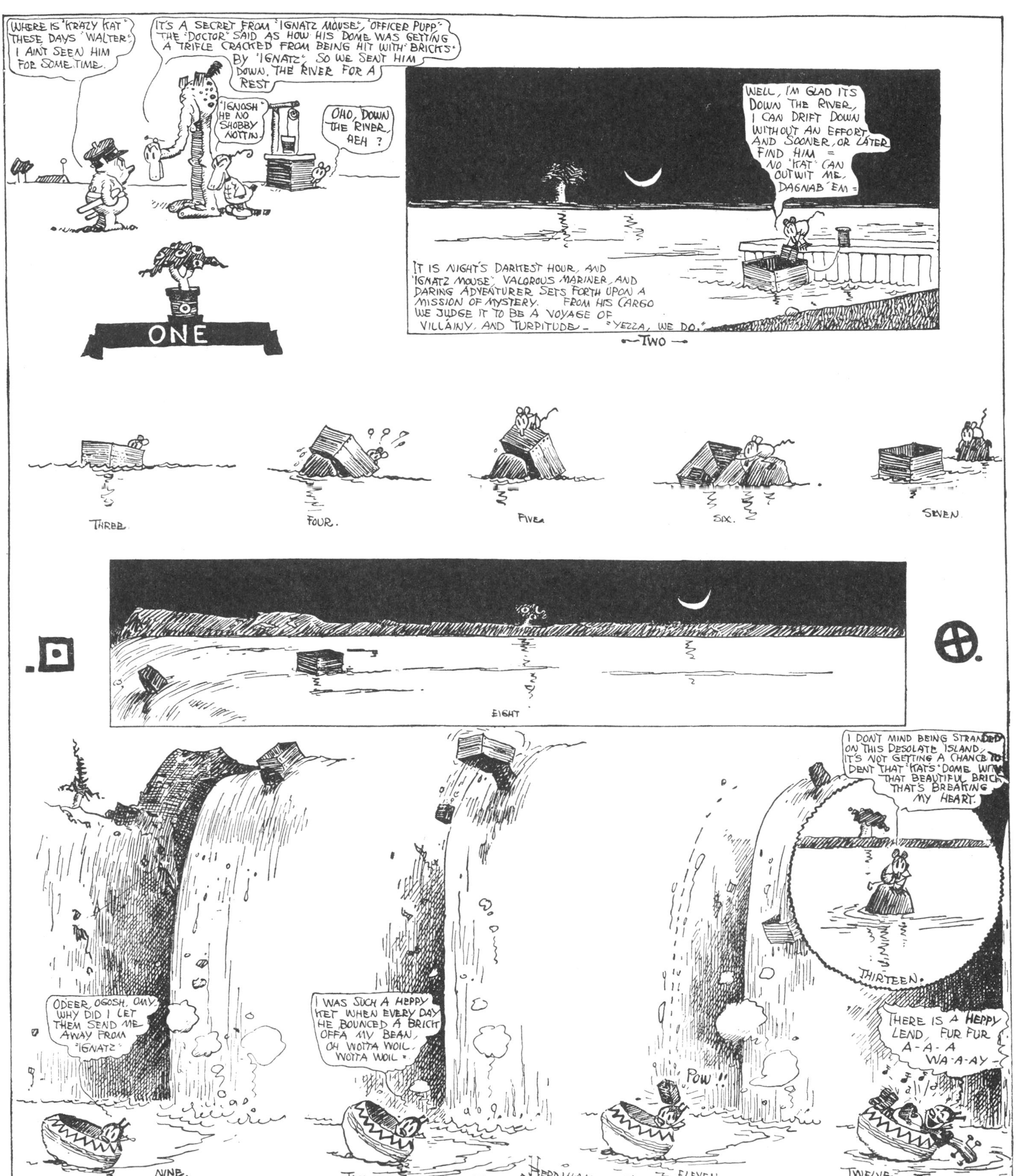
WHERE IS 'KRAZY KAT' THESE DAYS 'WALTER' I AINT SEEN HIM FOR SOME TIME.
IT'S A SECRET FROM 'IGNATZ MOUSE', 'OFFICER PUPP' THE 'DOCTOR' SAID AS HOW HIS DOME WAS GETTING A TRIFLE CRACKED FROM BEING HIT WITH 'BRICKS' BY 'IGNATZ', SO WE SENT HIM DOWN THE RIVER FOR A REST
'IGNOSH' HE NO SHOBBY NOTTIN.
OHO, DOWN THE RIVER, AEH ?
ONE
WELL, I'M GLAD ITS DOWN THE RIVER, I CAN DRIFT DOWN WITHOUT AN EFFORT, AND SOONER, OR LATER FIND HIM = NO 'KAT' CAN OUTWIT ME, DAGNAB 'EM =
IT IS NIGHT'S DARKEST HOUR, AND 'IGNATZ MOUSE', VALOROUS MARINER, AND DARING ADVENTURER SETS FORTH UPON A MISSION OF MYSTERY. FROM HIS CARGO WE JUDGE IT TO BE A VOYAGE OF VILLAINY AND TURPITUDE - "YEZZA, WE DO."
TWO
THREE.
FOUR.
FIVE.
SIX.
SEVEN.
EIGHT
I DON'T MIND BEING STRANDED ON THIS DESOLATE ISLAND, IT'S NOT GETTING A CHANCE TO DENT THAT 'KAT'S' DOME WITH THAT BEAUTIFUL BRICK THAT'S BREAKING MY HEART.
THIRTEEN.
ODEER, OGOSH, OMY, WHY DID I LET THEM SEND ME AWAY FROM 'IGNATZ'
I WAS SUCH A HEPPY KET WHEN EVERY DAY HE BOUNCED A BRICK OFFA MY BEAN, OH WOTTA WOIL, WOTTA WOIL =
POW!!
THERE IS A HEPPY LEND, FUR FUR A-A-A WA-A-AY -
NINE.
TEN.
HERRIMAN
ELEVEN.
TWELVE.

May 13th, 1917.

KORPORAL "KRAZY KAT," THERE'S SOMETHING SUSPICIOUS IN TRENCH NUMBER ONE, YOU ARE DETAILED TO SEE WHO IT IS, AND REPORT IF IT'S A "FRIEND," OR "FOE".

YEZZA, JENRIL, I WILL DO SO, FOR A FACK.

ZIB

POW.!!!

I DINT SEE NOBODY IN THAT TRENCH, "JENRIL".

AH, THEN YOU CAN'T SAY AS TO WHETHER IT'S A FRIEND, OR A FOE, CAN YOU?

OH, I ASSURE YOU "JENRIL," IT IS POSITIVELY A "FRIEND".

HERRIMAN.

May 20th, 1917.

I HAVE IN POSSESSION TODAY A COIN OF GREAT VALUE, WITH WHICH I WILL PURCHASE THE MOST MAGNIFICENT "BRICK" IN MR. KOLIN KELLY'S BRICK YARD = = KRAZY KAT, BEWARE !!!
PAUSE !! PAUSE, SIR "MOUSE", I WOULD WORD A WHILE WITH YOU =
BEHOLD, BEFORE YOU THE WONDER OF THE CENTURIES, THE MARVEL OF AGES, THE PERFECTION, AND PARAGON OF PHONOGRAPHY.
THIS INTERESTING INSTRUMENT WILL PLAY ANY SONG YOU WISH AT YOUR COMMAND = JUST TELL IT WHAT YOU WANT TO PLAY, AND IT WILL PLAY IT.
IT WILL, MY DEAR SIR, IT WILL FOR A THIN, FLAT "DIME" THIS LITTLE WIZARD OF HARMONY WILL TRILL THAT BEAUTIFUL BALLAD SWEETER THAN A FLOCK OF ANGELS WOULD.
WILL IT PLAY "SILVER THREADS AMONG THE GOLD", SIR ?
I HAD THOUGHT TO USE THIS DIME FOR ANOTHER PURPOSE, SIR, BUT IF THAT SONG IS RENDERED AS WELL AS YOU SAY, WHY I'LL NOT REGRET IT.
WHY, MY DEAR SIR, EVERY CROWNED HEAD IN EUROPE, AND EVERY POTENTATE IN INDIA HAVE HEARD THIS REMARKABLE MACHINE PLAY, AND NOT ONE HAS BEEN DISSATISFIED = - NOR WILL YOU BE - I ASSURE YOU
DAHLINK I AM GROWING OL-DUH SILVA TREADS A-MUNK THE GO-WULD - SHINE UPON MY BROWS TOOOO-NIGHT LIFE IS FADINK FAST A-WAAAY -
THATS WHAT I CALLS, EARNING A NEAT DIME
GRAND, TOUCHING, THRILLING, SOULFUL IT WAS WORTH THE SACRAFICE I MADE TO HEAR IT.
ALL DONE FOR THE DAY, "BOSS"?
YES "KRAZY", AND A VERY PROFITABLE DAY WE'VE HAD, TOO.
WELL, ADIOS, BE ON THE JOB EARLY TOMORROW -
MY DAY'S WOIK IS DONE, SO NOW I'LL GO FORT, AND SEEK "IGNATZ" L'IL AINJIL".
DAH-LINK, I AM GROWING OLDUH SILVA TREADS A-A-A-MUNK THE GO-WULD
SHINE UP-ON MY BROWS TOO-NI-HUH-HIGHT -
LI-I-IFE IS FADINK FA A-AST A-WAY
HERRIMAN

May 27th, 1917.

HA, HE THINKS HE'LL FOOL ME WITH THAT PHONEY PHONOGRAPH AGAIN -
YOU DECEIVED ME MOST CLEVERLY WITH THAT FAKE TALKING MACHINE LAST WEEK, DID'NT YOU ? - WELL I KNOW NOW HOW YOUR TRICK IS DONE -
DECEIVED YOU ? OSIRR - OSIRR !! HOW YOU SLANDER ME WITH SUCH TALK.
YOU'RE NOT FOOLING ME, I KNOW THAT IT WAS THAT "KRAZY KAT" IN THAT BARREL WHO DID THE TALKING.
OH, HOW IT GRIEVES ME TO HEAR YOU SAY SUCH -
WHERE, OH WHERE IS HIM ?
YOU GRIEVED ME, NOW IT'S ONLY FAIR THAT I SHOULD GRIEVE YOU - WRETCH -
OGOSH - OGOSH.
WHERE CAN "IGNATZ" BE ?
DID'NT I GIVE YOU A GOOD DIME TO HEAR YOUR MACHINE SING, DID'NT I ?
YES -
A-LASS - AND A-LAX.
AND WHAT DID I HEAR, HUH, WHAT DID I HEAR - ? - ONLY THAT FOOL "KAT" SINGING INSIDE OF THAT BARREL -
BUT YOU DON'T UNDERSTAND, AMIABLE SIR.
BOOM TERRERRA BOOM TEE YAY
BUT YOU GLASS EYED GOOFERS CAN'T FOOL ME TWICE - GET OUT OF THAT BARREL, "KAT" AND
L'IL HIDE, AND SICK -
KA-A-A-A MEER - YOU -
HA HA HA HA HA HA HA HA HA
HA - HA - HA
LISTEN TO IT MOAN, PEOPLE, LISTEN TO IT MOAN !!!! IT'S FREE - THE MOANING SOUL !!! AND IT'S ALL FREE !!
M-M-MO-HO M-M-MO-HO OO-OO
KEEP IT UP DA-A-GUNYA, KEEP IT UP !!
HERRIMAN

June 3rd, 1917.

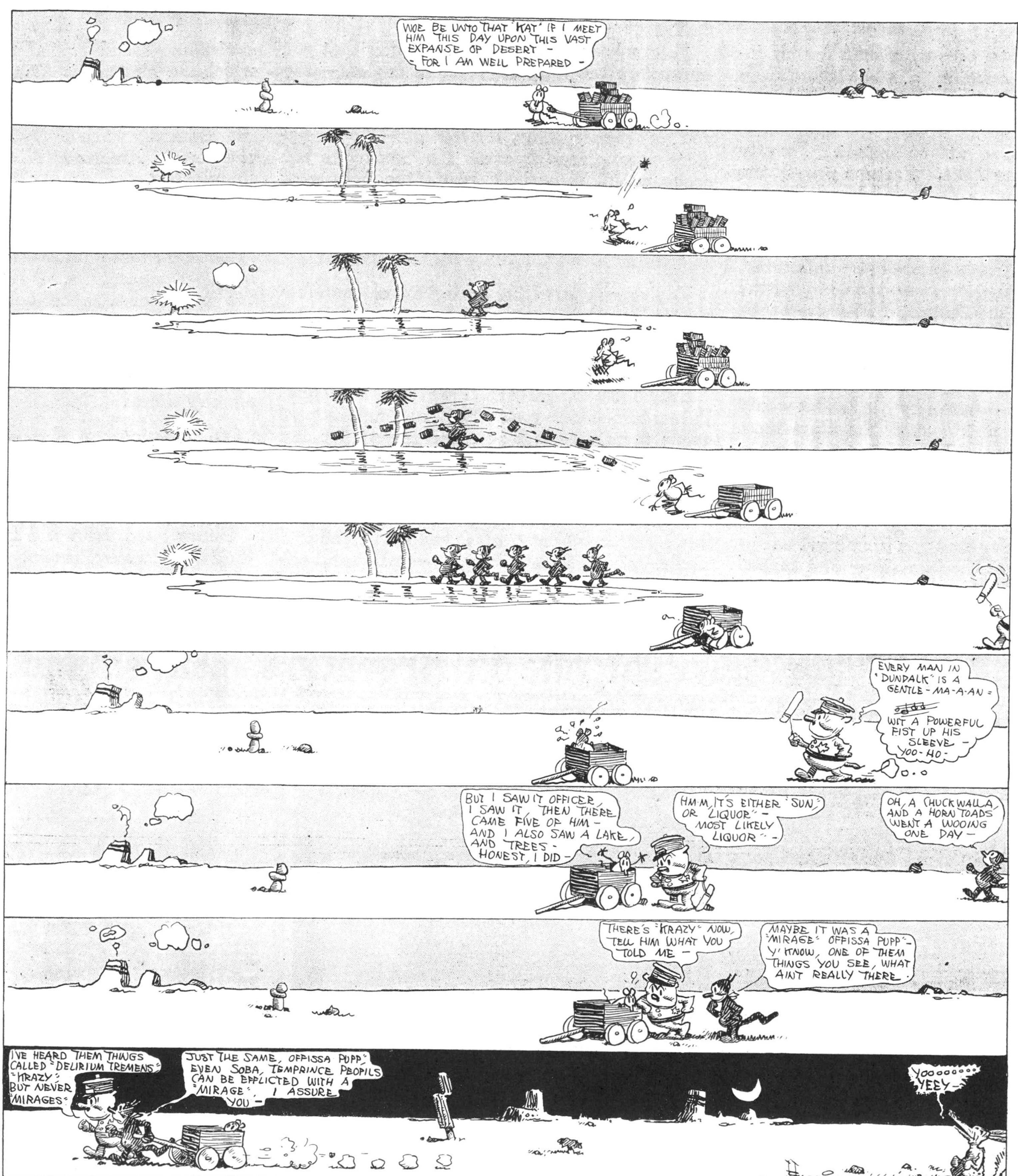

WOE BE UNTO THAT 'KAT' IF I MEET HIM THIS DAY UPON THIS VAST EXPANSE OF DESERT - - FOR I AM WELL PREPARED -
EVERY MAN IN "DUNDALK" IS A GENTLE-MA-A-AN = WIT A POWERFUL FIST UP HIS SLEEVE - YOO-HO-
BUT I SAW IT OFFICER, I SAW IT, THEN THERE CAME FIVE OF HIM - AND I ALSO SAW A LAKE, AND TREES - HONEST, I DID -
HM-M, IT'S EITHER "SUN" OR "LIQUOR" - MOST LIKELY "LIQUOR" -
OH, A CHUCKWALLA, AND A HORN TOADS WENT A WOOING ONE DAY -
THERE'S "KRAZY" NOW, TELL HIM WHAT YOU TOLD ME -
MAYBE IT WAS A "MIRAGE" OFFISSA PUPP - Y'KNOW, ONE OF THEM THINGS YOU SEE, WHAT AINT REALLY THERE -
I'VE HEARD THEM THINGS CALLED "DELIRIUM TREMENS" "KRAZY" BUT NEVER "MIRAGES"
JUST THE SAME, OFFISSA PUPP, EVEN SOBA, TEMPRINCE PEOPILS CAN BE EFFLICTED WITH A "MIRAGE", I ASSURE YOU -
YOOOOOOO YEEY -
HERRIMAN

June 10th, 1917.

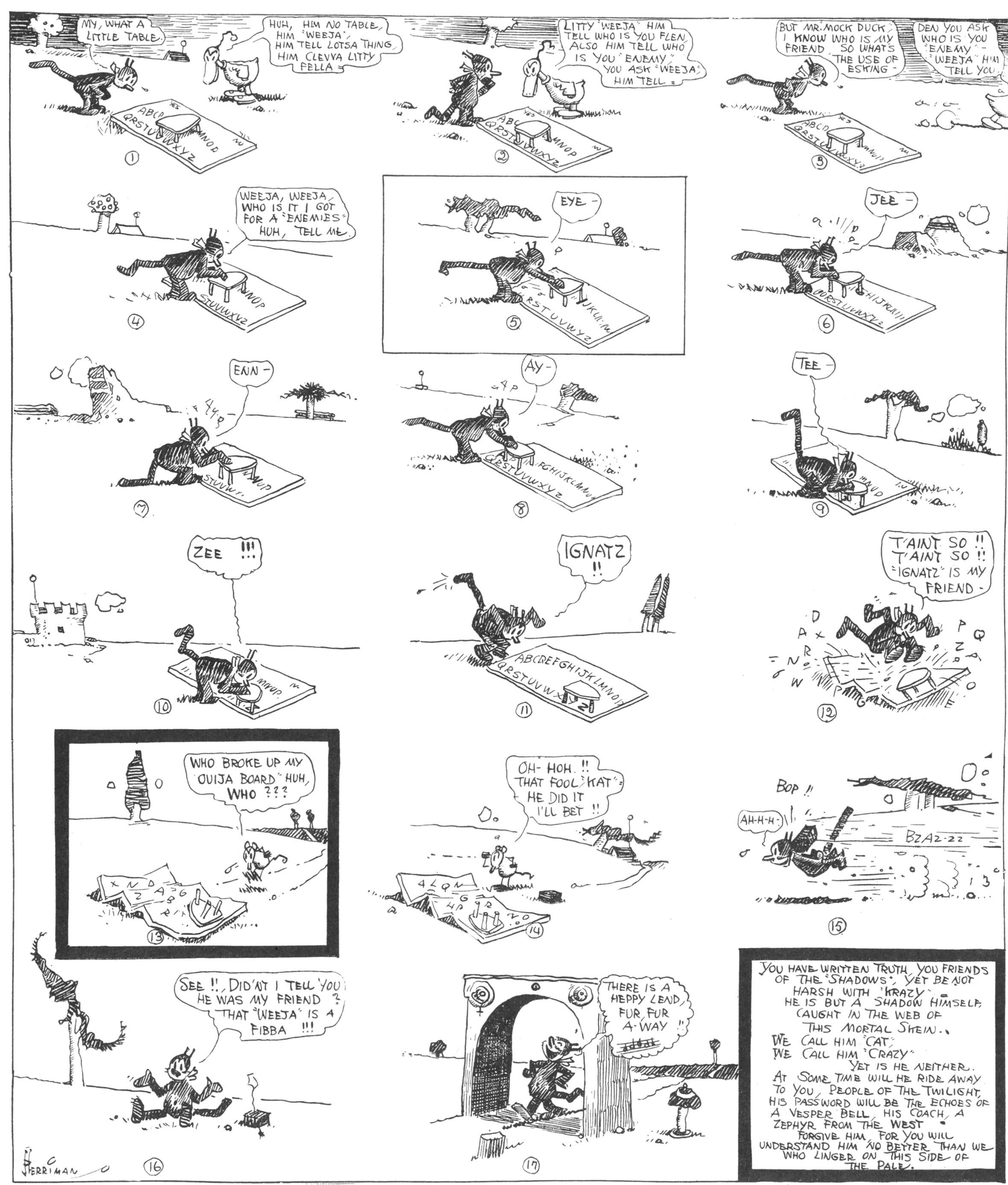

MY, WHAT A LITTLE TABLE.
HUH, HIM NO TABLE, HIM "WEEJA", HIM TELL LOTSA THING, HIM CLEVVA LITTY FELLA =
LITTY "WEEJA" HIM TELL WHO IS YOU FLEN, ALSO HIM TELL WHO IS YOU "ENEMY," YOU ASK "WEEJA" HIM TELL =
BUT MR. MOCK DUCK, I KNOW WHO IS MY FRIEND, SO WHAT'S THE USE OF ESKING -
DEN YOU ASK WHO IS YOU "ENEMY" - "WEEJA" HIM TELL YOU =
WEEJA, WEEJA, WHO IS IT I GOT FOR A "ENEMIES" HUH, TELL ME.
EYE -
JEE -
ENN -
AY -
TEE -
ZEE !!!
IGNATZ !!
T'AINT SO !! T'AINT SO !! "IGNATZ" IS MY FRIEND -
WHO BROKE UP MY OUIJA BOARD" HUH, WHO ???
OH- HOH. !! THAT FOOL "KAT" = HE DID IT I'LL BET !!
BOP !!
AH-H-H-
BZAZ-ZZ
SEE !!, DID'NT I TELL YOU HE WAS MY FRIEND ? THAT "WEEJA" IS A FIBBA !!!
THERE IS A HEPPY LEND, FUR, FUR A-WAY !!
YOU HAVE WRITTEN TRUTH, YOU FRIENDS OF THE "SHADOWS", YET BE NOT HARSH WITH "KRAZY" = HE IS BUT A SHADOW HIMSELF, CAUGHT IN THE WEB OF THIS MORTAL SKEIN.
WE CALL HIM "CAT".
WE CALL HIM "CRAZY"
YET IS HE NEITHER.
AT SOME TIME WILL HE RIDE AWAY TO YOU, PEOPLE OF THE TWILIGHT, HIS PASSWORD WILL BE THE ECHOES OF A VESPER BELL, HIS COACH, A ZEPHYR FROM THE WEST •
FORGIVE HIM, FOR YOU WILL UNDERSTAND HIM NO BETTER THAN WE WHO LINGER ON THIS SIDE OF THE PALE.
HERRIMAN

June 17th, 1917.

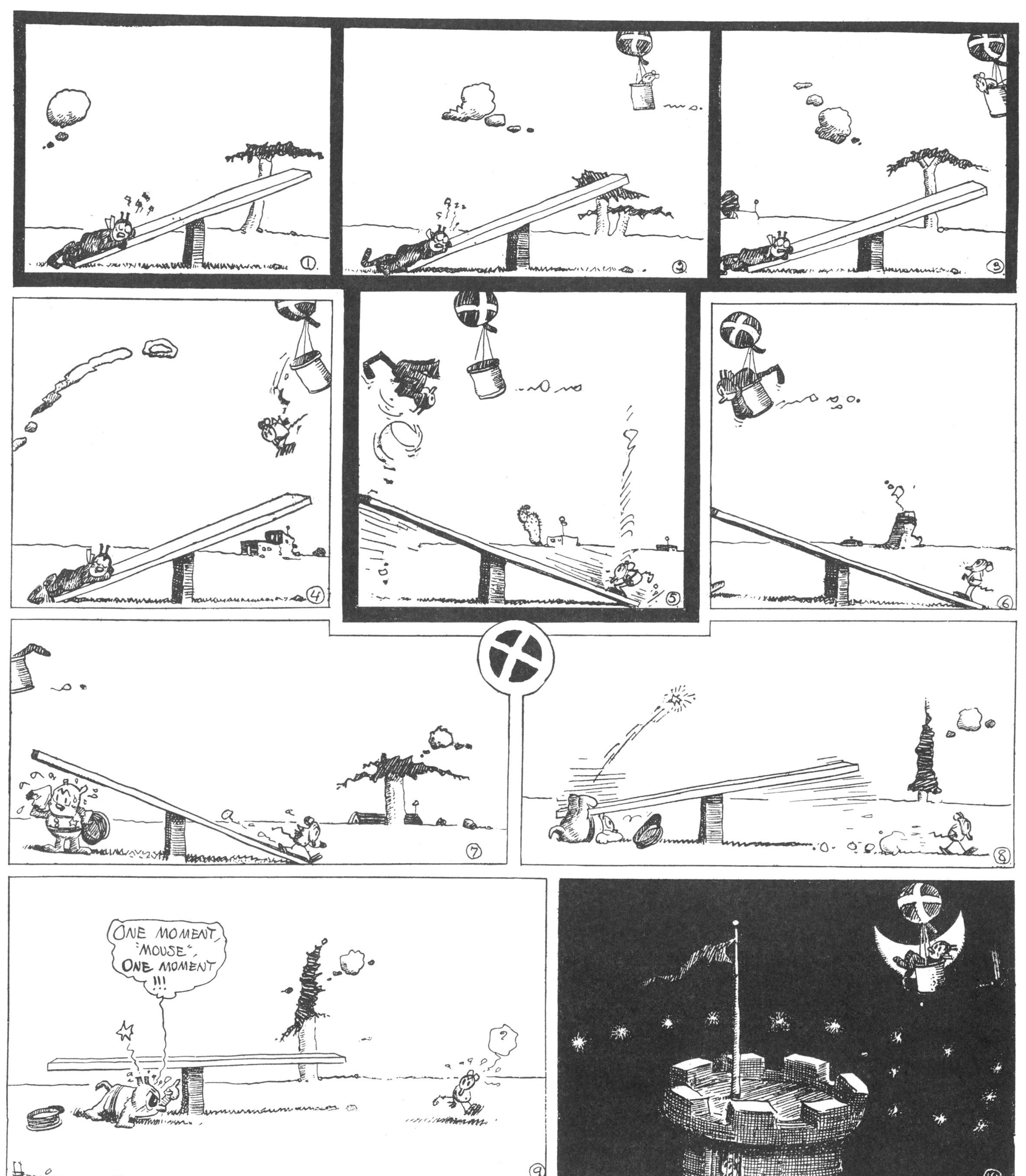

ONE MOMENT "MOUSE" ONE MOMENT !!!
HERRIMAN

June 24th, 1917.

BANG!!

POP

ZIZ

L'IL VIOLINCE.

S'ALL RIGHT, THE JUDGE'LL LISTEN TO YOUR STORY

LEDDA ZJIP ZINK WODDA I CARE ?

HERRIMAN

July 1st, 1917.

AH, UP IN THE FREE BLUE SKY, WITHOUT THE LEAST SIGN OF A "KAT" AROUND -
HELLO, "IGNATZ"
A KAT-BIRD -
I'LL DIVE FOR THAT FIELD - THERE'S NO "KAT" THERE
WHAT ARE YOU DOING IN MY KATNIP FIELD, HUH ?
I'VE GOT TO LOOK SOME OTHER PLACE
WA-AL, YOU - WHAT'S THE IDEA OF DISTOIBING ME "KATNAP" HEH ?
FWEEZY -
A DUCK-FIT IS IT ?
NO, ITS MORE LIKE A KATAPLECTIC FIT TO ME -
OOY -
RIGHT ON THE INSIDE, LADIES, AND GENTS, RIGHT ON THE INSIDE, THE ONLY WILD KAT-O-NINE-TAILS IN CAPTIVITY, THE MA-A-RVEL OF THE CENTCHRY =
S'NO USE -
THAT'S WHAT I SAID, YOUNG FELLA, I'M THE MEANEST, ORNERIEST KATAMOUNT IN THESE HERE HILLS, I AM -
GOLLIES -
THAT'S IT YOU BIG BRUTE PICK ON ME, JUST BECAUSE I'M ONLY A LIL BIT OF A "KATAPILLAR"
A-AH SHUT UP -
MEAN MOUSE
I AINT BEEN THE SAME SINCE I GOT THIS "KATARACT" ON ME EYE, "IGNATZ" - NO, NOT THE SAME A-TALL -
AT LAST = NOTHING HERE TO SUGGEST "KATS" TO ME
NICE WATER FALL, EH ?
SWELLEST "KATARACT" EVER I SEE
CAN I GET ABOARD OF YOUR BOAT, SIR ?
THIS AINT NO BOAT, ITS A "KATAMARAN"
A KATFISH -
SURE, I'M A "KATFISH" - KRAZY KAT'S KOUSIN -
I WUNDA WHERE IS "IGNATZ MICE" ALL THIS WET WEDDA ?
ASLEEPING IN THE RAIN, AND RETTLING ALL OVA WITH A CHILLS - POOR LIL "AINJIL"
THERE NOW - S'MO BETTA THUS
I HOPE HE HAS A PLEASANT DREAM.
HERRIMAN.

July 8th, 1917.

ALL THE DAY LONG MY SED, SED HEART HAS YEARNT FOR IGNATZ
AH-H-H
HE HAS SENT TO ME A TOKIN OF LOVE.
S'NO USE, WITH A "ROMEO" LIKE "IGNATZ" I'M A HEPPY, HEPPY "JULIUS"
COME ON, "JAKE" SHOOT IT OVER.
A-GAIN, HE TOSSES ME A MESSAGE OF TENDANISS
BZZEEE
OH LOVE, LOVE, LO-O-OVE WOTTA WONDAFIL THING YOU ADE
I WILL SIT HERE TO KONTEMPLATE UPON THE BLISSFIL MYSTERIES OF THE SOUL'S SUBLIME PESSION.
KUPID IS YODLING A SONG TO ME HOO-LEE-HOO-LEE HOO-OOO-OO HOO LEE HOOLEE HOOOO
I'LL REST HERE A WHILE, AND BESK IN THE SUNSHINE OF DEWOTION
DANGER
BAM
ALL DAY, "IGNATZ" YOU HAVE SHOWERED UPON ME, MENIFISTITIONS OF TENDANISS, BUT THAT LAST ONE, IGNATZES OLE TOPSY, THAT LAST ONE WAS THE GRENDEST OF THEM ALL
WHO, ME ??
WHY I HAVE'NT LAID EYES ON YOU, ALL DAY, FOOL
ZIB
MY DISH OF ROMENCE IS FULL AND I'M A HEPPY, HEPPY, HEPPY KET
KRAZY AS A "KOOT"
HERRIMAN.

July 15th, 1917.

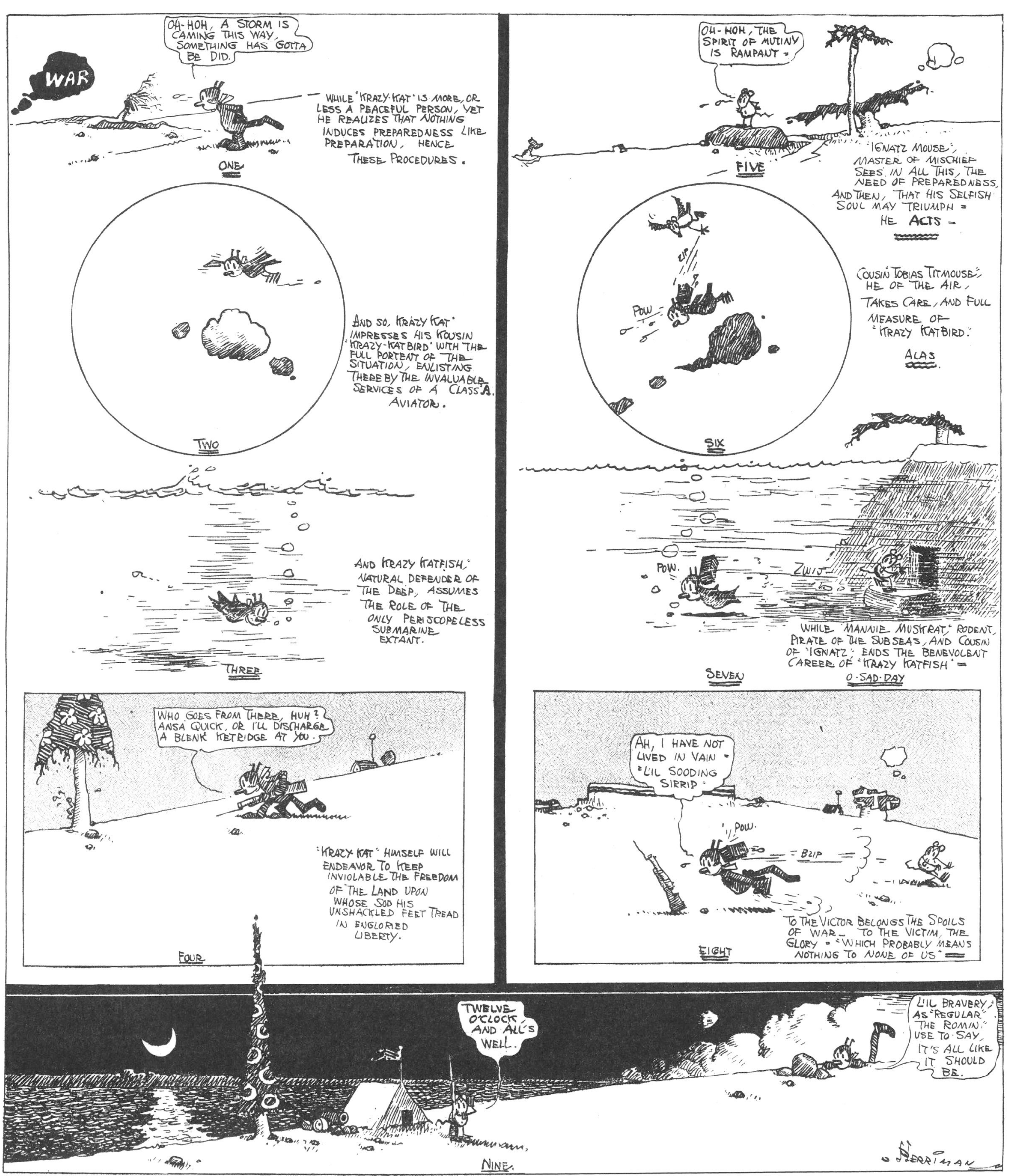
WAR
OH-HOH, A STORM IS CAMING THIS WAY, SOMETHING HAS GOTTA BE DID.
WHILE 'KRAZY KAT' IS MORE, OR LESS A PEACEFUL PERSON, YET HE REALIZES THAT NOTHING INDUCES PREPAREDNESS LIKE PREPARATION, HENCE THESE PROCEDURES.
ONE
AND SO, 'KRAZY KAT' IMPRESSES HIS KOUSIN 'KRAZY-KATBIRD' WITH THE FULL PORTENT OF THE SITUATION, ENLISTING THEREBY THE INVALUABLE SERVICES OF A CLASS A. AVIATOR.
TWO
AND 'KRAZY KATFISH' NATURAL DEFENDER OF THE DEEP, ASSUMES THE ROLE OF THE ONLY PERISCOPELESS SUBMARINE EXTANT.
THREE
WHO GOES FROM THERE, HUH? ANSA QUICK, OR I'LL DISCHARGE A BLENK KETRIDGE AT YOU.
'KRAZY KAT' HIMSELF WILL ENDEAVOR TO KEEP INVIOLABLE THE FREEDOM OF THE LAND UPON WHOSE SOD HIS UNSHACKLED FEET TREAD IN ENGLORIED LIBERTY.
FOUR
OH-HOH, THE SPIRIT OF MUTINY IS RAMPANT =
'IGNATZ MOUSE', MASTER OF MISCHIEF SEES IN ALL THIS, THE NEED OF PREPAREDNESS, AND THEN, THAT HIS SELFISH SOUL MAY TRIUMPH = HE ACTS =
FIVE
ZIP
POW
COUSIN 'TOBIAS TITMOUSE', HE OF THE AIR, TAKES CARE, AND FULL MEASURE OF 'KRAZY KATBIRD.'
ALAS
SIX
POW.
ZWIJ
WHILE 'MANNIE MUSKRAT', RODENT, PIRATE OF THE SUBSEAS, AND COUSIN OF 'IGNATZ', ENDS THE BENEVOLENT CAREER OF 'KRAZY KATFISH' =
SEVEN
O-SAD-DAY
AH, I HAVE NOT LIVED IN VAIN = 'LIL SOODING SIRRIP'
POW.
BZIP
TO THE VICTOR BELONGS THE SPOILS OF WAR_ TO THE VICTIM, THE GLORY = 'WHICH PROBABLY MEANS NOTHING TO NONE OF US' =
EIGHT
TWELVE O'CLOCK AND ALL'S WELL.
'LIL BRAVERY', AS 'REGULAR' THE ROMIN USE TO SAY, IT'S ALL LIKE IT SHOULD BE.
NINE
HERRIMAN

July 22nd, 1917.

TIC TIC TIC
ONE.
TIC TIC
TWO.
TIC TIC TIC
THREE.
AND SO, A BIT OF PILFERING WAS PERPETRATED !! INVOLVING AS IT WERE THE LOSS OF AN "EXPENSIBLE" WATCH, WHICH TICKED, TOCKED, AND TOLD TIME LIKE ANY OTHER OF THE CLOCK FAMILY = FROM A MONETARY VIEWPOINT A FULL DOLLAR'S WORTH OF HOROLOGE PASSED OUT OF THE POSSESSION OF "IGNATZ MOUSE" = YOU MAY NOW GO ON WITH YE TALE.
"IGNATZ" !! AH-H HOW QUEEN LIKE HE LOOKS — "LIL" SNAMBILISK"
FOUR.
FIVE.
? ? ? ? ? ?
SIX.
MY WATCH !! MY WATCH !! IT'S GONE.
SEVEN.
POLICE !! POLICE !!
EIGHT.
OFFICER, I DESIRE TO HAVE THIS "KAT" ARRESTED FOR STEALING MY WATCH !!!
WHO, ME ?
NINE.
"KRAZY," DID YOU TAKE HIS WATCH ?
OH, NO, OFFISSA "PUPP." OH, NO.
TEN.
WAL, "MOUSE," DO YOU PRESS THIS CHARGE ?
YOU BET I DO —
ODEER, ODEER
ELEVEN.
I HATE TO DO THIS, "KRAZY."
I KNOW MY RIGHTS, AND I INSIST UPON IT.
TWELVE.
TIC TIC TIC
? ? ?
THIRTEEN.
HARK !!
TIC TIC TIC
FOURTEEN.
HEY, YOU !! WAKE UP !!
TIC TIC TIC
FIFTEEN.
CANTCHA LET A FELLA SLEEP, AND DIGEST A "WATCH" IN PEACE, HUH ??
DO YOU HEAR THAT, "IGNATZ" ? DO YOU WISH TO SWITCH THE CHARGE OF THEFT TO HIM ?
TIC TIC TIC TIC
?!!?
SIXTEEN.
WAL, WOT ABOUT THAT CHARGE, HUH ?
N-N-N NOTHING S-S-SIR.
C'MON "KRAZY" LET HIM SETTLE IT WITH MR. OSTRICH
TIC TIC TIC TIC
SEVENTEEN.
TIC TIC TIC TIC TIC
OH-HM-M-M-
HERRIMAN
EIGHTEEN.

July 29th, 1917.

AH-H-
ALL'S SREEN
PLUP.
AH-H-
ALL'S WELL
SLUP.
EH-HEH-H-
ALL'S HUNKA DORA-
DLUP.
GLUP.
ZLUP.
ALL'S WELL.
ALL'S PUTTY GOOD.
YES, ALL IS AS IT SHOULD BE, "CALM" !!!
HERRIMAN

August 5th, 1917.

IT'S "IGNATZ'S" BIRTH-DAY, AND I'VE MADE A BIG CAKE, BUT THE "CANDLES" I ORDERED HAVE 'NT COME YET, AND I DONT KNOW WHAT TO DO.
AINT THAT TOO BAD NOW-
ONE.
TWO.
THE "TULE" GROVE, HOME OF MR. & MRS. "GLIMMERING GLOWERM", AND THEIR FAMILY.
THREE.
MR. GLOWERM, CAN I GET ABOUT FIVE OF YOUR BEST GLOWERS TO DO ME A FAVOR TONIGHT ?
YOU SURE CAN, "KRAZY"
FOUR.
FOLLA ME, BOYS, FOLLA ME.
FIVE.
?
I'LL ADMICK THESE STICKS DUNT LOOK MUCH LIKE "KENDLES" MRS. MICE, BUT HAVE A PATIENCE, AND ALL WILL BE WELL.
SIX.
??
NOW, SUSIE, JAKIE, HETTIE, MEGGIE, AND WALTA GLOWERMS TAKE YOUR SITS, AND REMEMBA WHAT I TOLD YOU. I'M GOING OUT TO TEND TO A L'IL BITTA BUSINESS
SEVEN.
MR. KELLY, I DESIRE TO PERCHIZ THE BEST "BRICK" YOU GOT FOR NINE CENTS, AS IT'S A BIRTH'S-DAY PRESENT FOR A MOST PITTICULA FRIEND OF MINE.
KOLIN KELLY DEALER IN BRICKS.
I'VE GOT THE VERY "BRICK" YOU WANT, "KRAZY"
NINE.
AND NEVER DID A CAKE RADIATE MORE CHEER THAN THIS ONE, WHICH ACCLAIMED "IGNATZ MOUSE" FIVE YEARS OF AGE.
EIGHT.
HERRIMAN

August 12th, 1917.

OH DOC, OH DOC. IF ONLY I COULD HAVE JUST A WEE BIT OF "CHEESE" -
NO "CHEESE" UNTIL YOU GET WELL -
I'LL SEE THAT HE DOES'NT GET ANY, "DOCTOR".
HOSPITAL
OH-H- POOR- POO-O-OOR LI'L "IGNATZ".
KRAZY, WHO IS AS NOSEY AS A SWORD-FISH, NOSES ABOUT A BIT, AND SO KNOWS MORE NOW THAN HE DID BEFORE.
ONE.
A CHEESE, A CHEESE, MY KING'S-DIM FOR A CHEESE !!
TWO.
O-HO-
"KRAZY," WHOSE INTELLECT IS ONLY A LITTLE BIT "THIS," AND A LITTLE BIT "THAT," BEHOLD'S THE RISING MOON - AND SO ENJOYS THE SENSATION OF AN "IDEA" IN PROCESS OF DEVELOPMENT.
THREE.
I'LL DESH UP TO THE TOP OF THE "HILL," AND WHEN THAT "MOON" GOES OVER IT, I'LL GRAB OFF A CHUNK OF IT = "IGNATZ" MUST, AND WILL HAVE "CHEESE".
FOUR.
HAIV-A-HO- !!
CHEESE
GOING UP THE SAME HILL WERE A NUMBER OF "SMUGGLER MICE" LADEN WITH CASEOUS BOOTY.
FIVE.
RUN FELLAS, RUN, THERE'S A "CAT" COMING UP THE "HILL," DROP EVERY THING, AND RUN !!!
CHEESE
SIX.
CHEESE
SEVEN.
GOSH !! WHY DONT "MOONS" GROW ON THE GROUND ENSTEAD OF UP IN THE AIR = IT WOULD BE SO MUCH EASIER TO GET "CHEESE" FOR LI'L SICK MICES THEN =
IN THE MEANWHILE "KRAZY" RESTS IN HIS LABOR OF LOVE.
EIGHT.
WOT'S AT, HUH, WOT'S AT
BZIZ
NINE
BZ-Z-ZEE-
HOSPITAL
TEN.
OH, HAPPY, HAPPY DAY !!!
POW
CHEESE
ELEVEN
TWELVE.
HERRIMAN

August 19th, 1917.

YOU WIP, MISSERS 'MICE': YOU WIP, FOR WHY MAY I ESK ?
OUR ALARM-CLOCK REFUSES TO ALARM, AND 'IGNATZ' MY HUSBAND CANNOT BE AWAKENED.
ONE.
TWO.
JEWELER AND CLOCKIST
YOUR CHOICE ALARM CLOCKS $1.98
$1.98
THREE.
$1.98. MY-MY. I HAD NO IDA ALARMING CLOCKS WAS SO EXPENSIBLE - STILL, I GOTTA GET ONE.
FOUR.
$1.98 = OGOSH, OGOSH !! OH WOULD THAT I WAS MORE MILLIONAIRISH IN MY FINENCES. OGOSH, ODEER OMY !!!
#1.98
FIVE.
HOWEVER IT DUNT COST NOTHING TO MOURN, AND MOAN OVER MY STATE OF POORISHNESS, SO I'LL MOURN, AND MOAN A BIT.
SIX.
MEE EE YOW !!!
?
SEVEN.
MR-R-R YOW- WOW WOW OW
EIGHT.
SKAT !! YOU SCOUNDREL SKAT !!
POW
NINE.
?
TEN.
GRRR RARR ING,
BING,
R-R-R
RRRR ZING ZING
BRRR RING
AH-H-
ELEVEN.
L'IL SNAMBLIST, HE IS NOW FULLY AWAKE, AND FULL OF HIS USUAL ECTIVITIES.
ZIF
AND IN DUE TIME MRS. MOUSE BECAME THE RECIPIENT OF MANY SLEEP DESTROYING CHRONOMETERS, AND 'IGNATZ' AROSE FROM A DEEP DREAM OF PEACE.
HERRIMAN

August 26th, 1917.

BREAKFAST !!!
IT IS MORNING TIME ON THE "DESIERTO PINTADO" AND "IGNATZ MOUSE" CLAMORS LOUDLY FOR FOOD =
ONE
WELL FOOL, WHAT ABOUT IT, HUH ?
OH, NOT SO MUCH ABOUT IT, "IGNATZ", Y'SEE I NEVER THOUGHT ABOUT IT =
TWO
HAM, AND EGGS MILK, AND TEA SUGAR, AND SALT, AND ALSO PEPPER BUT PARTICULARLY THE "HAM" - THAT'S WHAT I WANT FOR BREAKFAST.
I SHELL ENDEVVA TO PERKUE THEM -
THREE
AH-H - A "EGG'S-PLANT"
FOUR
AND A "MILK'S-WEED"
FIVE
A "TEA-ROSE", AND A "SUGAR'S-CANE" NOT BAD, DESS RIGHT
SIX
MY-MY-MY- THIS BREAD-FRUIT TREE HAS GOT SUCH A VARIETY OF "BREADS" ON IT, IT'S A DIFFICULTY TO KNOW WHICH KIND "IGNATZ" LIKES MORE BEST.
SEVEN
YES MR. MUTTINS, I'M LOOKING FOR SALTS, AND PEPPA
YOU'LL FIND THE "SALT-LICKS" "KRAZY", OVER THERE, UNDER THAT OLD "PEPPER-TREE"
EIGHT
AH-H - A UMBA-RELLA TREE -
NINE
BRECK-FISS !!
TEN
ELEVEN
L'IL AINJIL HOW SHOCKED WITH DELIGHT HE IS =
LOAFER !!
?
ZIP
POP.
TWELVE
HOW DID I EVER FURGIT THE "HAM" ?
THIRTEEN
HERRIMAN

September 2nd, 1917.

BLOP !!
ZIZZ
TAKE THAT, !!!
?
?
?
?
?
FOOL.
?
CAN IT BE POSSIBLE ?
IT CANT BE "KRAZY" - IT MUST BE SOME ONE DISGUISED LIKE HIM.
PERHAPS IT WAS A MIRAGE WE SAW -
MAYBE WE WERE ALL DREAMING
IT COULD'NT BE, NO-NO-NO - IT COULD'NT BE OUR "KRAZY", IT SIMPLY COULD'NT BE.
!
WE BEG PARDON SIR, BUT REALLY SIR, ARE YOU, OR ARE YOU NOT "KRAZY KAT" ?
WHO ME ? ME, "KRAZY KAT" ? ME ?
AH -
I'M "IGNATZ MOUSE", I AM - "IGNATZ MOUSE" - THAT'S WHO I AM.
AH, SIMBIL OF LOVE, OH, EMBLIM OF DEWOTION, OY, TOKIN OF ES-STEAM, FROM "IGNATZ", "IGNATZ" MOST GLORIOUS OF MOUSES.
WELL, NOW THAT ALL HAS BEEN SAID, AND DONE, YOU KNOW AS MUCH, IF NOT LESS THAN WE DO ABOUT IT. HOWEVER, "MOCK DUCK", HE OF THE MYSTERIOUS ORIENT MAY IN SOME SOON TIME BREAK THROUGH THIS OCCULT VEIL, AND LET IN THE LIGHT WHICH IS NOW DENIED TO OUR MEAGER VISION.
BIME BYE I TELL, BIME BYE EBBY TING BE PLAIN LIKE DAY TIME.
HERRIMAN

September 9th, 1917.

MBOB !
JAZZZZ
IF YOU REMEMBER, THIS INCREDIBLE SCENE HAPPENED A FEW DAYS AGO.
"MOCK DUCK", SAGE OF THE ORIENT,
HE WHO DEALS IN THE TREASURES OF THE OCCULT WORLD WILL NOW DRAG FROM IT'S MOST MYSTERIOUS RECESS THE INSIDE STORY OF THIS INEXPLICABLE DENOUEMENT.
TOOZDI NIGHT, LASH WEEK "IGNOSH MICE" AND "KLAZY KAT" HE GO TAKE BIG SLEEP TOGEDDA - YEZZA -
PIDDY SOON, "IGNOSH" HE DLEAM, SO HIM "SPILIT" GO OUT BYE-BYE - DEN "KLAZY" HE CATCH DLEAM TOO, AND HIM "SPILIT" HE GO BYE-BYE TOO - YOU SHOBBY ? YIZZA - VELLY WELL.
YOU SHOBBY WHAT PLACE "LIGHT" GO TO WHEN "LIGHT" GO OUT ? WELL, DASH SAME PLACE WHAT DEM TWO "SPILITS" GO TO - -YIZZA-
WELL, NOW COME TLEE, FO CLOCK MONNING TIME MISTA "SUN" HE GOT IDA IS TIME FO COME UP. AND WHEN "SUN" COME UP, IS TIME FO "SPILIT" TO COME BACK HOME - YIZZA.
SO SPILITS SEE "SUN" COME UP, AND GET HIP MUCH EXCITE, AND COME BACK HOME FAST LIKE EBBY TING - YIPPY, SHOO MIKE.
BUT, IGNOSH'S SPILIT MAKE BIG MISTAKE, HE COME BACK BY "KLAZY", AND "KLAZY'S" SPILIT HE MAKE BIG MISTAKE TOO, AND COME BACK TO "IGNOSH" - SO EBBY TING ALL LONG - EBBY TING ALL LONG - -YIZZA-
NOW, YOU SEE HOW IT IS - ?
L'IL AINJIL.
FOOL "KAT."
HERRIMAN

September 16th, 1917.

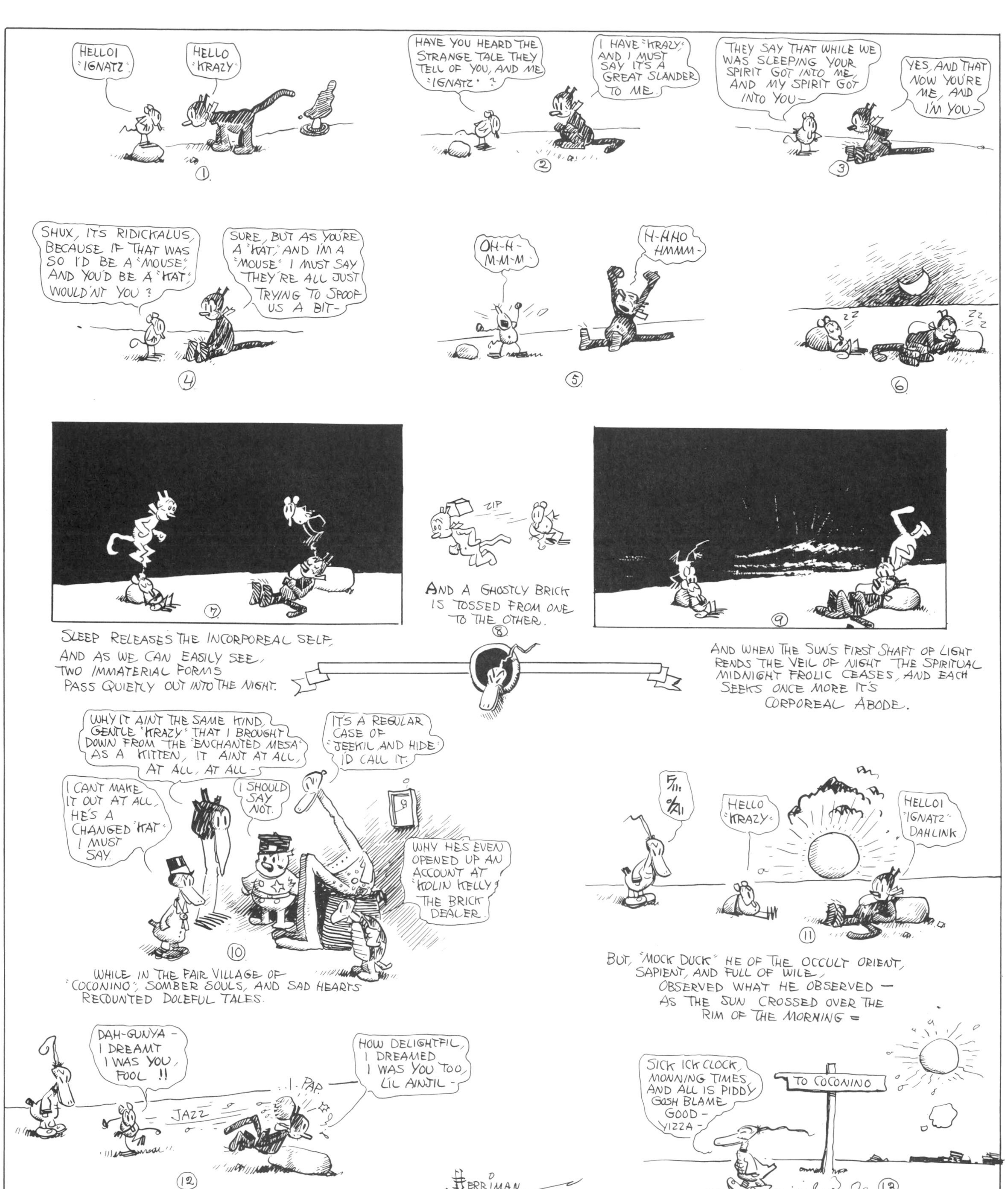

HELLO! "IGNATZ"
HELLO "KRAZY"
HAVE YOU HEARD THE STRANGE TALE THEY TELL OF YOU, AND ME "IGNATZ"?
I HAVE "KRAZY" AND I MUST SAY IT'S A GREAT SLANDER TO ME.
THEY SAY THAT WHILE WE WAS SLEEPING YOUR SPIRIT GOT INTO ME, AND MY SPIRIT GOT INTO YOU-
YES, AND THAT NOW YOU'RE ME, AND I'M YOU-
SHUX, ITS RIDICKALUS, BECAUSE IF THAT WAS SO I'D BE A "MOUSE", AND YOU'D BE A "KAT" WOULD'NT YOU?
SURE, BUT AS YOU'RE A "KAT", AND I'M A "MOUSE" I MUST SAY THEY'RE ALL JUST TRYING TO SPOOF US A BIT-
OH-H-M-M-M
H-HHO HMMM-
ZZ
ZZ Z
ZIP
AND A GHOSTLY BRICK IS TOSSED FROM ONE TO THE OTHER.
SLEEP RELEASES THE INCORPOREAL SELF, AND AS WE CAN EASILY SEE, TWO IMMATERIAL FORMS PASS QUIETLY OUT INTO THE NIGHT.
AND WHEN THE SUN'S FIRST SHAFT OF LIGHT RENDS THE VEIL OF NIGHT THE SPIRITUAL MIDNIGHT FROLIC CEASES, AND EACH SEEKS ONCE MORE IT'S CORPOREAL ABODE.
WHY IT AINT THE SAME KIND, GENTLE "KRAZY" THAT I BROUGHT DOWN FROM THE "ENCHANTED MESA" AS A KITTEN, IT AINT AT ALL, AT ALL, AT ALL-
IT'S A REGULAR CASE OF "JEEKIL AND HIDE" I'D CALL IT.
I CANT MAKE IT OUT AT ALL, HE'S A CHANGED "KAT" I MUST SAY.
I SHOULD SAY NOT.
WHY HE'S EVEN OPENED UP AN ACCOUNT AT KOLIN KELLY'S THE BRICK DEALER.
WHILE IN THE FAIR VILLAGE OF "COCONINO" SOMBER SOULS, AND SAD HEARTS RECOUNTED DOLEFUL TALES.
HELLO "KRAZY"
HELLO! "IGNATZ" DAHLINK
BUT, "MOCK DUCK" HE OF THE OCCULT ORIENT, SAPIENT, AND FULL OF WILE, OBSERVED WHAT HE OBSERVED — AS THE SUN CROSSED OVER THE RIM OF THE MORNING =
DAH-GUNYA - I DREAMT I WAS YOU, FOOL !!
JAZZ
PAP
HOW DELIGHTFIL, I DREAMED I WAS YOU TOO, LIL AINJIL-
SICK ICK CLOCK, MONNING TIMES AND ALL IS PIDDY GOSH BLAME GOOD - YIZZA-
TO COCONINO
HERRIMAN

September 23rd, 1917.

"KNODDING KORN" A VEGETABLE WHOSE INTELLIGENCE IS OFTEN DISPUTED.
"KRAZY," A "KAT" TO WHOM NO SINCERE CREDIT IS GIVEN IN MATTERS OF THE MIND.
"IGNATZ", A MOUSE, WHOSE ASTUTE ERUDITION IS NEVER DOUBTED.
NOW FOR THE DISPLAY !!!.
HERE IS IT TIMES FOR MY JOGRAPHY LESSON, AND I DON'T KNOW NOTHING ABOUT IT, ODEER, OGOSH, OSHUX.
WELL, AND WHITHER LIES THE "EAST" ?
M-M-M-M LESSEE, LESSEE
THATA WAY-
CORRECT.
AND WHERE IS THE "WEST" ?
ONA THIS'A WAY.
RIGHT.
M-M-M-AH-H-
WHERE IS THE NORTH ?
UP YON.
GOOD.
QUICK, QUICK - THE "SOUTH" WHERE IS IT ?
THERE.
WELL, I MUST GIVE YOU CREDIT, I DID'NT THINK YOU KNEW SO MUCH.
OH, DUNT GIVE ME CREDICK, GIVE IT TO YON "KORNS" 'TWAS HIS WUNDAFIL BRAINS WHAT DONE IT ALL.
JUST WHEN HE SHOWS A SPARK OF INTELLIGENCE, "BING" !! HE FALLS TO THE LEVEL OF A MERE "VEGETABLE" - "POOR FOOL"
PLOP
JAZZ-ZZ
WHAT A MARWILLIS FRUIT IS A "KORNS"
YES WE ARE VERY, VERY SUPERSTITIOUS.
HERRIMAN

September 30th, 1917.

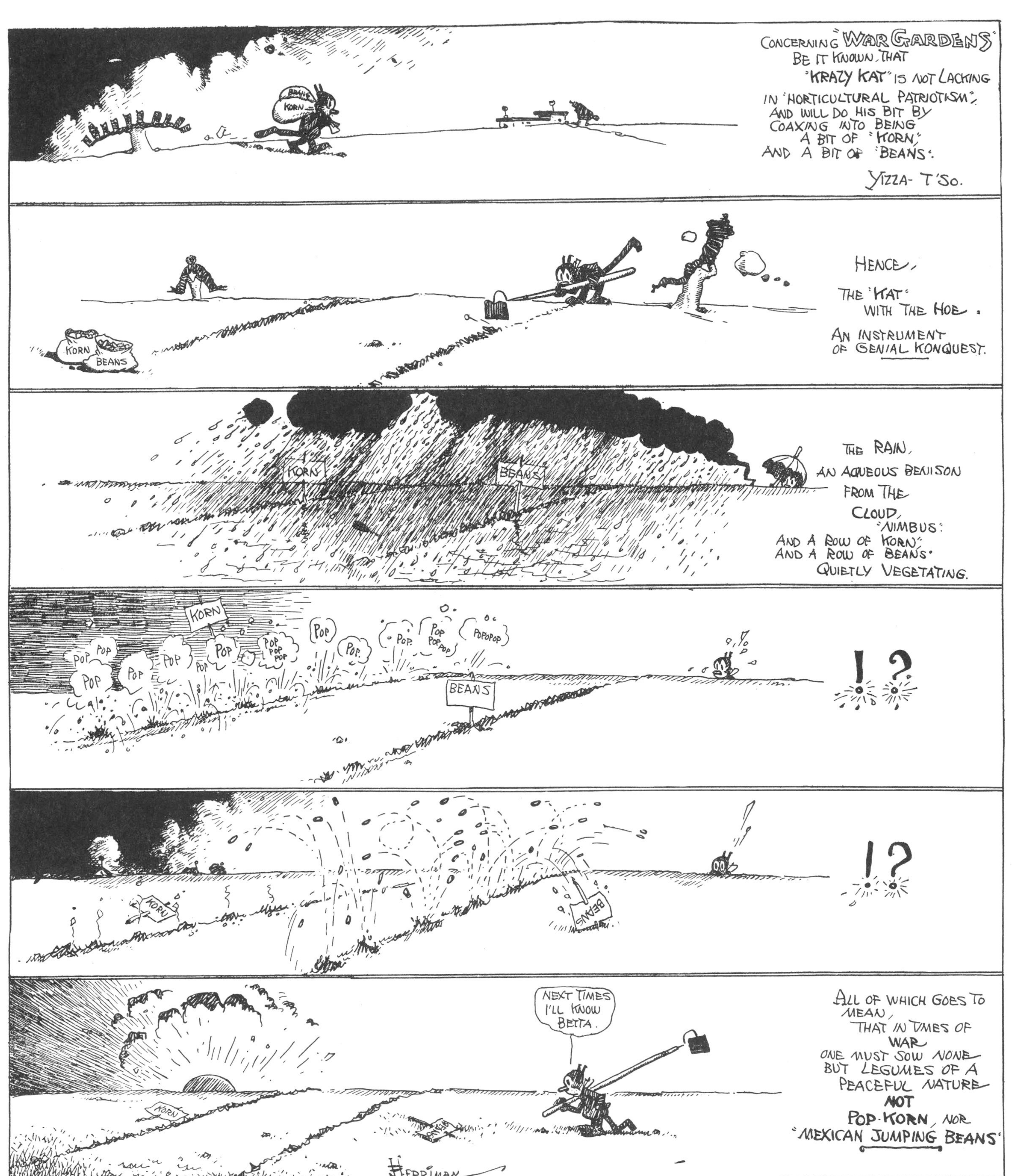

CONCERNING "WAR GARDENS"
BE IT KNOWN, THAT
"KRAZY KAT" IS NOT LACKING
IN "HORTICULTURAL PATRIOTISM",
AND WILL DO HIS BIT BY
COAXING INTO BEING
A BIT OF "KORN",
AND A BIT OF "BEANS".
YIZZA- T'SO.
BEANS
KORN
HENCE,
THE "KAT"
WITH THE HOE.
AN INSTRUMENT
OF GENIAL KONQUEST.
KORN
BEANS
THE RAIN,
AN AQUEOUS BENISON
FROM THE
CLOUD,
"NIMBUS".
AND A ROW OF "KORN",
AND A ROW OF "BEANS".
QUIETLY VEGETATING.
KORN
BEANS
POP POP
POP
POP
POP
POP
POP
POP POP POP
POP
POP
POP.
POP POP POP
POPOPOP
BEANS
!?
KORN
BEANS
!?
NEXT TIMES I'LL KNOW BETTA.
KORN
ALL OF WHICH GOES TO
MEAN,
THAT IN TIMES OF
WAR
ONE MUST SOW NONE
BUT LEGUMES OF A
PEACEFUL NATURE
NOT
POP-KORN, NOR
"MEXICAN JUMPING BEANS"
HERRIMAN

October 7th, 1917.

THERE WILL BE LOOT, AND BOOTY ENOUGH FOR ALL.
AND SO MY BRAVE MEN WHEN THE MANTLE OF NIGHT BLANKETS THE LAND WE SHALL MAKE THE RAID.
'TIS WELL.
FAIR ENOUGH.
GOOD.
IGNATZ: PLOTTING A PLOTS OY-OY-YOY.
ONE
TWO
PAINTS
THREE
FOUR
IN TIME !! THENX TO GOODNISS.
FIVE
INTERMISSION !!
DURING WHICH TIME WE WILL CUT BACK A BIT, AND MINGLE WITH THE CONSPIRATORS.
FOLLOW ME.
SIX
ALL'S WELL, APPROACH WITH CAUTION.
SEVEN
EIGHT
HE HE HE HE HE
NINE
QUIRQUE !!
DUNT WOIRY MRS. HENN; S'ONLY A L'IL BIT OF GRESS, AND A L'IL BIT OF PAINT - AND ALL'S WELL.
TEN
THERE IS A HEPPY LEND, FUR, FUR A-WA-AY
ELEVEN

October 14th, 1917.

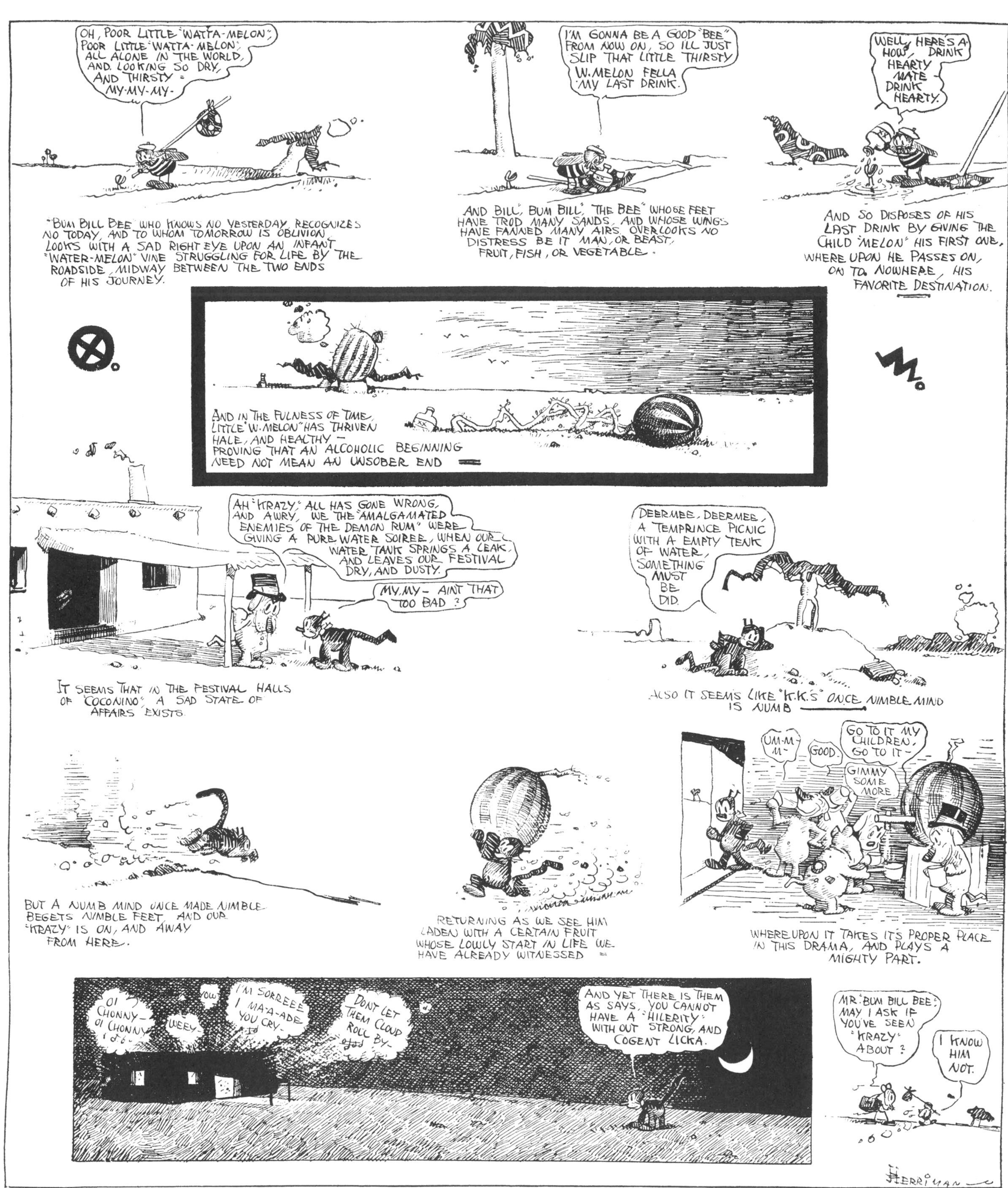
OH, POOR LITTLE "WATTA-MELON", POOR LITTLE "WATTA-MELON", ALL ALONE IN THE WORLD, AND LOOKING SO DRY, AND THIRSTY = MY-MY-MY-
"BUM BILL BEE" WHO KNOWS NO YESTERDAY, RECOGNIZES NO TODAY, AND TO WHOM TOMORROW IS OBLIVION, LOOKS WITH A SAD RIGHT EYE UPON AN INFANT "WATER-MELON" VINE STRUGGLING FOR LIFE BY THE ROADSIDE, MIDWAY BETWEEN THE TWO ENDS OF HIS JOURNEY.
I'M GONNA BE A GOOD "BEE" FROM NOW ON, SO ILL JUST SLIP THAT LITTLE THIRSTY W. MELON FELLA MY LAST DRINK.
AND BILL, "BUM BILL" "THE BEE" WHOSE FEET HAVE TROD MANY SANDS, AND WHOSE WINGS HAVE FANNED MANY AIRS, OVERLOOKS NO DISTRESS BE IT MAN, OR BEAST, FRUIT, FISH, OR VEGETABLE.
WELL, HERE'S A-HOW, DRINK HEARTY MATE DRINK HEARTY.
AND SO DISPOSES OF HIS LAST DRINK BY GIVING THE CHILD "MELON" HIS FIRST ONE, WHERE UPON HE PASSES ON, ON TO NOWHERE, HIS FAVORITE DESTINATION.
AND IN THE FULNESS OF TIME, LITTLE "W. MELON" HAS THRIVEN HALE, AND HEALTHY - PROVING THAT AN ALCOHOLIC BEGINNING NEED NOT MEAN AN UNSOBER END =
AH "KRAZY", ALL HAS GONE WRONG, AND AWRY, WE THE "AMALGAMATED ENEMIES OF THE DEMON RUM" WERE GIVING A PURE WATER SOIREE, WHEN OUR WATER TANK SPRINGS A LEAK, AND LEAVES OUR FESTIVAL DRY, AND DUSTY.
MY, MY - AINT THAT TOO BAD ?
IT SEEMS THAT IN THE FESTIVAL HALLS OF "COCONINO", A SAD STATE OF AFFAIRS EXISTS.
DEERMEE, DEERMEE, A TEMPRINCE PICNIC WITH A EMPTY TENK OF WATER, SOMETHING MUST BE DID.
ALSO IT SEEMS LIKE "K.K.'S" ONCE NIMBLE MIND IS NUMB
BUT A NUMB MIND ONCE MADE NIMBLE BEGETS NIMBLE FEET, AND OUR "KRAZY" IS ON, AND AWAY FROM HERE.
RETURNING AS WE SEE HIM LADEN WITH A CERTAIN FRUIT WHOSE LOWLY START IN LIFE WE HAVE ALREADY WITNESSED =
UM-M-M-
GOOD.
GO TO IT MY CHILDREN, GO TO IT -
GIMMY SOME MORE
WHERE UPON IT TAKES IT'S PROPER PLACE IN THIS DRAMA, AND PLAYS A MIGHTY PART.
OI CHONNY - OI CHONNY
WEEY-
YOW
I'M SORREEE I MA-A-ADE YOU CRY-
DONT LET THEM CLOUD ROLL BY-
AND YET THERE IS THEM AS SAYS, YOU CANNOT HAVE A "HILERITY" WITH OUT STRONG, AND COGENT LICKA.
MR. "BUM BILL BEE" MAY I ASK IF YOU'VE SEEN "KRAZY" ABOUT ?
I KNOW HIM NOT.
HERRIMAN

October 21st, 1917.

POOR LI'L 'IGNATZ', I DISLIKE SO MUCH TO INSPIRE A TERROR IN HIM, BUT THIS IS THE TIME FOR "JECK-LENTERNS", AND GOBLINKS", SO I'LL JUST SCARE HIM A WEE BIT, THEN APOLOGIZE TO HIM, LI'L GLESS EYB.
IT SEEMS TO US THAT THE HARVEST MOON IS ABOUT TO WITNESS A SCENE OF RUTHLESS FRIGHTFULNESS, DOES IT NOT ?
I'LL HAND THAT FOOL "KAT" SUCH A PANIC TO-NIGHT THAT HE'LL NOT STOP RUNNING THIS SIDE OF TIMBUCTOO" —
GEE, I HOPE I DUNT FRIGHTEN HIM TOO MUCH, LI'L AINJIL.
I HOPE I SCARE HIM OUT OF EVERY FOOL LIFE HE'S GOT.
HA'LO 'KLAZY,' HA'LO IGNASH' LONG TIME NO SEE YOU - LASH NIGHT I GO CELEBLATE 'HOLLY-WEEN' WIT LITTY CHINA GOBLIN LANTLUN, BIME-BYE COME TWO PUNKUN LANTLUN WOT GIT VELLY FLIGHTEN MY CHINA LANTLUN AND LUN AWAY ALL SAME JACK LABBIT — NOW I CATCHUM = YIZZA.
OH, WELL, HERE'S A HARVEST BRICK.
LI'L INDIAN'S SPRING TIMES.
POW.
JAZZ
HERRIMAN
AND SO, IN THE LIGHT OF NEXT MORNING'S MORE, OR LESS HARVEST SUN, WE FIND WE WERE NOT SO VERY FAR FROM BEING MISTAKEN =

October 28th, 1917.

LOAFER, INGRATE, LOW-LIFE, BUMMER !!! YOU CAN WELL AFFORD TO BUY BRICKS, CAN'T YOU ? BUT WHEN IT COMES TO KEEPING YOUR FAMILY SUPPLIED WITH "POTATOES" YOU'RE NOT THERE, HUH - YOU WRETCH" -
BUT "MATILDA" MY OWN - LISTEN -
IT SEEMS LIKE "IGNATZ MOUSE" HAS IN A MEASURE FAILED TO PROVIDE, AND RATHER THAN PREMATURELY DUBBING HIM A CONNUBIAL, OR HOUSEHOLD SLACKER, LET US FOLLOW FURTHER THE DEVELOPMENTS OF THIS TALE.
WE ARE NOT MR MOUSE'S MORAL GUARDIAN, HENCE WE REFRAIN FROM BEING CAPTIOUS ABOUT HIS CONSCIENCE - HOWEVER, WE FEEL THAT HIS MIND IS FULLY MADE UP TO PROCURE A POTATO OR TWO =
YES, I GOT IN MY CELLAR 12 BIG, FET "PITATOES" WHAT I AM KEEPING IN CASE A HARD TIME COMES, THEN I WILL GIVE THEM TO POOR WIDOW LADIES, AND ORFINS - YES -
OH-HOH - IN HIS CELLAR, HUH -
GOOD BOY, "KRAZY"
KIND HEART.
FINE
SAM SPANYIL'S GROCERY STORE. THE COMMUNITY'S UNOFFICIAL CIVIC CENTER - WHERE SCANDAL, AND EULOGIUM, CALUMNY, AND PRAISE, EBBS, AND FLOW - EBBS, AND FLOW =
SHUX !! THOSE WIDOWS, AND ORPHANS WONT MISS A SPUD, OR TWO -
NOW, WE DONT KNOW WHETHER THESE ACCUSING EYES ARE THE VEGETABLE ORBS OF KRAZY'S POTATOES, OR MERELY THE PERVERTED VISION OF A GUILTY CONSCIENCE =
GOSH !! I KNOW THOSE FOOL POTATOES HAD "EYES," BUT I HAD NO IDEA THEY COULD SEE WITH THEM -
WELL, I'LL GO SEE HOW THE COMPANY WHAT I GOT IN MY PITATO BIN IS COMING A-LONG.
WELL, HOW DID YOU L'IL KET CHILDS INJOY SLIPPING WITH THEM PITATOES LEST NIGHT, HUH ?
FINE, UNCLE "KRAZY" FINE.
FINE.
CAN WE SLEEP THERE AGAIN TO-NIGHT ?
REMEMBER, WE MADE NO BOAST THAT THOSE WERE POTATO EYES - WE WERE AS MUCH IN THE DARK ABOUT THEM AS "IGNATZ MOUSE".
HERRIMAN

November 4th, 1917.

November 11th, 1917.

AY CHINITA QUE SI, AY CHINITA QUE NO-O-OO-
?
VENTE CONMIGO CHINITA - A DONDE VIVO YO —
I'M TIRED "WALT"
WELL, SIT ON THIS ROCK AND REST A BIT.
AREN'T YOU TIRED TOO ?
ME ? NA-A-A-
YOU, AND ME IS GOING TO BE PRETTY WEARY BEFORE WE FINISH THESE TEN MILES, "IGNATZ".
YES - ESPECIALLY ME.
OH, THE BLECKBIRD, AND A TRUSH THEY WAS SITTINK ON A BUSH, MAKING LOVE LIKE "ROMEYET," AND "JULIO."
SAID THE BLECKBIRD TO THE TRUSH LET US NOW THE GROWLA RUSH, LEND ME A JIT, AND I'LL GIVE YOU A "U.I.O."
BUT THE BLECKBIRD BY THE TRUSH GOT THE GREND OLD HOBO'S RUSH, AND THE BLECKBIRD LEFT THAT NIGHT FOR "TOKIO"
SO-N-N-NOW
????
?
?
SNAP
KURIOUS KAT
OH HOHO
HUH, I PASSED ALONG THE OLD "TULE" ROAD TODAY, AND I DIDN'T SEE ANY SNAPPING TURTLE.
NEITHER DID I.
NOR I
THAT "SNAPPING TURTLE" YARN IS PRETTY FLIMSY - HE'S BEEN HITTING THE "CATNIP" AGAIN.
NOW GENTS BE LENIENT. REMEMBER THE PATIENT HAS HAD A SEVERE SHOCK, AND HIS MIND IS A BIT HAZY YET.
BUT DOCTA, IT WAS A SNEPPINK TURTIL.
HERRIMAN

November 18th, 1917.

OH HOH !! A "DIME", A NICE NEW "DIME"

BLIND

ONE.

IT'S A DERN GOOD THING THIS DIME WAS LYING IN FRONT OF OLD "SANCHO PANSY" THE BLIND PIG, OR ELSE I WOULD'NT BE A DIME RICHER RIGHT NOW – GEE, I WISH IT WAS A $10. INSTEAD OF .10¢.

BLIND

TWO.

DO YOU MEAN TO TELL ME, "DON KYOTY" THAT "SANCHO PANSY" IS NOT BLIND

I SURE DO, "IGNATZ"

THREE.

WELL HOW IS IT HE DID'NT SEE THIS "DIME", HUH, HOW IS IT ?

THAT, I CANT ANSWER, BUT WERE I A BETTING MAN I'D WAGER HE WAS NOT BLIND –

FOUR.

BUT IF I WERE YOU, "IGNATZ" A PLUNGER, A GAMBLER, A SPORT, I WOULD PLACE A $20. BILL BEFORE "SANCHO PANSY" THE BLIND PIG WHO CAN'T SEE, AND THEN WOULD I WAGER $10. WITH THAT SMALL WIT "KRAZY KAT" WHO ALSO BELIEVES THAT PIG IS NOT BLIND.

FIVE.

GOOD, NOW GO GET TEN MORE FROM THAT SILLY "KAT".

BLIND

HERE'S THE $20 BILL

$20.

SIX.

SANCHO PANSY IS THE BLINDEST PIG IN THIS TOWN, "KRAZY"

WHY "HASH-DINGIT" "IGNATZ" HE AINT NO SUCHA THING, HE'S GOT A GREAT SENSE OF EYE I'M THINKING

SEVEN.

I'M STAKE HOLDER.

$10. SAYS HE'S BLIND !!

AND $10 SAYS HE AINT –

$10

$10

EIGHT.

LET US NOW GO FORTH TO PROVE IT.

MAY THE BEST MAN WIN.

NINE.

BLIND

?

TEN.

NO CONTEST, ALL BETS OFF !!

BLIND

T'IS WELL

ZIP

ELEVEN.

TEN FOR YOU, "DON," AND TEN FOR ME

YEP "SANCHO" TEN FOR YOU, AND TEN FOR ME –. MIGHTY GOOD HUNTING I CALL'S IT TOO

BLIND

TWELVE.

Herriman

November 25th, 1917.

GAH-SHANGIT !! HAVE'NT I SAID A THOUSAND TIMES TO THROW AWAY THAT FOOL PICTURE OF ME HEH ? IT'S OLD FASHIONED AND I DONT WANT IT IN MY HOUSE !!
VERY WELL, IT'LL GO OUT TO-DAY, IT SCARES THE CHILDREN ANYWAY
ONE
THERE, THAT'LL NEVER BOTHER ME ANY MORE
PLOP
TWO
A BIT OF A ROOKUS IS OCCASIONED IN THE HOUSE OF "MOUSE".
AND SO THERE'S A NEW FACE IN THE ASH HEAP TODAY
IT'S A PITCHA OF 'IGNATZ', A OLD FESHIONED PITCHA OF HIM AS A YOOT — L'IL KENDY KID
THREE
AT LAST I GOT A JEWEL MORE PRECIOUS THEN A $20 PIECES OF GOLD
FOUR
AH, I CAN LOOK UPON HIM WITH A HEPPY, HEPPY EYE, AND A SOUL SINGING LIKE A LINNET BIRD
FIVE
YOU TOOK IT WITHOUT ASKING
IT IS'NT YOURS
WHERE IS YOUR TITLE TO IT
WHO GAVE IT TO YOU ?
DID YOU GET IT HONESTLY ?
BUT A HEAVY THUMB HAS FALLEN UPON A CERTAIN 'KAT', AND THE VOICE OF THE TONGUELESS TALKER HAS ASSAILED HIM — FOR "KONSCIENCE" HAS COME TO ABIDE AWHILE WITH HIM
SIX
I'VE COME TO GIVE IT BECK — I'M SO S-SORRY —
OH, IS THAT SO !!
SEVEN
AND DONT YOU DAST BRING IT BACK AGAIN, FOOL !!!
CLENK
EIGHT
L'IL AINJIL
NINE
HERRIMAN

December 2nd, 1917.

PLOP
POW
POW
ZIZ
FOR TO NIGHT I AM A WEE-E-E-DO IN A COT-TUDGE BY THE SEA
HERRIMAN

December 9th, 1917.

IF I WERE AS TALL AS YOU 'WALTER' I'D BE ABLE TO EXPLORE THAT 'JAM' CLOSET UP THERE.

SHUX, I HATE 'JAM' I DO, I LIKE CIGARS BETTER

AH-

AH-

AH?

?

?

NOW UP, KRAZY UP.

REEL IT UP, REEL IT UP.

ARE YOU UP THERE, 'IGNATZ'?

I AM

GOOD !!

SEEMS I HEARD A NOISE.

BUT I GUESS I WAS MISTOOK.

SLAM

KAPLOOP

R-R-R REVENGE !!!!

HERRIMAN

December 16th, 1917.

AH-H-H, "IGNATZ" IS NIGH -
POW
ZIZZZ
L'IL "AINJIL" HE HIDES -
AHDEER, WHAT A DELIGHTFIL BOONS IT IS TO BE SO CONSTINTLY REMINDED OF LOVE LIKE THAT - MAKES ME SO HEPPY
AH-H ONCE MORE, AGAIN.
POW
ZIG
L'IL HIDE, AND SEEKA, WHERE IS YOU ANY WAY ?
RIGHT HERE SILLY RIGHT HERE !!!
WHERE ?
HERE !!!
SPOOX !!!
ART DEPT.
OH-HOH
INVISIBLE INK
NO WUNDA I DINT SEE HIM -
ART DEPT
"IGNATZES," OY "IGNATZES" L'IL INWISIBIL, IS YOU AROUND, AND ABOUT, IF SO SAY IT - !!!!
POW
ZIJ-J
I'M RIGHT HERE !!
GOOD !!
ALL'S WELL, LIKE IT SHOULD BE.
HERRIMAN

December 23rd, 1917.

LOOKS LIKE A BURGLAR'S LANTERN.
OFFICER "PUPP" IT LOOKS LIKE A JOB FOR YOU.
IT'S OFFA MY BEAT
A MYSTERIOUS LIGHT DANCING OVER A "DISMAL TULE SWAMP AT TWILIGHT HAS MADE THEM QUITE CAUTIOUS
YEZZA, QUITE CAUTIOUS.
BUT YOU KANT KEEP KAUTION IN A KAT, THEY'RE TOO FILLED UP WITH "KURIOSITY."
SHUX, IT'S ONLY AN "IGNIS FATUUS" THAT'S ALL, I'VE SEEN HUNDREDS IN MY TIME
A "IGNATZ FATTIS" YOU SAY MR. STORK, A "IGNATZ FATTIS" ?
"JOE STORK", WISE, AND FULL OF YEARS IMPARTS A BIT OF INFO
ANY THING BY THE NAME "IGNATZ" I GOTTA FIND OUT ABOUT.
AH-HA-AH
ARE YOU RILLY A "IGNATZ FATTIS" L'IL LIGHT. ARE YOU ?
ZIZ-Z
POW !
AH-H, ANUDDA "IGNATZ" IS NIGH - THE GREATEST OF HIS KIND.
BY THE LIGHT OF A "IGNATZ FATTIS" I FOUND MY DAHLINK "IGNATZ MICE" I FOUND HIM IN A DIZMIL TOOLY SWUMP - OY-YOI - IN A DIZMIL TOOLY SWUMP I FOUND MY DA-A-AH-LINK
HERRIMAN

December 30th, 1917.

# 1918.

I REALIZE THE ERROR OF MY WAYS, AND SO, CONTRITE AND HUMBLE I PROMISE TO HURL NO MORE "BRICKS" AT THAT KRAZY KAT'S DOME.
1918
WITH THE BIRTH OF THE NEW YEAR WE ALSO CELEBRATE THE BIRTH OF A "RESOLUTION" - "IGNATZ MOUSE", SINNER - AND RESOLVER.
GOOD FOR YOU, "IGNATZ" YOU'RE A "BRICK"
LOOK OUT BELOW
DANGER
GANG WAY !!
THIS STREET BEING PAVED BY THE DOBY BRICK
KOLIN KELLY DEALER IN BRICKS
YES "IGNATZ" I'M CLOSING OUT MY LINE OF CHOICE BRICKS AT A VERY LOW FIGURE
ICE-CREAM "BRICKS" NICE ICE-CREAM "BRICKS"
BRICK TOP-
OH-HO- BRICK TOP
AAH- WA-A-A
JUST TO SHOW YOU MY HEART'S HANGING ON THE RIGHT PEG, AND BECAUSE MY GRAND-PA LIKED YOUR GRAND-PA SO MUCH - I'M GONNA LET YOU HAVE THIS $82. - 18 KARAT SOLID GOLD "BRICK" FOR FOUR BITS YEZZA FOUR BITS -
OY "IGNATZ", AINJIL, LOOK A NICE LI'L LOVE TOKINS I GOT FOR YOU, A NICE, NEW, FRESH 1918 MODELS "BRICK".
IT'S A HEPPY, HEPPY NEW YEAR AND I'M A HEPPY, HEPPY "KET"
THANK GOODNESS I DID'NT SWEAR OFF ON "KOBBLE ROCKS"
HERRIMAN

January 6th, 1918.

I'M GOING FOR A SPIN, GET THE CAR READY.
YEZZA.
HAVE YOU ALL THE GAS, AIR, AND WATER YOU NEED ?
YEP.
TAIL LIGHT
SOUND YOUR "STARTER"
GRA-A A-A
GET INTO "LOW"
GRA-A-A
NOW INTO INTERMEDIATE, AND DONT STRIP YOUR GEARS.
GRAAA
NOW INTO HIGH
GRAAA AA
GET UP TO 40 MILES QUICK. I'M OUT FOR SPEED.
A-AH, THE HIGH COST OF SPEEDING HAS PUT THE BUSINESS ON THE BLINK.
OH-HOH A CUSTOMER - HE'S DOING AT LEAST "40," TOO
I'LL GET HIM IF MY WIND HOLDS OUT -
HOHO, LOOK WHATS TRYING TO CATCH ME - THINKS HE'S A "GREYHOUND" - HAA-HAA -
KAA PLOP
WA-AL - I GOTCHA HEY ?
POOR LI'L SPEEDIST.
SPEEDING YOUR HONOR
30 DAYS.
HERRIMAN

January 13th, 1918.

A BOOMARENG, "IGNATZ" ?
THAT'S WHAT I SAID, A "BOOMERANG"
ONE.
YOU TOSS IT AWAY FROM YOU ?
I DO, "KRAZY," I DO, BUT IT SHALL RETURN, REMEMBER, IT SHALL RETURN.
BZEE
TWO.
YOU WAIT RIGHT WHERE YOU ARE, AND THAT "BOOMERANG" WILL COME BACK TO YOU.
THREE.
AND WHEN IT COMES BACK SOMEBODY'S GOING TO GET SOMETHING THEY DON'T EXPECT - AND I'LL WATCH THE CIRCUS FROM BEHIND THIS BOULDER WITH GREAT IMPUNITY, AND SAFETY.
FOUR.
DOWN IN MY MOST INSIDE SOUL I SEEM TO FEEL A SISPICION THAT "IGNATZ" IS SPOOFERING ME - HOW-EVVA I'LL LET HIM THINK HE IS GETTING BY WITH HIS LIL GAME - LIL JOKIST HE MUST HAVE HIS FUNS.
FIVE.
WHY OFFISSA "PUPP," WHERE-EVVA DID YOU COME FROM ?
OH, JUST HAMMERING THE OLD BEAT, "KRAZY," AT'S ALL - HOW'S THINGS ?
SIX.
I'M KEEPING A DATE WITH A "BOOMARENG" - "IGNATZ" TOSSED IT AWAY, BUT HE WISHES I SHOULD STAY HERE TILL IT COMES BECK.
SHUX, AINT YOU NEVER GONNA QUIT LETTING THAT FOOL MOUSE PLAY HORSE WITH YOU, AINT YOU ?
SEVEN.
KOP !!
ZJIZZ-Z-
EIGHT.
HERRIMAN
NINE.
TEN MILES OUTSIDE OF COCONINO COUNTY, AND STILL GOING STRONG, YEZZA, AND WITH NO THOUGHT OF ABATING HIS SPEED

January 20th, 1918.

YOUR TREASURE CHEST IS ABOUT FULL.
GOOD, - IT'S AS IT SHOULD BE, AS 'IGNATZ' WILL NEED A GREAT WEALTH TO KEEP HIM PROPALY WHEN HE IS OLD OF AGE.
SH-H- QUIET-
THERE'LL BE GOLD ENOUGH FOR ALL
ON THE RIM OF THE "DESIERTO PINTADO" STANDS THE "MESA PEQUENA" ON WHOSE INACCESSIBLE CREST "KRAZY KAT" BANKS HIS WEALTH — IT DRAWS NO INTEREST, BUT IT LIES SAFE FROM THOSE WHO SEEK TO MARAUD, AND PILFER
WHILE, IN THE SHADOWY UMBRAGE OF THE OLD SMOKE TREE "IGNATZ MOUSE", AND HIS BAND OF ROBBER RODENTS PLOT A SINISTER SCHEME.
GOSH, THERE'S A WORLD'S RANSOM IN THIS CHEST - AT LEAST $2.62¢.
YES, AND THERE'LL BE THREE DOLLAS IN IT BEFORE MY LIFE'S WORK IS DID.
AND IT IS THAT HONEST FELINE VOLANT, "KRAZY KATBIRD", KRAZY'S KOUSIN WHO MAKES POSSIBLE THE USE OF THIS INVULNERABLE REPOSITORY OF GREAT RICHES.
HOO-ROOR !!! THE TREASURE IS OURS !! HOO ROAR !!
AFTER A NIGHT OF WICKED WORK, THE DAWN BRINGS A SINFUL SUCCESS
AINT IT TOO BAD YOU, AND YOUR L'IL FRIENDS WENT TO SO MUCH "TROUBIL" 'IGNATZ'? - IF ONLY YOU HAD ESKED ME, I'D A TOLD YOU THAT THAT WAS THE SLIPPERIEST "SLIPPERY ELMS" TREE IN COCONINO COUNTY - YEZZA.
HERRIMAN

January 27th, 1918.

ONE.
OH-HOH-HOH !! EITHER SOMEBODY HAS BROKE OUT, OR ELSE SOMEBODY HAS BROKE IN -
OFFICER "PUPP" FINDS THAT A DOBY BRICK IS MISSING FROM THAT ONCE IMPENETRABLE BASTILE - THE COUNTY JAIL OF COCONINO —
TWO.
HERE.
PRESENT.
NOT ABSINT.
JOHN FINBERG - ALOYSIUS GREYHOUND - MANNIE MEEYOW - ALL HERE OFFICER NO BREAK-OUTS AS FAR AS I CAN SEE.
S'FUNNY.
AND SO WARDEN "WUFF" LINES UP THE INMATES, CALLS THE ROLL, AND FINDS ALL PRESENT - THEREBY DEEPENING THE MYSTERY ——
THREE.
YES "DON" IT'S A BIG MYSTERY IN FACK IT'S GOT THE WHOLE POLICE FORCE BAFFLED.
AH, CONSIDERING THAT THE POLICE ARE BAFFLED I SHOULD SAY IT'LL PROVE NO MYSTERY AT ALL — HEH "SANCHO" ?
QUITE SO, "DON" - QUITE SO.
"DON KYOTI", GENTLEMAN OF INVISIBLE MEANS, AND SUB-CONSCIOUS MIND PAUSES IN PASSING, WITH HIS "MAN" "SANCHO PANSY."
FOUR.
HAVE YOU SOLD ANY "BRICKS" TO-DAY MR. KELLY ?
NOT TODAY SIR - THIS IS A "BRICKLESS DAY" YOU KNOW.
"KOLIN KELLY" DEALER IN "BRICKS" OF A VINTAGE
DROPPING A "?" HERE, AND A "?" THERE WE SEEM TO ARRIVE NOWHERE IN THIS TALE.
FIVE.
OH, WHAT A UNHEPPY "KET" I AM, THESE "BRICKLISS" DAYS - OY-YOI-YOI
FOLLOW HIM !!
WHAT, FOLLOW "KRAZY" ? WHY HE'S THE MOST HONEST PERSON IN THESE PARTS
ANYWAY FOLLOW HIM.
WILD "SUSPICION" RUNS RAMPANT IN THIS STANZA ——
SIX.
"HIST !!!
SEVEN.
OFFICER "PUPP" DO YOUR DUTY !!!
SIC 'IM
AH-H- ALL IS YET WELL !!
POW
ZIB
FINIS -
EIGHT.
VERY CLEVER CAPTURE YOU MADE THERE OFFICER "PUPP", THERE'S A REWARD OF "FOUR-BITS" IN IT YOU KNOW.
IT WAS A MERE NOTHING, WARDEN, A MERE NOTHING.
TWO BITS OF THAT REWARD FOR MY MASTER "DON KYOTI" Y' KNOW, OFFICER.
GIVE ME THEM 80 CENTS, "KRAZY", I'LL SEE WHAT I CAN DO WITH THE "JUDGE".
I DO HOPE THE JUDGE WILL FORGIVE HIM.
POST-FINIS —
HERRIMAN

February 3rd, 1918.

SENOR PEDRO RAFAEL DE LOS HUEVOS Y JAMBON" OF GUADALAJARA, AND OTHER MEXICAN PARTS, SCULPTOR, AND DILETTANTE ARRIVES AT, AND ESTABLISHES IN COCONINO COUNTY, A STUDIO AL FRESCO, AND HAS MOLDED FROM THE RADIANT DOBY OF THE "DESIERTO PINTADO" MANY PLASTIC MASTERPIECES
NO. 1. AJAX DEFYING THE COOK.
NO. 2. THE WELCOME.
NO. 3. THE DAWN OF AN IDEA.
NO. 4. THE MAIDEN'S APPEAL.
NO. 5. THE GROGGY GLADIATOR.
NO. 6. REGULAR, THE ROMAN.
IN DUE TIME, THE SENOR, WITH THE TRUE ARTIST'S SIMPERING MODESTY PERMITS THE ELITE, AND THE GENTEEL OF COCONINO TO BASK IN THE GLORY OF HIS ART —
BUT AMONG THEM IS ONE WHO ENTHUSES NOT.
CUTE
WONDERFUL
AH, IT PLEASES ME.
ALLAGINT ALLAGINT.
ROTTEN.
QUICK "KELLY," THE MOST POWERFUL BRICK YOU HAVE, PRICE NO OBJECT.
I'VE GOT JUST THE BRICK YOU WANT.
KOLIN KELLY, DEALER IN BRICKS
POP
BZEE-EE
MR. PEDRO" CAN I BE YOUR MODEL AGAIN TODAY ?
I AM VERRA VERRA SORRY SENOR "KAT," BUT I NOW FIND IT MORE PRUDENT TO HAVE THE SENOR "B. PUPP" FOR MY MODEL.
OH WELL, ART IS SO FLEETINK THAT I MIGHT AS WELL POSE MYSELF AS A WOONDID GEZELLE.
"MANYANNA", OR WE MIGHT SAY, THE "MORROW" — THE MODEL'S RETURN
HERRIMAN

February 10th, 1918.

THAT WE MAY ALL KNOW -
THAT SIGN CALLS UPON EACH GOOD CITIZEN, AND PATRIOT, (AND 'KRAZY' IS BOTH) TO KEEP A HOG, PACK HIS OWN PORK, AND HELP HIS COUNTRY -
1.

BY GOLLIX, MR HERBIT HOOVA "IS RIGHT, AND AS I PERSINILLY KNOW A NUMBA OF HOGS I'LL ADOPT ONE.
2.

I WILL NOW LOOK UP A 'HOG' WHAT SUITS MY FENCY BEST -
3.

WHY MRS. HEDGE-HOGG, HOW IS IT BY YOU, AND YOUR CHILDS ?
AH, 'KRAZY,' DISMAL DAYS HAVE COME UPON US - MY HUSBAND HAS GONE WE KNOW NOT WHERE, AND WE BE ORPHANS, AND WIDOW - A-LAS -
4.

GO MY CHILDREN WHERE THIS GOOD 'KAT' LEADS, AND MAY THE ANGELS' BENISONS BE SHOWERED UPON HIM -
MY HEARTH, AND HOME SHALL BE YOUR'S, AND YOURS, SO CONSIDDA YOURSELFS ADOPTED. FOLLA ME.
5.

NOW MAKE YOURSELVES TO HOME, I'M GOING ON A WISIT.
AND SO, MRS. H. HOGG, AND BROOD NOW BASK ON THE BOSOM OF BLISS.
6.

WHILE 'K.K.' RETIRES TO THE SOLITUDES, ALONE WITH HIS DREAMS.
7.

?
HELP !!
8.

I'M CAMING.
9.

WHY MR. HEDGE-HOGG' WHAT'S HEPPENED ?
I FELL OFF THE CLIFF, AND LANDED ON MY SPINES - AND EEN NOW MY POOR FAMILY PROBABLY SEEK ME MOURNING, THINKING ME DEAD -
10.

HEEVA-HO HOOVA-HI
POP
11.

WE'LL NOW GO SEE YOUR WIFE, AND CHILDS WHERE THEY IS SAFE IN MY HOUSE.
HOW CAN I EVER REPAY YOU.
12.

WHAT BUSINESS HAS HE GOT TO HAVE HIS HOUSE ALL LIT UP LIKE A ROOF GARDEN - BUT I'LL DARKEN IT, DAA-GUN HIM.
'IGNATZ MOUSE,' FULL OF SIN, AND CONCEIT, PREPARES TO END THE SIGNS OF CHEER WHICH 'KRAZY'S' BRILLIANT HOME DISPLAYS.
13.

DON'T BE AFRAID CHILDREN, IT'S ONLY A CHEESE FACED MOUSE - I'LL ATTEND TO HIM -
14.

NOW MR. 'IGNATZ,' YOU'LL BE GOOD FOR A WHILE - JAB HIM IF HE MOVES KIDS.
AH-H, WHAT HAVE I EVER DONE TO YOU, MRS. HOGG ?
15.

HERE THEY IS MR. HOGG
MY DEAR WIFE
MY LOST HUSBAND -
PA-PA -
AH-H MY CHANCE
16.

17.

HERRIMAN

February 17th, 1918.

BUT "PAUL" MY OWN –
BUT, ME EYE. THESE BISCUITS ARE AS HARD AS DORNICKS — WHAT DO YOU THINK I AM A ROCK-CRUSHER ?
"PAUL POODIL" FULL OF PETULANCE, AND IRASCIBILITY, DENOUNCES WITH VIOLENT VEHEMENCE THE "BISCUITS" WHICH "PAULINE" HIS WIFE HAS MORE THAN BAKED FOR HIM.
AND SO THEY (THE BISCUITS) GO THE WAY OF ALL FINITE CREATION.
PLOP PLOP PLOP PLOP
JIB
ENDING THEIR EXODUS UPON THE PROUD FRAME OF "IGNATZ MOUSE".
WHO DID THAT !!!
HUH, THEY'RE NOT ROUND ENOUGH TO BE CANNON-BALLS, AND THEY'RE TOO HARD TO BE ROCKS, I WONDER WHAT THEY CAN BE ?
OH-HOH
MISSED HIM, B'GOSH !!!
ZIJ
KO-VADIS, LI'L "KETTA PILLA" KO-VADIS ?
PLOP. PLOP. PLOP
GUIDED BY FATE, "BISCUITS" LIKE "POULTRY" OFTEN COME HOME TO ROOST.
GO GET HIM "PAUL" – MY OWN –
I'LL GET HIM IF I RUN ALL THE FUR OFFA MYSELF – THE BALD FACE GAZOONI –
I'LL CARRY YOU TO YOUR DESTINATION, "KETTAPILLA", AND SAVE YOUR FEETS.
HERRIMAN

February 24th, 1918.

GOSH! MR. SANCHO PANSY, WHAT'S THE RISSON YOU WIP, HUH? IS IT A UNHEPPINISS YOU GOT?
AH, KRAZY, I AM INDEED UNHAPPY. "DON KIYOTI," MY MASTER HAS JUST FOUND OUT ABOUT MR. HOOVER'S ORDER FOR EVERY ONE TO KEEP A "PIG" - AND I FEAR THAT IN AN EXCESS OF PATRIOTISM HE WILL CONVERT ME INTO PORK, PIGS-KNUCKLES, OR SPARE-RIBS - OMY-OMY-OMY.
1.
OOHOOO-OOOOO
DA-A-GUNNIT, NO "PIG" CAN SUFFA LIKE THAT WHILE I GOT A MEANS, OR TWO AT HEND TO MAKE HIM HEPPY. NOZZA.
2
IT'S MIGHTY NICE OF MR. HOOVA TO HAVE US KEEP A PIG, BUT TO MAKE A "PIGS-NICKEL" OUT OF ONE AINT NO PROPPA KIND OF BUSINESS.
K.K.
3
NOW PUT ON THE BEARD, AND RIGHT AWAY YOU WILL BE BEYOND ALL RECOGNIZMENT.
MY, WHAT A KLEVER, KLEVER KAT YOU ARE, "KRAZY"
4
THESE MANY YEARS HAVE I MAINTAINED THAT "PIG" IN LUXURY OF FOOD, HABITATION, AND RAIMENT, AND NOW HE LEAVES ME FLAT AS A LETTUCE SANDWICH - I WILL GIVE A REWARD OF $2. FOR HIS RETURN - "$2."
$2. GOSH -
5
"IGNATZ MOUSE" IS DEEPLY MOVED BY "DON KIYOTI'S" ELOQUENT APPEAL - PARTICULARLY WITH THE LAST PART OF IT - WHERE-IN $2. IS MENTIONED
I'LL FIND THAT "PIG" IF IT TAKES A MONTH OF SUNDAYS -
$2. $2 $2 $2 $2 $2
6
LIKE THE CONQUISTADORES OF OLD, "IGNATZ" GOES FORTH TO SHAKE A DOLLAR, AND HIS TWIN OUT OF THE OLD TREE OF CHANCE.
I'LL NEVER FORGET THIS DAY'S KINDNESS, "KRAZY" NEVER.
SHUX, MR. PANSY, DUNT MENTION IT.
7
AH-HAH!!
POW.
ZIP
EVEN $2. IS'NT IMPORTANT ENOUGH TO MAKE ME PASS UP ANY CHANCE TO BEAN THAT FOOL "KAT."
8
CORN-SARN YOU - "MOUSE" YOU CANT INSULT MY PAL, AND LIVE TO CHEER ABOUT IT -
$2.
9
OH, I'LL GET YOU -
10
"SANCHO," MY DEAR OLD SANCHO PANSY - COME BACK TO ME, AND ALL WILL BE FORGIVEN -
11
L'IL SPEN-TRIFF.
OGOSH - I GUESS IT'S ALL FOR THE BEST.
I'M A MAN OF MY WORD, "IGNATZ"
I WILL NOW BUY A FLOCK OF "KOLIN KELLY'S" CHOICEST BRICKS
$2
12
HERRIMAN

March 3rd, 1918.

NEED WE SAY THAT THIS A 'STAR'S' DRESSING ROOM, A 'STAR' WHOSE SALARY IS KINGLY TO THE AMOUNT OF $1.98¢ PER WEEK -

NOR, NEED WE INFORM YOU THAT IN THIS LOWLY UNPRIVATE SPOT ROBES, AND DIS-ROBES THE MENIAL 'EXTRA' WHO CRASHES THE CASHIER TO THE NOBLE FIGURE OF 30¢ PER WEEKLY,

THE 'STAR' COME'S FORTH -
. THE STAR —— IGNATZ MOUSE.

'KRAZY KAT' —— 'EXTRA'.

'STAR' ME FOOT!! EITHER YOU TAKE A 'PIE' IN THIS SCENE, OR YOU'LL BE 95¢ SHORT IN YOUR SALARY NEXT WEEK, SAVVY?

BUT MR. HENNIT, AS A 'STAR' AND AN ARTIST I SIMPLY CAN NOT DEAL IN 'PIE' COMEDY, I SIMPLY CAN NOT.

BUT THERE IS A POWER WHO GUIDES THE DESTINIES OF 'STARS', A POWER, PULCHRITUDINOUS, AND POTENTIAL, AND THAT FORCE IS, 'MAX HENNIT,' DIRECTOR, SUPERVISOR, & PRODUCER.

GOOD, YOU TOOK IT NOBLY

SKWIJ

ZAP

AND SO, FOR THE SAKE OF 'ART'.... STILL ——

GO TAKE A BATH, AND I'LL LET YOU KNOW WHEN YOU CAN SEE THIS REEL IN THE PROJECTING ROOM

WELL, ANYWAY, I'LL BET YOU, JOHN DREW, OR LOUIE MANN COULDN'T HAVE DONE IT MORE ARTISTICALLY -

SNAP

FOR EVERY WOUND, A BALM,
FOR EVERY SORROW, CHEER,
FOR EVERY STORM, A CALM,
FOR EVERY THIRST, A BEER —
('BILL KIRK').

GREAT WORK, KRAZY, VERY, VERY ARTISTIC, — Y'GET .10¢ EXTRA FOR IT.

THENX MR. HENNIT.

ZIP

PROJECTING ROOM

LI'L PROJECTA

ZING

POW

AND THIS —— IN THE PROJECTING ROOM, WHERE 'STARS' OF THE FIRST MAGNITUDE SOMETIMES FALL TO EARTH ——

HERRIMAN

March 10th, 1918.

BEAN
IGNATZ MOUSE" HAS PLANTED A "BEAN", TRUSTING IT WILL YIELD A CROP OF BOUNTIFUL, UNCTUOUS, AND OLEAGINOUS AMPLITUDE.
BEAN
I'M SO THIRSTY
BUT NATURE, FICKLE MISTRESS OF OUR FORTUNES NEGLECTS TO POUR IN AQUEOUS BOUNTY THE "RAIN" SO NECESSARY TO THE GROWTH, AND HEALTH OF A CHILD BEAN.
BEAN
WATER, WATER
WHICH IN A MEASURE, PERTURBS THE MIND OF "IGNATZ MOUSE" WITH A GREAT FEAR FOR THE FUTURE OF HIS FRETFUL LEGUME
WATER, OR I PERISH
BEAN
AND SO COMES A SAD HOUR WHEN THIS GENTLE BEAN SOUL, PARCHED, AND WITHERED BY A TOO ARDENT SUN IS ABOUT TO PASS OUT INTO A LEGUMINOUS LIMBO, UNMOISTENED, UNBAPTISED, AND MUY SECO. "ALAS.
TELL THEM NOT TO GRIEVE WHEN I AM GONE
BEAN
AH, WHAT FATEFUL SHADOW IS THIS WHICH FALLS UPON THIS EXPIRING BEANLET, THE SHADOW OF MORTALITY, THE SHADOW OF LIFE, THE SHADOW OF WEAL, OR THE SHADOW OF WOE = "OY, INJIBO, INJIBO"
?
AT LAST AT LAST — A BENISON.
BEAN
A THROB, A THRILL, A SPASM OF ANIMATION, THE FULL FLOW OF A TOSSING TIDE REVIVIFIES THE DROOPING PLANTICLE, AND CHEATS THE REAPER OF A PURE YOUNG SOUL.
AT LAST THE EMBITION OF MY LIFE IS REALIZED, I'VE BEEN A "JUPITA PLOOVIS" TO IGNATZ'S LI'L BEAN CHILD.
AND I WILL NOW GO DOWN, AND GIVE THE RESULT OF MY CLOUD EFFECK THE ONCE OVA THE TOPS.
BEAN
?
HIS GRETITUDE IS MEGNIFICINT, LI'L PINK-EYE, AND MY DISH OF JOY IS FULL
POW
ZIP
AH
EPILOGUE.
HERE LIE THE BONES OF "ASTRINGIA BEAN" HER LIFE WAS SHORT BUT VERY SERENE SHE SUFFERED MUCH ILL THOUGH NEVER INFIRM SHE MADE A GREAT FEED FOR "KASPER KUTWORM".
FINIS.
HERRIMAN

March 17th, 1918.

AH-H- JWEE-EE
ONE.
AH-H- JWOO-OO
AH-H- A CELESTIAL SYMPHONY-
TWO.
THE HOURS I SPEND WITH THEE DEE-E-E-ER-R-R HOT
K-JWA-A-ANG
THREE.
IS LIKE A STRING OF PUR-R-R-R-UH-HULLS TO MEEEE
AH- JWONG
FOUR.
ODEER-ODEER NO MATTA HOW MUCH I SEEK TO DROWND MY SORROW IN MUSIC, THOUGHTS OF "IGNATZ" GIVES ME A SADNISS
FIVE
OGOSH IF MUSIC WONT DO IT MAYBE A HOOKA OF STRONG BUTTA-MILK WILL.
SIX
IT'S HIM.
SEVEN.
L'IL TOOTSA-WOOTSA HE SLEEPS IN SLUMBA.
EIGHT.
SMACK
NINE
OH-HOH, SO T'WAS YOU WHO WOKE ME UP OUT OF MY DREAM HUH?
TEN
BLOP
ZIP
JUST AS THE ANGEL KISSED ME TOO -FOOL-
ELEVEN
EACH PEARL A PRAYER-
AH- JWANG AH
ONE DOZEN.

March 24th, 1918.

OH, TREAT MY DOTTA KINDLAY – KEEP HER SAFE FROM HOM – AND WHEN I DIE I'LL GIVE TO YOU-U-U
NO, THEY'RE NOT BOWLING-BALLS THEY'RE KO-KO-KNUTS – NOW, GO ON WITH THE STORY
AH-HA-HA – EGG ROBBAS, A PLOT IS BEING HETCHED –
HER HUSBAND IS AWAY AND THERE'S NOBODY FOR MILES AROUND, AND THE NEST IS FULL OF NICE FRESH EGGS – AND YOU BOYS KNOW HOW DELICIOUS A "STOCKING BIRD'S" EGG IS – HEY ?
WE'RE WITH YOU –
OH, YOU EGGS.
LEAD US TO IT –
TO THE LAST EGG, LET NONE ESCAPE
POOR MRS. STOCKING-BIRD, I MUST LEND HER A HELPING HEND.
YOUR KINDNESS WILL NEVER BE FORGOTTEN, "KRAZY"
I'LL DO THE BEST I CAN TO HELP YOU, MRS. "STOCKING-BIRD"
ONWARD BOYS, THE LOOT LIES BEFORE US – LET US AT IT.
HM-M, LOOKS LIKE SOMEBODY HAS EXPECTED US – GIVE THEM THE SHRAPNEL, BOYS, AND A ROUND FROM OUR MOUSERS, THAT'LL SETTLE THEM – UP, AND AT THEM !!!
BUT, MY BRAVE MEN, THINK OF THE EGGS
EGGS, OUR FOOT, YOU SAID HER HUSBAND WAS AWAY.
D'YOU THINK WE ARE BOLSHEVIKI ?
YOU FOOLED US.
YOU SAID IT WOULD BE A CINCH.
DOWN WITH HIM.
LOOKA THEM HARD NUTS.
BUT BOYS LET ME EXPLAIN !!!
TRAITOR !!
DOWN WITH HIM !!
FIBBER !!
SOAK HIM –
WE WIN –
OH, WAKE ME, MUDDA, – EARLY IN THE MOR-R-R-N-INK –
FINALLY WE RAN OUT OF AMMUNITION, BUT DID THE MONSTERS DAUNT US, NO, HAND, TO HAND WE FOUGHT THEM MAN TO MAN UNTIL –
UNTIL WHAT ?
YES, WHAT, "IGNATZ" ?
AND THAT DAY, AT VESPERS, IN "BARNEY BORRACHO'S" PULQUERIA, A PRODIGIOUS TALE WAS TOLD – A TALE WITH AN INTERRUPTED CLIMAX
HERRIMAN

March 31st, 1918.

A STRAY STAR FALLS UPON THE TOP OF THE "ENCHANTED MESA" WHICH IN A MANNER EXCITES OUR KURIOSITY.
EEEY YEEEEE EOOOOO
AND FOR EACH STAR THAT FALLS UPON THE "ENCHANTED MESA" "DON KYOTI," PSALM SINGER OF THE "DESIERTO PINTADO" LILTS AN ANTHEM. NOW, AS THERE BE MANY STARS WHICH FALL UPON THAT "MESA OF MYSTERY" "DON KYOTI" IS A FREQUENT TRILLER OF "SONGS."
ALL OF WHICH AWAKENS "KRAZY KAT" ASLUMBERED BENEATH THE OLD SMOKE TREE, AND "KURIOSITY," A KAT'S PET PASSION, MOVES INTO, AND TAKES PROUD POSSESSION OF HIS SOUL.
A "KAT" FULL OF "KURIOSITY" IS CONSIDERABLE DRY PACKAGE. WE ASSURE YOU.
WHY DO YOU SING SO LATE IN THE NIGHT, DONS KYOTI" - HUH ?
CALL IT SONG IF YOU WILL, "KRAZY," BUT I TERM IT "HYSTERICAL KURIOSITY" - EVERY TIME A STAR FALLS ON THIS "MESA" MY NERVES GET ALL A-TINGLE, AND I MUST NEEDS GIVE VENT TO MY AGITATION IN VOICE.
BUT WHEN A KURIOUS KAT IN KWEST OF KURIOSITY MEETS A KOYOTE FULL OF KURIOSITY, WE MUST SAY AS HOW IT IS SOME KLASH OF KURIOSITY.
I MUST BE KAUTIOUS - THERE ARE SO MANY KURIOUS KUSSES ABOUT -
WHILE IT IS KURIOSITY WHICH SO OFTEN INSPIRES A KAT, IT IS THAT FROM WHICH IT ALSO OFTEN EXPIRES. HOWEVER, WITH "JOSE CIGUENO," OR JOE STORK" AS WE KNOW HIM BETTER, HE WHO LIVES ON THE TOPSIDE OF THE "ENCHANTED MESA," IT IS KAUTION, NOT KURIOSITY WHICH IS THE HIGH NOTE IN THE GAMUT OF HIS VIRTUES.
T'IS HE WHO GATHERS THE STRAY STARS WHICH FALL IN HIS FRONT YARD - FOLDS THEM IN A KNITTING BAG, - AND WHEN NO ONE IS LOOKING ——
WE REPEAT, WHEN NO ONE IS LOOKING ——
OH-HO-HO NO WUNDA "DON KYOTI" GETS THEM HYSTERICS -
SHUX. DID WE SAY, NO ONE ? DID WE ? BUT WE HARDLY FIGURED ON THE INSIPID ENDURANCE OF A "KATS" KURIOSITY - WHICH AT THIS MOMENT LURKS IN THE UMBRAGE OF A SHELTERING PIE PLANT ——
KINGRETULATIONS, "IGNATZ"
?
?
L'IL PROUD FODDA.
IN FRONT OF BARNEY BORRACHO'S PULQUERIA A FERVENT FELICITATION COMES TO PASS.
AND NOW, THE MANTLE OF KURIOSITY FALLS UPON OTHER SHOULDERS, WHILE "KRAZY KAT" GOES FORTH SEEKING NEW PASTURES OF INQUISITIVENESS.

April 7th, 1918.

PROLOGUE
"A BUCKET OF WATER".
OH, KRAZY, WHAT A MORNING OF BLISS IT WAS TO ME TO FIND THAT "JOE STORK" HAD GIVEN INTO MY CARE, SIX KITTENS, SIX GEMS, JEWELS MOST PRECIOUS TO ME
AINT THAT NICE -
THE SENORA "ANITA GATA BLANCA" SHE WHO MOURNS IN HER BARREL OF SORROW - TO HER IS ALLOTTED THE OVERTURE OF OUR TALE.
BUT THAT VERY NIGHT MY JOY WAS MADE GRIEF FOR "MARMADUKE" HE WHOM I CALLED HUSBAND WAS STRUCK DOWN IN THE FLOWER OF HIS KATHOOD BY A FLAT-IRON, AS HE VOICED HIGH HIS HAPPINESS ON THE BACK ALLEY FENCE
OH LADY, LADY, AINT THAT TOO BAD.
HER INTERLUDE OF SORROW.
AND NOW, BEFORE THIS DAYS SUN HAD RISEN, BEHOLD, MY SIX KITTENS WERE TAKEN FROM ME, AND I AM LEFT A CHILDLESS WIDOW IN SOLITUDE, AND SORROW.
S'AWFIL, S'AWFIL.
THE CLIMAX, ANGUISH.
POOR WIDDA - OMY-OMY-OMY.
"A HEART BOWED DOWN -
BUT MR. BARQUE CAN SUCH BE ?
I HAVE SEEN MUCH - AND AMONG THAT MUCH, THAT OF WHICH YOU SPEAK. AH, IF BUT YON BUCKET OF WATER COULD GIVE TONGUE, WHAT A TALE IT COULD UNFOLD -
"B. BOSWELL BARQUE" THE FAMOUS MOON HATER WHO SLUMBERS WITH BUT ONE EYE, TELLS A THING, OR TWO
FROM THIS BUCKET OF AQUEOUS DOOM, KRAZY BEHOLDS IN HIS MIND'S EYE THE WRAITHS OF MANY KITTENS ARISING FROM IT'S HORRIPILATING DEPTHS.
BUT WHY SHOULD THEY BECOME KETFISHES MR. OWL ?
THINK WHAT MUSSY SPIRITS THEY WOULD BE, WET, AND DRIPPING ABOUT ON LAND - THEIR'S WAS A MOIST END, HENCE, WATERY MUST BE THEIR AFTER LIFE, AND IN WHAT BETTER WAY THAN THAT OF FISH -
AND THE FOOLISH KITTENS WHICH GET LOST IN HIGH TREES, DONT THEY MAKE NICE PUSSY-WILLOWS ?
THIS HAS NOTHING TO DO WITH OUR STORY
OWEN OWL, SUN HATER, SEER OF THINGS WE NEVER SEE, ADDS A BIT OF INFO.
"IGNATZ", OY "IGNATZ" !!!
I'VE FOUND OUT, I'VE FOUND OUT !!!
FOUND OUT WHAT FOOL ?
WHAT MAKE'S US "KETS" SO DERN AFRAID OF WATER !!!
HERRIMAN

April 14th, 1918.

WHAT DO YOU THINK, GIRLS? MRS. "DODO" TOLD MRS. "PIGEON" WHO TOLD MRS. "HENN" THAT SHE THOUGHT THAT LOW MRS. "KITTY KOTTENTAIL" WAS THINKING OF TRYING TO JOIN OUR CLUB.

IS THAT SO?

MERCY.

WELL, DID YOU EVER?

THE VERY IDEA.

WHY SHE'S A MERE NOBODY.

HOW DARE SHE THINK SUCH A THING.

AS "CHOLLY KOKONINO" WOULD PUT IT – THE WHOEST OF THE WHOS WERE THERE. THE DIMLESS DAMES OF COCONINO, THE MERRY WIVES IN FULL GALAXY, THE REPRESENTATIVES OF THE "DESIERTO PINTADO'S" SOCIAL APEX.

FROM LEFT TO RIGHT THEY BE. MRS. MOCK DUCK, WIFE OF COCONINO'S LAUNDERER DE LUXE, MRS. IGNATZ MOUSE, MRS JOSEPHINE TURTLE, MRS. WALTER C. AUSTRIDGE, MRS B. PUPP, MRS. KOLIN KELLY, MRS. SPRIG, THE DUCK DUCHESS, THE SENORA MARIQUITA PELONA, OF GUADALAJARA, MEX. AND THAT ARISTOCRAT OF SPINSTERS, MISS. TABBY KAT – AND SO, AS LADIES WILL, THEY TALKED OF THIS, OF THAT, AND NOTHING MUCH.

DRIFTING NOW TO A LOWER SOCIAL LEVEL, WE FIND "KRAZY KAT" PROPELLED BY A GREAT SENSE, AND URGE OF KURIOSITY ON HIS WAY TO THE ENCHANTED MESA, ON WHOSE TOPSIDE, "JOE. STORK" THE BIRD OF DESTINY MAKES HIS HOME.

OH-HOHO – AND HE'S GOING TOWARDS "COCONINO" TO LOOK FOR A CUSTOMER TOO –

I MUST SEE THIS THROUGH.

WELL, I'VE VISITED EVERY HOUSE IN TOWN, AND NOT A SOUL AT HOME – THIS LOOKS LIKE A DARN DULL DAY FOR ME.

"MRS. KITTY KOTTENTAIL" WAS "AT HOME".

QUIET NOW CHILDREN, DON'T DISTURB YOUR NEW LITTLE BROTHER.

WELL GIRLS, I'M GLAD THE "CLUB" HAS RULED THAT SHOULD THAT MENIAL MRS. "KOTTENTAIL" EVER DARE TRY TO JOIN OUR "CLUB", SHE WILL BE PROPERLY TURNED DOWN.

IMAGINE SUCH AS SHE TRYING TO MIX WITH SUCH AS US.

DREADFUL.

OUR SOCIAL LIFE IS THREATENED.

WHILE AT THE LADIES' CLUB, THE DIVINITIES STILL CHATTER OVER THEIR "DISH OF TEA", OF THIS, OF THAT, AND NOTHING MUCH.

HERRIMAN

April 21st, 1918.

FOR WHY, "MADRE MIA," DO YOU WEEP ?
AH, MY "PEDRO," IF I AM SAD TODAY, IT IS BECAUSE OF THE "KOOKOO KLOCK," FOR TRULY DO I TELL YOU THAT SOME ONE HAS STOLEN THE "KOOKOO-BIRD" FROM IT, ALAS.
AINT THAT TOO BAD, NOW ?
THE WIDOW "MARIQUITA PELONA," KNOWN TO THEY OF "COCONINO," AS THE "VIUDA DOLOROSA," SHEDS AN EXTRA TEAR OR TWO, FOR AN ADDED SHADOW OF SORROW HAS SETTLED IN DAMP, AND DEPRESSING UMBRAGE UPON HER ALREADY AFFLUENT AFFLICTION.
TODAY, "PEDRO," HE FROM WHOM I AM BUYING THIS "KLOCK" COMES TO COLLECT THE LAST INSTALLMENT WHICH I OWE UPON IT - BUT ALAS, THE "KOOKOO-BIRD" BEING GONE, HE WILL TAKE BACK THE KLOCK, AND ALSO DO I LOSE ALL THAT WHICH I HAVE ALREADY PAID ON IT.
EVEN THOUGH THE KOOKOO BE SILENT, MY "PEDRO," AN HOUR OF GRIEF HAS STRUCK FOR US.
AND THAT THE BURDEN OF WOE BE NOT MORE THAN SHE CAN BEAR, SHE SHARES WITH HER ELDEST SON, "PEDRO," THE WEIGHT OF IT.
DAWGUNNIT !! NO "WIDDA" CAN LOSE A "KOOKOO-BIRDS" WHILE I'M AROUND - Y'BETCHA !!!
THE WHOLE PURPOSE OF "KRAZY KAT'S" EXISTENCE IS ONE OF GENTILITY, BUT NOW, WE ARE NOT SO SURE THAT SOMEWHERE IN THE OLLA-PODRIDA OF HIS CORPOREAL CONFINES A SEED OF SIN HAS NOT FOUND FERTILE SOIL. THE GODS GRANT THAT OUR SUSPICION BE GROUNDLESS, AND THE EVIL THEREOF FALL UPON OUR OWN SINFUL SOUL.
IGNATZ !!!
I WANT YOU TO TAKE A "KOOKOO-KLOCK" OUT OF THE "WIDOW PELONA'S" HOUSE, JOE, HERE'S A DIME FOR YOU - BE THERE IN A HALF HOUR
I'LL BE RIGHT THERE, BOSS.
PRETTY SLICK JOB I CALL IT, TAKING THE "KOOKOO BIRD" OUT THAT CLOCK JUST AS SHE WAS ABOUT TO MAKE HER LAST PAYMENT - BEING DAMAGED, IT COMES BACK TO ME, AND ALL THE PAYMENTS SHE'S MADE ON IT TOO - I'M CONSIDERABLE PROFITEER, I AM -
IS IT POSSIBIL !!
KOOKOO - KOO KOO - KOO KOO- KOOKOO KOO KOO
OH-HOHO-
DON'T HOLLA, I AINT GONNA HURTCHA !!
KOOK !!
NOW YOU BE A SWEET LIL "KOOKIE," AND GET IN THERE, AND WHEN IT'S TIME TO KOOKOO, YOU KOOK FOR ALL YOU'RE WORTH, OR I'LL BE ENGRY AT YOU.
OH, SENOR "MOUSE" DO NOT TAKE AWAY MY KLOCK, TRULY I TELL YOU I KNOW NOT HOW THE BIRD WAS LOST OUT OF IT - HAVE PITY SENOR -
PITY, ME NECK, YOU'VE RUINED THAT CLOCK, SO IT REVERTS TO ME AS PER CONTRACT - JOE, TAKE IT AWAY !!
ALL RIGHT, BOSS.
ALL'S WELL - ALL'S WELL - HERE IS YOUR LAST PAYMENT, GIVE ME A RECEIPT, AND THE CLOCK IS MINE -
KOOKOO - KOO KOO - KOOKOO KOO KOO KOO KOO
S'ALL OFF, JOE.
SO, I SEE.
YES, SENOR "KRAZY," THE CLOCK IS NOW MINE, THANKS TO A WONDERFUL MIRACLE WHICH HAPPENED JUST AS HE WAS ABOUT TO TAKE IT FROM ME IF YOU PROMISE NOT TO LAUGH I'LL TELL YOU ALL ABOUT IT.
LADY, I PROMISE.
HERRIMAN

April 28th, 1918.

"JOE STORK" HE OF THE "ENCHANTED MESA" HAS ANNOUNCED THAT IN THE NAME OF "CHARITY" HE WOULD BE PLEASED TO MEET THE BENEVOLENT CITIZENS OF "COCONINO" IN THE LITTLE GREEN SCHOOL-HOUSE ON THE "MESA ESPIRAL" —.
NOW, IN THIS GENERATION OF GENEROSITY, (AND GENERALS) IT IS ONLY OUR BEST PEOPLE WHO DEAL IN "CHARITY" WHICH IS WHY WE SEE THE ELITE OF THE DESIERTO PINTADO BETAKING THEMSELVES TO THIS INSTITUTION OF LEARNING —
"HOOZOO, BY "CHOLLY KOKONINO".
OFFICER B. PUPP" - LAW, AND ORDER.
GOOSEBERRY SPRIG" - THE DUCK DUKE.
TERRY P. TURTLE" - DIAMOND BROKER.
DON KIYOTI" - CASTILLIAN NOBLEMAN OF A MOST SOAPY NATURE.
"SANCHO PANSY" - HIS AMANUENSIS.
KOLIN KELLY" - THE BRICK MAGNATE.
"WALTER CEPHAS AUSTRIDGE" - A "DICKEY BIRD"
"IGNATZ MOUSE" - POSSESSOR OF OBSCURE WEALTH.
"BARNEY BORRACHO" - PROPRIETOR OF THE "PALOMA BLANCA PULQUERIA"
MOCK DUCK" - LAUNDERER DE LUXE.
PARA LA ESCUELITA VERDE
WHERE IS EVERY BODY TO-DAY L'IL KETTAPILLA ?
"JOE STORK" IS HAVING A BIG CHARITY AFFAIR IN THE SCHOOL-HOUSE ON THE MESA, AND THEY'RE ALL UP THERE.
"KRAZY KAT," AND "KRISTOPHER KATAPILLAR" A WORM, BOTH HARDLY CONSIDERED "PERSONAGES" ARE NECESSARILY NOT AMONG THOSE PRESENT.
BUT, IF "SOCIETY" INVITES HIM NOT HIS "KURIOSITY" BIDS HIM GO.
BEFORE I BRING FORTH THE LITTLE ORPHANS WHO WILL BE THE BURDEN OF YOUR BENEVOLENCE, DEAR PEOPLE, I WILL SAY THAT THEY BE TWINS - AND THEY ARE NAMED "NORTH," AND SOUTH" - I WILL NOW PRESENT THEM TO YOU -
"NORTH," AND SOUTH" SOUNDS LIKE MR. STORK WAS GIVING A LESSON IN JOGRAPHY
LA ESCUELITA VERDE
MAKE WAY - MAKE WAY.
ONE SIDE -
MAS PRONTO, "PUERCO," MAS PRONTO.
WA-AL, AINT I MAS PRONTOING, Y'BIG "CHOLO"
MORE SPEED "DUCK"
I'M DOING MY BIT, "DON"
EXCUSE ME.
LA ESCUELITA VERDE
THEY BE TWIN KATS OF THE POLE VARIETY, "KRAZY," WHICH IS WHY WE CALL THEM "NORTH," AND "SOUTH" - THEY ARE ORPHANS, AND THERE BE NONE IN "COCONINO" TO GIVE THEM SHELTER.
OH, YES THERE IS MR. STORK - YES THERE IS - Y'BETCHA.
AND SO THEY LIVED HEPPY EVVA EFTA-WIDS.
FAIRY TALES
AND SO, "CHARITY," TO WHOM MAMMON ERECTS SUPER-TEMPLES FINDS SANCTUARY IN THE HEART OF THE PROLETARIAT.
HERRIMAN

May 5th, 1918.

HAH, THAT 'KAT' HAS A GRUESOME GLEAM IN HIS EYE, HE MEANS EVIL - I'M SURE OF IT.
AH, SENOR 'KRAZY' IT IS YOU AT LAST WHO COME TO ME, NO?
YES, MRS PELONA, IT'S ME - JUST LIKE I SAID I WOULD.
AH, A WOMAN IN THE CASE TOO, THAT MAKES IT WORSE -
AND THIS IS WHAT 'IGNATZ' HEARS 'KRAZY' TELL THE SENORA 'PELONA'
FIRST, MRS. PELONA YOU GOUGE IT'S EYES OUT, THEN YOU SCRAPE ALL OF IT'S SKIN OFF, THEN YOU TOSS IT INTO BOILING WATER, EFTA WHICH YOU BEAT IT, AND BEAT IT UNTIL IT IS LIKE A PULPS - THEN THE DEED IS DID - AND THAT'S ALL THEY IS TO IT.
DAW GAWN HIM!! THE MISERABLE SCOUNDREL IS PLANNING MURDER, MAYHEM, AND MASSACREE ON SOME ONE, BUT I WILL FOIL HIM -
I MUST AROUSE THE VILLAGERS THEY MUST KNOW OF THE MONSTER WHO PLOTS IN THEIR MIDST, AND BRING HIM TO JUSTICE.
YOU WILL ALL NOW AGREE WITH ME THAT THIS 'KAT' BEEN A VILLAIN IN CAMOUFLAGE RIGHT ALONG.
POOR 'KRAZY' MAYBE IT'S MILD INSANITY
HE WAS ALMOST SANE WHEN I LAST SEEN HIM.
MAYBE THE HEAT'S GOT HIM.
OR MAYBE 'VINO'
WE'LL SEE - WE'LL SEE
AH, SENOR 'KRAZY', IT WAS SO NICE OF YOU TO TELL ME HOW TO COOK THAT DELIGHTFUL DISH OF 'SMASH POTATO' - I THANK YOU MUCH.
DUNT MENTION IT MRS. PELONA. BY ME IT'S A PLEASURE TO TELL YOU.
SO THEMS THE EYES, HEH?
AND THE SKIN.
AND THE BOILING ALIVE.
AND THE BEATING
?
STOP HIM!! STOP HIM!!
MAKE WAY, MAKE WAY!!!
HERRIMAN

May 12th, 1918.

AT ONE GLANCE 'KRAZY,' YOU WILL NOTICE THAT I AM NOW POINTING TO THE NORTH POLE
AND UNLESS YOUR EYE BE DEFECTIVE, YOU WILL OBSERVE THAT I MAKE NO MISTAKE IN CALLING YOUR INSIPID ATTENTION TO THE 'SOUTH POLE'.
THE GEOGRAPHY CLASS WILL NOW GO INTO A STATE OF RECESS.
KOUSIN 'KRAZY KET-BIRD,' WILL YOU DO ME A FAVA, AND TAKE ME TO LOOK AT THE NORTHS POLE ?
I WILL DO SO WITH PLEASURE
SO THIS IS THE 'NORTHS POLE' ?
THIS IS IT
NOW, WOULD IT BE TOO MUCH TROUBLE TO TAKE ME TO THE 'SOUTHS POLE' ?
NO TROUBLE AT ALL.
AND THIS IS THE SOUTHS POLE. ?
IT IS INDEED.
THE GEOGRAPHY CLASS WILL NOW GET TOGETHER AGAIN
NOW, TO CONTINUE OUR STUDY OF THE 'POLES'—
WELL 'KRAZY' WHAT DO YOU WISH ?
OH TEACHA, IT'S ALL WRONG
THE 'SOUTHS POLE' AINT UPSIDE DOWN — I SEEN IT WITH MY OWN EYE
HIS CAREER OF KNOWLEDGE ENDS RIGHT HERE.
ANY WAY I WAS EXPELLED WITH ONNA
HERRIMAN

May 19th, 1918.

THE OLD HOME AINT THE SAME NO MORE. I'VE LINGERED TOO LONG ON THIS HOBO "SKYE TERRIER"
"TIDDY WEEWEE" THE VAGABOND FLEA LILTS A LACHRYMAL LAMENT. THE GRASS HAS GROWN SHORT IN HIS PASTURE, AND NOURISHMENT RUNS LOW.
AH-H-
FOR I'M TO BE KWIN OF THE MAY - YAY, I'M TO BE KWIN OF THE MAY -
"KRAZY," A SAD KAT WITH A LIGHT MIND, A HAPPY HEART, AND A NEW COAT OF SPRING FUR AMBLES INSIPIDLY INTO OUR STORY.
LET'S GO -
SANS TEARS, SANS REGRET, AND SANS FAREWELL, "TIDDY WEEWEE" THE FLEA LEAVES THE OLD HOME FOR THE NEW.
ZIP
ZIG
ZAG
GOOD HUNTING
L'IL AINJIL, HOW HE LOVES ME
AND HOW UNERRINGLY HE DELIVERS HIS DAILY MESSAGES OF EDMIRATIONS -
DAILY !!!
THIS IS NO PLACE FOR A PEACE LOVING FLEA -
I'M A HEPPY, HEPPY KET.
BE IT EVER SO-O-O-O HUMBLE - THERE AINT NO PLACE LIKE HOME -
HERRIMAN

May 26th, 1918.

OY, I'M HEPPY - I'M HEPPY - AND I HOPE THAT EVERY BODY'S HEPPY TOO.
HELLO!, 'IGNATZ', HOW IS EVERYTHINGS BY THOU ?
USUALLY, MR. STORK, HE GREETS ME WITH A 'BRICK' BUT TODAY HE DID'NT NOTICE ME A-TALL - I WUNDA IS HE MED AT ME.
MAD AT YOU, ? NO. HE HAS DECIDED TO SAVE ALL HIS 'BRICK' MONEY TO BUY 'LIBERTY BONDS' WITH - SO YOU SEE -
HOO-ROO HOO-RAA HO-ROR -
LI'L DIMOCRACY DEFENDA -
POW
ZIP
THANK GOODNESS KOBBLE ROCKS DONT COST ANYTHING
- AND - THE LAST ONE .
HERRIMAN

June 2nd, 1918.

OH, MY KLOCK, OH, MY "KOOKOO KLOCK" IT NO MORE TELLS THOSE TIME-
ONCE AGAIN THAT DOLEFUL DAME, THE WIDOW MARIQUITA PELONA, OR AS SHE IS KNOWN IN COCONINO THE VIUDA DOLOROSA - IS IN A STATE OF TEARS.
AND THIS IS THE "KOOKOO KLOCK" WHICH GIVES THIS WEEPING WIDOW HER DAY OF ILL REST.
ALAS, THEY HAVE STOLEN THE KOOKOO-BIRD FROM OUT OF MY KLOCK.
CAME A DAY WHEN THE BIRD WHICH KOOKED WITHIN THE KLOCK WAS STOLEN, AND THE MOIST MELANCHOLY INTO WHICH THIS LACHRYMOSE LADY PASSED WAS ASTOUNDING.
AH, SENOR KAT, HOW CAN I, A WIDOW, EVER REPAY YOU?
AW-F'GITIT.
KOO. KOO. KOOKOO KOO KOO
"KRAZY KAT" IT WAS WHO LAID THE ASHES OF SADNESS BY KOAXING A REAL "KOOKOO-BIRD" TO KOOK THE HOURS IN THE WIDOW'S KLOCK.
OH - WILL MISFORTUNE NEVER CEASE TO HAUNT ME?
KOO KOO
BUT JOY DIES YOUNG - FOR. WHILE THE "KOOKOO-BIRD" STILL KOOKS - THE KLOCK TELLS NO MORE TIME
SO, THAT SOOTHER OF SADNESS - "KRAZY," THAT BENEVOLENT BLUNDERER AGAIN WALKS INTO OUR STORY AS A SUPER-HOROLOGIST.
NO SPOOFING NOW, MRS. KOOKOO; I WANT TO KNOW WHY THIS KLOCK HAS STOPPED - TELL ME, OR I'LL BE PRETTY DAWGUN MAD AT YOU.
WELL "KRAZY," I'LL TELL YOU -
IN HIS EXPERT WAY HE SETS FORTH TO FIND OUT THE WHY OF THINGS.
OH-HO-HO - SO THAT'S IT? WELWELWEL
YES, THAT'S WHY = AND NOW, I DO HOPE YOU WILL RESPECT MY POSITION IN THIS MATTER -
THE CONVERSATION TURNS FROM THIS, AND THAT, TO A DELICATE SUBJECT - WHICH CONCERNS NEITHER YOU, NOR ME.
NOW MRS PELONA, YOU SEE HOW IT IS, SO BE RISSONABLE - IT WAS RILLY TO BE EXPECTED, SEEING LIKE HOW MRS. "KOOKOO-BIRD" IS SO VERY, VERY DOMESTIC IN HER HEBITS - SO DUNT WOIRY, ALL WILL BE WELL AGAIN -
AFTA THEY HETCH OUT, THEN THE KLOCK WILL RUN AGAIN - - ADIOS -
THERE IS A HEPPY LEND, FUR-FUR - A-WA-A-AY
HE'S SHINING UP TO THAT WIDOW TOO MUCH LATELY
HERRIMAN

June 9th, 1918.

I'M ON MY WAY TO THE "CORN" DOCTOR -
YOU POOR L'IL SINNA, IT'S A LONG LONG WAY TO THE "KORNS DOCTA" -
BUT -
BUT, NOTHING, I AIN'T GONNA LET YOU ABUSE YOUR SICK FEETS - NOT WHILE I GOT HEALTHY ONES - YOU AIN'T.
BUT LISTEN, FOOL
I WOULD N'T DO IT -
DR. POODIL EXPERT ON WARTS, WENS, KORNS, AND KALLOUSES
RAP RAP RAP
DOC I JUST DROPPED IN TO TELL YOU THAT MRS MOUSE'S CORN IS DOING FINE, AND SO YOU NEED N'T CALL ANY MORE
GOOD.
HERRIMAN
IF YOU WAIT TILL THE "DOCTA" FIXES MY FEETS, "IGNATZ", I'LL CARRY YOU BECK.
4 BUNIONS, 6 KORNS, 8 KALLOUSES, 3 STONE BRUISES, 12 PUNCTURES, A VERY, VERY INTERESTING CASE.

June 16th, 1918.

THE HOUR IS LATE; THE NIGHT IS DARK, THE AIR IS CHILL, AND "IGNATZ MOUSE" FEARS TO GO HOME.
IT IS MORAL SUPPORT HE WANTS, "KRAZY" IF ONLY SOME DOMINANT SOUL WOULD ADVISE HIM TO GO HOME, AND TELL HIM THAT ALL IS WELL - HE'D GO.
IN UDDA WORDS HE NEEDS A "CHASER" FOR HIS FEAR - IS THAT IT MR. STORK ?
"IGNATZ" DAHLINK - FEAR NOTHING, GO HOME, ALL IS WELL !!!
DAGAMBYA !! I NEVER TAKE ADVICE FROM "KATS", BEAT IT !!!
PLUP
ZIP
WELL, I DID THE BEST WHAT I COULD, SO NOW I'LL GO TO A PLACE OF GREAT SOLITUDE, AND COGITATE A BIT
THEY TELL ME THAT WHEN ONE IS IN DOUBT, AND IN NEED OF ADVICE, ONE SHOULD GO TO THE "WHISPERING JUG" IN THE CAVE UNDER THE "RED MITTEN," IT ALWAYS TELLS WHAT ONE SHOULD DO -
SO I'VE HEARD TELL.
GOLLY.
OH JUG! - ADVISE ME - WHAT MUST I DO GO HOME, OR NOT GO HOME ?
GO HOME, "IGNATZ," GO HOME - ALL IS WELL.
L'IL SOUPISTITIOUS.
WELCOME, DEAR HUSBAND, WELCOME
GOSH, THE JUG WAS RIGHT
THE NEXT DAY
WELL, I SEE YOU TOOK MY EDVICE, "IGNATZ," AND LIKE I TOLD YOU ALL WAS WELL - WAS'NT IT ?
YOUR ADVICE ?!!?
DID'NT I TELL YOU I NEVER TOOK ADVICE FROM "KATS."
BLAAM.
JIZ
AND THAT'S ALL.
HERRIMAN

June 23rd, 1918.

ZIZ
POW
TWELVE O'CLOCKS AND ALL IS WELL !!
GOOD HUNTING.
HERRIMAN

June 30th, 1918.

I'M GLAD YOU'RE WHERE YOU CAN'T PESTER THAT POOR "KRAZY KAT" — HE'LL BE SAFE FROM YOUR "BRICKS" NOW, FOR A FEW DAYS AT LEAST.
DAW-GAWNIT — THIS IS A BUM VACATION FOR ME.
SPANICLA
MR. & MRS. IGNATZ MOUSE, WITH THEIR THREE CHARMING CHILDREN, "MILTON," "MARSHAL," AND "IRVING," ARE SOJOURNING IN THE COOL HILLS OF "TUSAYAN," VACATIONING A BIT.
YES, "KANG," OLD BOY, MY WIFE HAS FERNIGGLED ME INTO COMING OUT HERE WITH HER, AND THE KIDS — AND HERE I'VE GOT A NICE "DOBY" BRICK, AND THAT "KAT" SAFE BACK IN TOWN.
S' TOO BAD TO WASTE SUCH A SWEET WEEPON — WE MUST COOK UP A SCHEME TO MAKE GOOD USE OF IT.
"IGNATZ MOUSE'S" LAMENT REACHES THE EARS OF HIS DESERT COUSIN, THE HON. KANGAROO RHATT, — WHO IS FULL OF MORE THAN USUAL WILE, AND WISDOM
DEAR BOY, HE'S THROWING THAT "BRICK" AWAY —
GO FORTH —
ZIPP
NEXT MORNING TIME — IN A MANNER SUGGESTING MYSTERY, "IGNATZ" CASTS AWAY HIS IDLE "BRICK".
AH —
AND, WE MIGHT SAY, IT IS A MATTER OF STRANGE CO-INCIDENCE THAT THE HON. KANGAROO RHATT SHOULD BE JUST WHERE THE DORNICK FELL.
CARRY ON.
ZIP.
AND IN AS MILD, AND INSIPID A WAY HE TOO TOSSES THE BRICK ONWARD —
ENDING ITS FLIGHT NOT MANY MILES FROM THE WELL KNOWN MR. WOOD RATT.
AH-H —
CARRY ON.
ZIZ
AND HE, IN A STYLE NO LESS QUAINT THAN HIS RELATIVES PUNCHES THE MISSILE ON —
AY —
IT LIGHTS IN THE VICINAGE OF "SENOR SAND MOUSE."
CARRY ON —
ZIP
WHO GIVE'S IT FURTHER IMPETUS.
FALLING WITHOUT A TRACE OF MALICE NEAR THE OLD SMOKE TREE WHERE-IN ROOSTS MR. FIELD MOUSE.
CARRY ON.
ZIG
IT MOVES ON
AH —
ENDING IT'S MOMENTUM FERNINST "JOE HEAUBEAU," A RAT OF THE WHARVES, AND GUTTERS
FOR TO-NIGHT — I AM A WEE-DO, IN A KOTTIDGE BY THE SEA —
POW
ZIP
OY — A MESSAGE OF LOVE
A BRICK, LIKE ALL THINGS HAS IT'S — "JOURNEY'S END"
ALL'S WELL —
ALL'S WELL
ALL'S WELL
ALL'S WELL
BACK OVER THE DESERT GOES THE GOOD NEWS.
ALL'S WELL !!
T'IS WELL
TO THE JOURNEY'S BEGINNING.
I DO BELIEVE HE'S REFORMING THE WRETCH
GOOD HUNTING.
HERRIMAN

July 7th, 1918.

"MADAME KAMOUFLAGE"
BEAUTY PARLOR
I.
WHERE THERE BE WOMEN THERE BE THESE TEMPLES OF "HENNA". THESE SHRINES OF "PATCHOULI". OUR DEAR ONES ENTER ONE THING, AND COME OUT ANOTHER. "ROMEO TODAY IS ONLY SURE OF HIS "JULIET BY HER BIRTHMARK.
AH, A KOOKOO, AND THE LITTLE DEAR IS GOING TO HAVE HERSELF MADE MORE BEAUTIFUL
II.
WHILE OUTSIDE FLUTTER THE STERNER SEX, LIKE MOTHS TO THE CANDLE. STAR-DUST IN THE WAKE OF VENUS.
I'LL LOOK LIKE THE KWIN OF SHIBBA WHEN I COME OUT.
DAW-GAWN !! LOOK WHAT'S GOING IN THAT BEAUTY PARLOR. THE NERVE OF THAT "KRAZY KAT"
III.
WAIT TILL HE COMES OUT - OH-H-H- WAIT !!!
IV.
WAITING - WISTFULLY WATCHFULLY AND VIGILANTLY.
V.
OOOH-H.
VI.
THE DEUCE WITH THAT "KAT" - I CANT WASTE TIME ON HIM, WITH BEAUTIFUL BLONDES LIKE THIS RUNNING WILD -
VII.
WOULD'ST DIP THY BEAK IN A BEAKER OF SASSPRILLA WITH ME, "SNOW MAIDEN," OR WOULD'ST TAKE A TRIP IN MY AIR-SHIP ? HUH ?
WHO, ME, SIR ?
VIII.
OY, "IGNATZ" DAHLINK, I DINT THINK YOU'D KNOW ME, NOW THAT I'M A "BLEACHES BLONDE"
IX.
GOSH !! I HOPE THAT "BRICK" IS STILL THERE !!
LIL "DONS JOOWAN"
X.
HERRIMAN

July 14th, 1918.

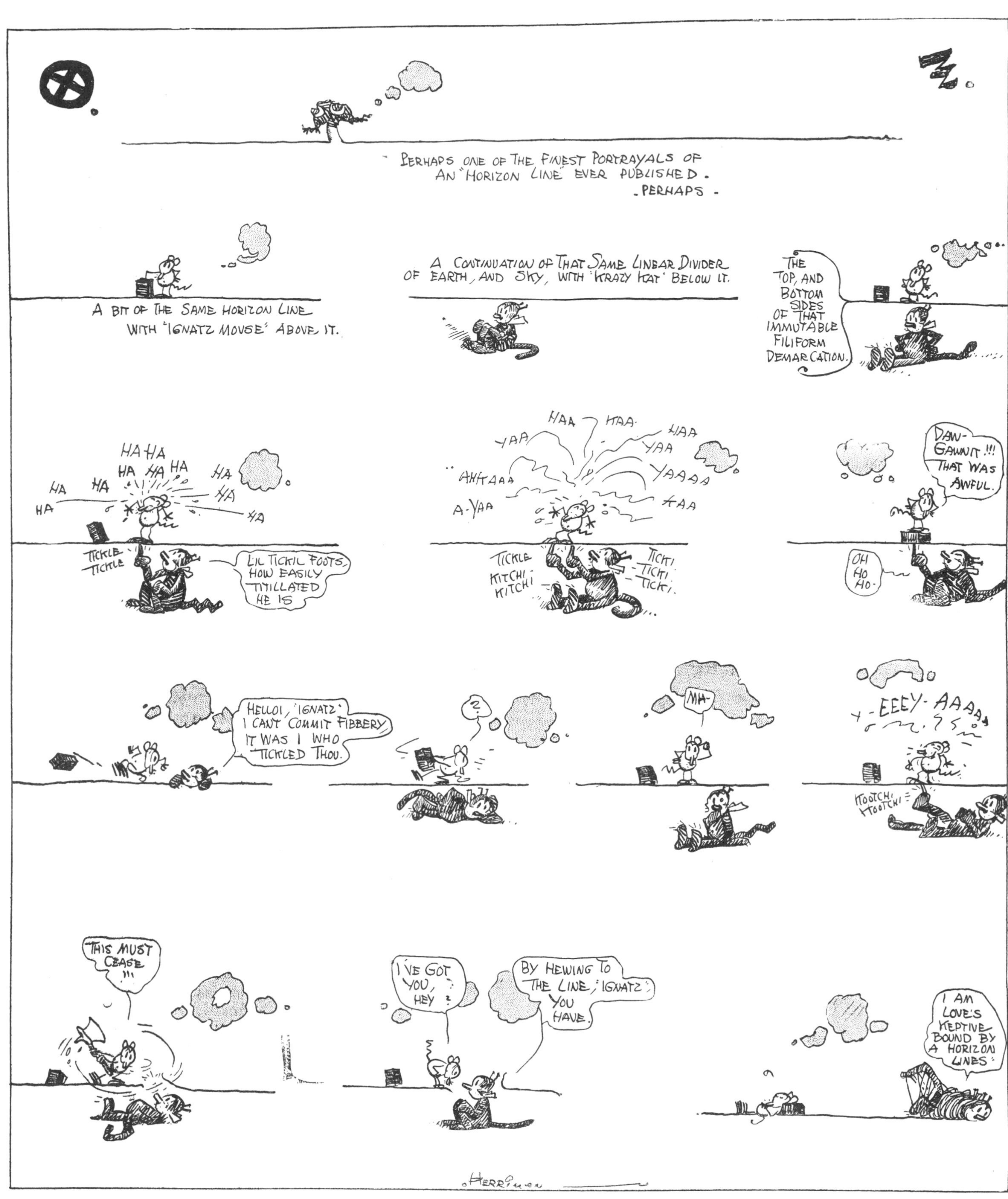

PERHAPS ONE OF THE FINEST PORTRAYALS OF AN "HORIZON LINE" EVER PUBLISHED. -PERHAPS-
A BIT OF THE SAME HORIZON LINE WITH "IGNATZ MOUSE" ABOVE IT.
A CONTINUATION OF THAT SAME LINEAR DIVIDER OF EARTH, AND SKY, WITH "KRAZY KAT" BELOW IT.
THE TOP, AND BOTTOM SIDES OF THAT IMMUTABLE FILIFORM DEMARCATION.
HA HA HA HA HA HA HA HA HA HA
TICKLE TICKLE
LI'L TICKIL FOOTS. HOW EASILY TITILLATED HE IS
HAA HAA HAA YAA YAA AHHAAA YAAAA A-YAA HAA
TICKLE KITCHI KITCHI
TICKI TICKI TICKI
DAW-GAWNIT!!! THAT WAS AWFUL.
OH HO HO.
HELLO!, "IGNATZ" I CAN'T COMMIT FIBBERY IT WAS I WHO TICKLED THOU.
?
MA-
EEEY-AAAA
TOOTCHI TOOTCHI
THIS MUST CEASE !!!
I'VE GOT YOU, HEY ?
BY HEWING TO THE LINE, "IGNATZ" YOU HAVE.
I AM LOVE'S KEPTIVE BOUND BY A HORIZON LINES.
HERRIMAN

July 21st, 1918.

OH-HO-HO-
A HOT-WATER
BOTTLES-
HOW FLET IT IS,
HOW INEEMIC,
HOW DIPSPEPTIC -
PFOOO
NOW IT'S A
HOT-AIR
BOTTLES.
YOI-HOI-HOI -
AND A BOTTLE
OF RUMS -
HOOY, THE GOOD SHIP
"HOT-WATER-BOTTLES"
IS NOW LUNCHED.
O'ER THE DE-E-EEP
BLO-OOOOO SEA -
SAIL ON -
SAIL ON.
OY, I'M FREE AS A
HOTTENTOTTLES
ON BOARD THE GOOD SHIP
HOTWATTA-BOTTLES
YES THAT'S HIM
ALRIGHT -
I MUST FIND A
MEANS OF
APPREHENDING
HIM.
I UNDERSTAND
"IGNATZ" -
I'LL GET
HIM.
YOU DO, MR. SORDFISH
AND THE REWARD
WILL BE MOST
MUNIFICENT.
S.O.S S.O.S. S.O.S
S.O.S.
S.O.S.
S.O.S
POP
ALL'S
WELL
GOOD -
A L'IL BIT FURDA
KOUSIN KRAZY KETFISH
A L'IL BIT FURDA.
I WUNDA WHAT
HE'S SO HEPPY
ABOUT.
GOOD
HUNTING.
HERRIMAN

July 28th, 1918.

FORTUNE FAVORS ME - A BRICK
A "BRICK," THE HARDEST, AND MOST WICKED, AND TRUCULENT OF IT'S KIND - AND THAT IT SHOULD FALL INTO THE HANDS OF "IGNATZ MOUSE" - ALAS, THE PITY OF IT.
WELCOME, SWEET MOON - YOUR CHASTE LIGHT WILL SURE HELP ME IN MY WORK THIS NIGHT.
AND THE "MOON", Y' KNOW THE "MOON", QUEEN OF THE NIGHT - THAT SHE TOO SHOULD LEND AID TO THIS CONTEMPLATED MASSACREE - N-N-NAAAA-HAAAA
FOR TONIGHT - I YAMMA WIDOW
AND "KRAZY KAT" - THE VICTIM - OY-OY-OY -
DAN-GANN THAT CLOUD -
THEN CAME A CLOUD - HAMPERING HIS EVIL VISION.
DAG-NABBIT !!!
THEN CAME TO OUR "MOON" AN ECLIPSE - THE DARKNESS OF WHICH NOT EVEN AN OWL'S EYE COULD PIERCE.
IT'S ALL OFF - NOW - MY NIGHT'S WORK HAS GONE TO POTS.
THEN, AS MOONS WILL DO, SHE GO DOWN - "JUSS LIKE THAT".
BUT THIS RESOURCEFUL MOUSE, AND HIS VIOLENT BRICK QUIETLY SLUMBER, AND AWAIT THE "DAY," AND THE SUN - IN WHOSE LIGHT THE DEADLY WORK WILL GO ON
YES, THE SUN ROSE, BUT WITH IT ROSE A FOG -
GAH-SHANGIT !!!
THEN DID A CLOUD OF THE NIMBUS VARIETY ENSHROUD IT
WHAT A WORLD, WHAT A WORLD !!
THEN, LIKE IT'S SISTER, THE "MOON" - IT IS ALSO LAID LOW IN DARKNESS BY AN ECLIPSE
THIS IS THE END !!!
AND THE "SUN," LIKE THE "MOON" - WILL GO DOWN - AND SO IT DOES -
LOOK, MR. FIRE-FLY IT SEEMS LIKE "IGNATZ" OVA-LOOKED A PRETTY NICE "BRICK", HEH
HERRIMAN

August 4th, 1918.

AH-H, A BEAUTIFUL DAY, A BEAUTIFUL BRICK, AND TO MAKE IT ALL PERFECT I WISH BUT TO MEET UP WITH THAT FOOL "KRAZY KAT."
THUNDER
BR-R-R BROOOOM
APPROACHING STORM
IGNATZ MOUSE" EXPRESSES A BEAUTIFUL, AND BENEVOLENT SENTIMENT, AND A VIOLENT WISH.
AND UNDER THE STRESS OF HIS EMBATTLED EMOTIONS HE PASSES INTO A STATE OF QUIESCENT SLUMBER.
OMY - OMY -
MY GOODNISS, THE LIGHTNINK HAS STRUCK UPON HIS "BRICK," AND BURSTED IT ALL TO A SMIDDARINS -
AH-H. ALL'S WELL -
THE STORM IS OVER, HIS BRICK IS USELISS, SO I SHALL LINGA NO LONGA, A LET HIM SLUMBA IN PEACE, LIL DAHLINK -
AN EVIL FATE HAS BEEN AT WORK WHILE I SLEPT - AND MY PLANS ARE ALL AWRY -
WHAT A DISMAL, DOLEFUL, DREARY DAY OF WOE THIS HAS BEEN FOR ME -
'IGNATZ MOUSE,' LIKE ANY DAY, ANY WEATHER, ANY CLIME, IS A CHILD OF MOODS, AND MOODS WILL CHANGE.
ADIOS.
HERRIMAN

August 11th, 1918.

THE MOON IS FULL TO-NIGHT -
AS IT HAS BEEN MANY A NIGHT IN THE PAST, AND WE TRUST IT WILL BE MANY A NIGHT TO COME.
WHICH MAY, OR MAY NOT INTEREST YOU -
.HOWEVER.
WITH A BACK ALLEY FENCE.
OMOON !! OMOON !!! OMOON !!!! WHAT IS IT IN THEE WHAT MAKES IN ME A GREAT DESIRE TO SING.
AND A "KAT" -
IT SEEMS THE WORLD'S GREATEST TRIO IN HARMONICS BE GATHERED TOGETHER IN FERVENT DISCORD.
TWUNK
K'MON KLIO - TUNE UP THE OLD HARP, AND LET'S GO.
FUR-R-R-R - TO-NIGHT
SKAT
ZIP
A OLD SHOE.
I YAM A WEEDOH -
SKAT
ZIP
A ROLLING PINS
IN A KAH - TUDGE -
SKAT
A KLOCK.
BY THUH
SKAT
ZIP
A FLET-IRON.
SEA -
POW -
ZAZ
AH - AT LAST A 'BRICK'
'IGNATZ' IS NIGH
L'IL TENTALIZA - YUN, MOON HAS NOT STIRRED MY SOUL TO SONG IN WAIN - MY DISH OF JOY IS FULL.
AND SO WITH THE LOWERING MOON "KLIO" FOLDS HER HARP, AND WITH THE WRAITH OF THE LAST NOTE IN KRAZY'S KONCERT PASSES OUT WITH THE EXPIRING NIGHT.
HERRIMAN

August 18th, 1918.

DAW-GAWN !! SHE'S DISCOVERED MY AMMUNITION DEPOT !!
AH-HAH !! SO HERE IS WHERE YOU KEEP IT, HEH ?
BUT "MAGNOLIA" MY DOVE IT'S ONLY TO LAMBASTE A FOOL "KAT" WITH A MOST WORTHY PURPOSE !!
WORTHY PURPOSE ME NECK, I FOR ONE WILL NOT STAND BY AND SEE THAT POOR "KRAZY KAT" GET MASSACREED !!
WOMAN, HAVE A CARE, DONT YOU DARE INTERFERE WITH MY PURSUIT OF HAPPINESS -
OH-HO-HO - I DONT DARE HEH ? - IS THA-A-AT SO ?
GOSH !! MY BLUFF DID'NT WORK -
NO DISH-FACED MOUSE CAN TALK TO ME LIKE THAT, AND LIVE TO WIGGLE A WHISKER - VILLAIN, YOUR DOOM IS NIGH -
AW "MAGNOLIA" BE CHARITABLE BE CHARITABLE
ZUP
ZEB
ZIB
ZAB
ZUP
ZOP
ZIB
YOU MONSTER !! YOU WOLF !! YOU LOAFER YOU BUMMER !!
MY GOODNISS, SEEMS LIKE THERE IS A RUMPIS IN "IGNATZ'S" HOUSE -
THAT AND THAT AND THAT
ZIP
ZIP
ZIP
ZIB
AH-H- LIL DAHLINK - NO METTA WHAT BETIDES, HE FORGETS-ME-NOTS.
THERE IS A HEPPY LEND, FUR-FUR A-WAAAAAY
OH WOTTA-WOIL - WOTTA-WOIL !!
WELL, I FEEL THAT I'VE SPARED THAT POOR "KRAZY KAT" A LOTTA MISERY TODAY -
HERRIMAN

August 25th, 1918.

COMES A TIME, THIS TIME, EACH YEAR WHEN NATURE IN HER WILFUL WAY SENDS INTO THIS WORLD AN HUMBLE VEGETABLE.
AH-H-H MY FAVORITE TIPPLE A WATTA-MELON VINES.
AND HUMBLY DOES IT PUT FORTH IT'S TENDER LEAVES IN SEARCH OF HEALTH, WEALTH, AND HAPPINESS.
I WILL NURSE IT INTO A MOST STURDY MEN-HOOD -
AND HUMBLY DOES THE HUMBLIEST OF HIS KIND LAVISH HIS CARE UPON THIS MODEST VINE, AND GENEROUSLY DOES IT RESPOND IN GROWTH, AND VEGETABLE COMLINESS.
OH-HO-HO, A BLOOM IS HERE, OH, HARBINGER OF DELIGHT, OH, FO-RUNNA OF BLISS.
SOON THERE DAWNS A SUMMER DAY WHEN AN HUMBLE BLOSSOM NESTLES IN THE LEAFY ARMS OF THE NOW PARENTAL VINE.
WEEY. A CHILD MELON - AND DOINK WELL - HOOROO !!
FROM THE HUMBLE PARENT TO THE HUMBLE OFFSPRING - WE NOW MUST TURN.
OH, HASTE THEE HASTE THEE - AND GET RIPE.
BATHED IN THE DEWS OF SUMMER DAWNS, FANNED BY THE SUMMER BREEZE, WARMED BY THE RAYS OF THE SUMMER SUN - ADROWSED BY THE SUMMER MOON -
"LOR-DELPUS."
AT LEST THEE IS RIPE.
"SANDIA," GODDESS OF MELONS, BE PRAISED !!! — OUT OF THE MISTS OF HUMILITY, BEHOLD, THIS PARAGON OF VEGETABLES !!!
"IGNATZ," MOST DAHLINK OF MICES, T'IS HIM WHO SHALL FIRST SIP OF THIS AMIABLE FRUIT
BEHOLE, AT THY FEETS I PLACE A PRICELISS PEARL
AT LAST A SIGN OF INTELLIGENCE DAWNS UPON YOU, FOOL.
ARE YOU PREPARED FOR THE FIST, "IGNATZ" ?
AM I - MMMM - YMMM YMM
A CITRON !!!
PLOP !!
ZIB
FOR TO-NIGHT, I YAMMA WIDOW IN A HAH-TUDGE BY THE SEA.
HERRIMAN

September 1st, 1918.

"KRAZY KAT" HAD A DREAM THE OTHER NIGHT — 'TWAS OF A BULL-FIGHT" —
THE NEXT MORNING HE AWOKE WITH "SPANISH INFLUENZA" — WHICH MAY, OR MAY NOT DISPROVE THE "GERM" THEORY
WEDDA, OR NOT I GOT A "SPANISH INFLIENZA", I'VE GOTTA KEEP MY DATES WITH "IGNATZ" — THAT'S ALL THEY IS TO THAT.
I WAS THINKING, MR. KELLY IF YOU COULD TELL ME WHERE IS "IGNATZ MOUSE" ?
I HAVE N'T THE LEAST IDEA "KRAZY" — HE HAS N'T BEEN AROUND TODAY.
KOLIN KELLY. DEALER IN BRICKS
GOLLIX, IT'S SURE SOMETHINGS SERIOUS WHEN HE DONT GO BY MR. KELLY TO BUY A BRICK.
IGNATZ MOUSE.
NOK NOK NOK
IGNATZ MOUSE
I DONT THINK YOU'D BETTER COME IN "KRAZY" HE HAS THE "SPANISH INFLUENZA", AND IT'S SO CATCHING —
NOW I CAN ENJOY MY SPANISH INFLIENZA WITH A EASY CONSCIENCE.
HERRIMAN

September 8th, 1918.

L'IL' WATTA-WOIX, HE WIPS, CAN YOU TELL ME FOR WHY MR. STORK ?
WELL 'KRAZY', IT'S THIS WAY, MR. HOOVER HAS ORDERED EACH, AND ALL OF US TO ADOPT A 'HOG', AND 'IGNATZ' BEING OF AN INCONSIDERABLE STATURE IS NOT MAN ENOUGH TO SUFFICIENTLY INTIMIDATE A PIG INTO HIS SERVICE. HENCE, HE WEEPS.
?
BEFORE THIS DAY IS OVER, 'IGNATZ' WILL NOT BE PIGLISS.
MASQUERADE COSTUMES.
WIGS & FALSE FACE FOR HIRE.
NOT ONLY WILL I DELIGHT 'IGNATZ', BUT ALSO WILL MR. HERBIT HOOVA' BE PLEASED BY ME.
AS A 'PIG' YOU ARE PERFECT 'KRAZY' - ALL BUT THE TAIL, WHICH SHOULD HAVE A MARCEL WAVE IN IT.
GOLLUX, I FORGOT THAT.
THERE, THAT'LL FETCH IT.
THANX, MR. SKYTERRA YOU DID ME A GOOD TURNS.
DONT MENTION IT, 'KRAZY', TURNS IS WHAT YOU NEEDED IN THAT TAIL.
OYNQUE. OYNQUE.
HOORAY !! A PIG - A PIG - PROVIDENCE HAS PROVIDED.
WHEN, OUT OF A CLEAR SKY, LIKE THIS
COMES A RAIN, LIKE THIS
RAINBOW
OH-HOH, THERE'S ONLY ONE TAIL IN THE WORLD LIKE THAT, ONLY ONE, AND I KNOW THAT ONE TOO.
MY DISH OF HEPPINISS IS ALMOST FULL.
AND WE ALL KNOW WHAT AN EXCESS OF MOISTURE WILL DO TO A "MARCEL WAVE", DONT WE ? ASK 'MA', SHE KNOWS, AND SO DOES 'IGNATZ'
ZIP
AND NOW IT IS.
AS LONG AS IT'S A 'HOG' WHY SHOULD I WORRY -
A GROUND HOG'S HOUSE
HERRIMAN

September 15th, 1918.

"KRAZY" IS NOW THE OWNER OF AN "AUTOMOBILE", A SPEEDSTER OF GREAT VELOCITY, FORCE, ENDURANCE, AND MECHANICAL INTELLIGENCE.
1.
2.
HAWNK KAWNK AWNK
3.
HAWNK KWAWNK GAWNK
4.
5.
A DOLLAR'S WORTH OF YOUR BEST "CATNIP" MR. KASKARA
NUX VOMICA
DOOLOOROO
HABBAS CORPUS
GUMBUTUS HUDSONIA
TASTA ERL
6.
7.
SNIFF-FA
8.
9.
"KRAZY" NO LONGER HAS THAT NEW AUTOMOBILE, MR STORK. THAT SPEEDSTER, OF GREAT VELOCITY, FORCE, ENDURANCE, AND MECHANICAL INTELLIGENCE — NO — HE HAS IT NO LONGER.
10.
HERRIMAN

September 22nd, 1918.

OOY I DUNT KNOW WHAT'S IN MY HEAD WHAT CAN GIVE SUCH A PAIN - ITS IN MY HEAD SO IT MUST BE A HEAD ACHE.
AND ITS MY SINCERE WISH THAT 'IGNATZ' WOULD REFRAME FROM BINNING ME BY A BRICK OR TWO TODAY - OY -
IF YOU'VE GOT A HEAD ACHE "KRAZY" I'D ADVISE YOU TO GO INTO HIDING QUICK I'VE JUST SOLD "IGNATZ MOUSE" A FINE MESS OF BRICKS AND I FEAR FOR YOUR POOR SICK HEAD -
THEAX 'MR. KELLY' I WILL EXCEPT THE INFIMATION WITH SPID AND ALECKRITTY.
GOSH NO METTA WHERE I'LL HIDE HE'LL SEEK ME OUT - I WISH I COULD THINK OF A WAY TO OUT-WHITTLE HIM.
AND SO OUR NIMBLE LIMNER WITH NIMBLE WIT DELINEATES AN UNFAVORABLE DESIGN WITH HOPES OF A FAVORABLE RESULT.
OKDULEEVA VOTS ISSIT ?
L'IL PATRIOTICS.
"KRAZY KAISERS" ARE AS BAD AS "KRAZY KATS" TO ME. DERNEM !!!
HERRIMAN

September 29th, 1918.

October 6th, 1918.

ALL DAY I'VE BEEN HOPING, SOME BODY WOULD 'GO THERE', AND STILL NO BODY HAS YET-
ONE.
DAW GUNNIT !! WHO GOES THERE !!!
TWO.
HEY !! WHAT'S THE IDA, AINT NO BODY NEVER GONNA 'GO THERE' ?
THREE.
WHO 'GOES THERE, OVER HERE, HUH ?
FOUR.
I'LL DESH BECK - MAYBE SOME BODY'S OVER HERE NOW -
FIVE.
AT LAST, IT'S SOMEBODY - TELL ME RIGHT AWAY, IS YOU 'IGNATZ MICE' ?
I AM OFFICER 'B. PUPP'
SIX.
AND, I WANT TO TELL YOU, YOU NEED HAVE NO FEAR OF 'IGNATZ' BOTHERING YOU WHILE ON DUTY - I'VE GOT MY EYE ON HIM.
SEVEN.
OGOSH, TWENNY MINUTE TO TWELVE, AND ALL AINT SO GOOD - JEEWIZZ !!
EIGHT.
HERRIMAN
ONE FALSE MOVE, WRETCH
NINE.

October 13th, 1918.

YOU SAY, MY HUSBAND, MR. IGNATZ MOUSE, ORDERED THAT BATH-TUB BROUGHT HERE ?
YES LADY HE SURE DID.
WE DONT KNOW WHAT HE WANTS IT FOR, BUT HERE IT IS.
HE'LL PROBABLY PUT SAILS ON IT, AND USE IT FOR A BOAT.
MAYBE HE WANTS IT FOR AN ORNAMENT.
IT WOULD MAKE A NICE FOLDING BED.
OR A PILL-BOX.
I MUST GET TO THE BOTTOM OF THIS.
THE FIRST "BATH-TUB" IN ALL TIMES, ARRIVES AT "COCONINO," AND CITIZENS "T. TURTIL," "WALTER C. AUSTRIDGE," "JOE STORK," "KOLIN KELLY," AND "DON KIYOTI" ARE MUCH IMPRESSED, AND DULY DUMBFOUNDED
THE DAY ROLLS ON, AND "KURIOSITY" FADES AWAY FROM ALL BUT IN THE SOUL OF "KRAZY KAT," WHERE-IN "KURIOSITY" ONCE PLANTED FINDS FERTILE SOIL, AND SO GROWS, AND GROWS, AND GROWS
ODEER - ODEER IF ONLY I COULD REASON IT OUT, THIS SISPENSE IS MORE THAN I CAN BEAR.
"KRAZY" RETIRES TO THE SHADE OF THE OLD UMBRELLA TREE, TO DWELL IN A BLISSFUL FEVER OF KURIOSITY, UNTIL HE PASSES INTO THE LIMBO OF USELESS UNCONSCIOUSNESS.
OH HO-HO-
YES "KELLY" IT'S A BIG ORDER, BUT YOU SEE I'M LAYING IN A SUPPLY FOR THE WINTER.
THEY SHALL BE DELIVERED AT ONCE "IGNATZ"
SHOWING HERE-IN THAT "KURIOSITY" WHICH SO DIMS THE WIT OF A "KAT" WILL FAN INTO A GREAT BRIGHTNESS THAT OF A "KOYOTE".
SHUX, IT CAN'T BE COAL, BECAUSE Y' DONT ORDER COAL IN A "BRICK-YARD," SO IT MUST BE "BRICKS".
THUS —
WELL, I'M FIXED FOR THE WINTER NOW LET THAT FOOL "KAT" HAVE A CARE.
AND SO IT IS, SO IT IS.
I'VE DECIDED THAT THE ONLY WAY TO FIND OUT IS TO GO, AND ASK "IGNATZ".
HERRIMAN

October 20th, 1918.

I ASK YOU AS A FAVOR "KRAZY" TO WATCH OVER THEM - MY "PEARL" AND "RUBY."
MRS. WREN I'LL WATCH OVER THEM GOOD, AND FAITHFIL
OH-HO-HO "GEMS" -
ONE.
GUARD THEM WELL THIS NIGHT "KRAZY" THEY ARE MY JEWELS SEE THAT NOTHING BEFALLS THEM I SHALL RETURN AT SUNRISE.
WITH ALL OF MY NINE LIVES MRS. WREN I WILL PROTECK THEM.
"JEWELS" HOHO -
TWO.
AND SO OFF INTO THE NIGHT A MOUSE SETS FORTH WITH A SOUL LADEN WITH EVIL INTENT.
THREE.
THERE'LL BE LOOT FOR ALL - "KRAZY" IS GUARDING THE JEWELS ALONE - WE'LL BE MORE THAN A MATCH FOR HIM —
AH-H IH-H HI!!!
AH-H HAAA AH-H HA-H
FOUR.
FOLLOW ME MEN !!!
PEARLS & RUBIES LEAD ON KAP - WE FOLLOW -
OVER THE HILLS THEY GO — MARAUDER MICE, BENT ON MAYHEM, MASSACREE, AND PLUNDER —
FIVE.
AH-H - L'IL RUBIES AH-H - L'IL PEARLS YOU IS JEWELS INDEED —
DO YOU HEAR MEN ? - SPAKE I NOT TRUTH ?
AYE-AYE KAP LET US AT THE LOOT - BEFORE SHE WHO OWNS THEM RETURNS AT THE RISE OF SUN.
SIX
NOW RUBY, AND PEARL, YOU BE GOOD L'IL "WREN-BIRDS" - YOUR MUDDA WILL BE BECK SOON AS THE SUN MAKES A RISE ON THE YEAST.
KWEE KWEE KWEE KWEE
SEVEN.
ROCKY RYE RUBIES ROCKY RYE PEARLS - BE GOOD LITTIL BIRDIES BE GOOD LITTIL GIRLS. WHEN DE MOMMA COMES BECK A BIG WORM SHE'LL BRING AND DEN LITTIL RUBIES AND PEARLIES WILL SING -
DOWN WITH HIM -
HE'S A LIAR -
SHOOT HIM -
TRAI-TOR -
BUT MEN - LET ME EXPLAIN.
EIGHT.
HERRIMAN

October 27th, 1918.

OVER WITH IT.
NOW FOLLOW IT.
GOOD, DID IT GATHER ANY MOSS ?
WELL, I FOLLOWED IT, 'IGNATZ'
PLOP.
NO.
THAT'S WHAT I THOUGHT.
L'IL FILLOSSIFFA, ALWAYS HE SEEKS THE TRUTH, AND ALWAYS HE FINDS IT.
HERRIMAN

November 3rd, 1918.

HA-A- IT RAINS.
I MUST SEEK SHELTER
YON TREE WILL GIVE ME PROTECTION.
THESE UMBRELLA TREES ARE SURE A WISE PROVISION OF NATURE.
IT SLACKENS -
IT IS OVER -
THAT UMBRELLA TREE SURE SAVED MY LIFE.
HO-HMM- I GUESS I WONT SEE 'KRAZY' TODAY KATS NEVER COME OUT IN RAINY WEATHER - POOR FOOLS.
DAW-GUNNIT !! S'RAINING AGAIN.
BLESS MY EYE ANOTHER UMBRELLA TREE - JUST WHEN I NEED IT AGAIN -
ONCE MORE I MUST THANK NATURE FOR PROVIDING ME WITH SHELTER
IT HAS CEASED RAINING -
WELL, I'M ALMOST HOME NOW -
MY "OLD LADY" WILL BE SURPRISED TO FIND ME DRY, AFTER PASSING THROUGH TWO SHOWERS.
I TELL YOU THERE ISN'T AN UMBRELLA TREE WITHIN TWO MILES OF HERE
BUT 'MAGNOLIA', MY OWN, I KNOW, BECAUSE I SOUGHT SHELTER UNDER TWO OF THEM -
OH-HMM- I CANT SAY THAT THIS DAY HAS BEEN IN WAIN - IT HAS BEEN FROTH WITH EDWENTURE
HERRIMAN.

November 10th, 1918.

Old "King Kole" abdicates his throne, and is now tossing wheat poultices in Joe Brown's Broadway Bean Stube. The well known King of Klubs was black-balled, and run out of town. King Dumkum was assassinated by a saxophone jazzist. King "Pinn", is now a sock mangler in Mr. Pee Wee's Select Oriental Laundry. Forecast for "Kings" today - dark, and stormy.
A close up of that which "Krazy" reads..
My goodniss, this is awfil.
While keeping a date with "Ignatz Mouse", "Krazy Kat" dips his mind into a bit of news, and is much disturbed there at.
To think I never took the adwantage us "Kats" has of looking at "Kings" and now they is all getting put out of business
And so decides to somewhere find a "King" to look upon — before the last of these royal kooties pass away from earth.
Oyez - oyez - ye King holds court today - oyez oyez -
Ye King's Kourt.
I wish to look at the "King"
Two bits is the fee - sir.
Two bits, my feet - "Kings" was made for us "Kets" to look at. You warlet !!
So, that's a "King" !!
Golly, I always had a ida they was grend, and megnifishint, and wondafil, and mejestic like King Richid the Lime Heart, but my goodniss !! It aint so.
And here I passed up a date with "Ignatz", just to look at a fake like this - ogosh - ogosh - ogosh.
Get out of my way !!!
Daw-gunnit !! Raus with this ermine. I abdicate !!!
Oh, for one look at "Ignatz", now - most demi-krettic of mices.
Rear entrance to ye King's palace.
Herriman

November 17th, 1918.

MY GOODNISS !! A KEPTIVE KANARY BIRDS IN A KAGE.
I WILL RESKUE YOU.
THERE NOW, GO FOURTH TO LIBITTY.
TWEE ?
YOU IS NOW FREE, FREE, FREE - TO FLITTA HIDDA, AND YUN IN YOUR NATIVE ELIMINT ONCE MORE.
PWEE.
BUT WHAT PROFITS IT TO A "CANARY" TO GAIN IT'S FREEDOM IF THAT FREEDOM BE BOUNDED BY A WORLD UNKNOWN, STRANGE, AND MYSTERIOUS ???
HO-HO-HO - IT'S FIRST TIME OUT - I'LL GIVE HIM A SCARE
HELP !! HELP !! HELP - !!!
WAF-WAF-WAF IM A "TIGER" - WAP WAP -
WA-AL WHAT'S THE IDEA HUH ?
I-I-I-I-I W-WAS ONLY FOOLING, OFFICER
YOU FADE !!!
YOU FOOL CAGE BIRDS AINT GOT NO BUSINESS TO BE OUT IN THE WIDE WORLD A-TALL -
OH, JUST GET ME BACK IN MY CAGE, SIR, AND I WILL NEVER ROAM AGAIN - NEVER !!
GET IN, AND CLOSE THE DOOR AFTER YOU.
MY GOODNISS !! HE'S IN AGAIN, AND ONCE MORE I GOTTA SET HIM FREE !!
YOU VILLAIN, DONT YOU DARE SET ME FREE AGAIN, DONT YOU DAST LURE ME FROM MY GILDED CAGE NO MORE - GO 'WAY, OR I'LL "TWEET" FOR HELP !!
TWEE TWEE-EE WEE-EE
"KRAZY KANARY"
KRAZY KAT
HERRIMAN

November 24th, 1918.

THERE IS A SINISTER FULNESS TO THE MOON TONIGHT AN INSIDIOUS LUNAR AMPLITUDE REPLETE WITH SEBACIOUS GUILE AND ARTFUL WILE.
OH-H-MMMM - WELL, I'VE HAD A GOOD DAY'S SLEEP, AND I'M FULL OF 'PEP' AND READY FOR MY NIGHT'S KONCERT
ALL OF WHICH HAS ITS EFFECT UPON SENOR 'KARUSO KAT' FIRING HIS SINFUL SOUL WITH A MALIGNANT DESIRE TO CELEBRATE IN SONG.
AINT YOU GOT NO DISSINCY, GOING OUT TO MAKE NOISES AT THIS HOUR OF THE NIGHT - HUH - I'M ASHAMED FOR YOU -
A-AAH - SHUT UP
BUT, DESPITE THE WORDS OF ADMONITION ADMINISTERED BY HIS WISER RELATIVE, 'KRAZY KAT', THIS KAT, 'KARUSO KAT' PERSISTS IN HIS AIM TO BLAST THE SAINTED NIGHT WITH HIS MAUDLING MINSTRELSY, AND SHIVER THE VERY STARS WITH HIS IRRELIGIOUS CAROLING -
AND SO, AT THE STROKE OF TWO, A.M. - HE LETS FORTH HIS OVERTURE OF AGONY - THEN WITH MAGNIFICENT SPLEEN HE BESTOWS UPON THE WORLD A YODLING OF THE MOST EXQUISITE DESPAIR - RUNNING THE GAMUT OF MAYHEM, MURDER, AND MASSACREE.
SKAT !! SKAT !!! SKAT !!! SKAT !!
SKAT !! SKAT !! SKAT !!! SKAT !! SKAT !
BOUNTY & LARGESS - WITH MALEDICTIONS.
AS USUAL MY KONCERT WAS A GRAND SUCCESSFUL FAILURE
I GIVE THEM ART, I GIVE THEM SONG - AND THEY ABUSE ME
OF-COURSE YOU DO, 'KARUSO,' BUT YOU GIVE IT TO THEM AT THE WRONG TIME - LOOK AT ME, I STAY HOME AT NIGHT AND NOBODY ABUSES ME - NOBODY THROWS THINGS AT ME - Y BETCHA
NO-BODY, 'KRAZY' ?
NO BODY - 'KARUSS'
POW
ZIZ
LUCKY 'KAT'
LUCKY IS RIGHT !!!
L'IL DAHLINK MICE
HERRIMAN

December 1st, 1918.

IT MAY INTEREST YOU, "MR. MOUSE" TO KNOW THAT MR. PERCIVAL PURP THE MILLIONAIRE PRESIDENT OF THE BONE TRUST HAS ALSO PROMISED ME A PEARL NECKLACE
OH, FAIREST ONE, DO NOT ACCEPT IT, FOR I WILL GET YOU ONE THAT WILL MAKE HIS LOOK LIKE A STRING OF CHALK PILLS.
BEING A BIT OF MORE, OR LESS AMOROUS PERSIFLAGE TAKING PLACE IN THE PARLOR OF THE GAY MISS. PAULINE PULLET, THE BELLE OF COCONINO
ANY TIME THAT "PERCIVAL PURP" CAN GET AHEAD OF ME "PAULINE" WILL HAVE THAT NECKLACE EVEN IF THE WIFE AND KIDS GO WITHOUT CHEESE FOR A MONTH.
AH, EACH ONE A GEM OF THE FIRST MAGNITUDE
Jeweler
AND WITH THE JEWELS — A DAINTY CARD SAYING —— "TO THE MOST CHARMING OF CHARMERS".
IF ONLY I HAD DIME TO BUY 'IGNATZ' A PRESENT OF A ALL DAY SUCKA, OR SOME OTHER DELICACY - BUT, GOLLIX, I AINT - SO I AINT HEPPY LIKE I SHOULD BE
OH WELL, I WILL SLUMBA, AND FORGET.
I SAW HIM BUYING THEM TODAY, MEN, THEY ARE WORTH A FORTUNE.
T'IS WELL.
ROBBER RATS CONSPIRE —
BEHIND THIS SNOW PILE, MEN, T'IS AN IDEAL PLACE TO LAY FOR HIM.
AYE AYE CAP
SH-H-H- HE COMES
STAND, "IGNATZ MOUSE" AND DELIVER !!!
TAKE THE JEWELS, BUT SPARE MY LIFE.
WE'RE GIVING YOU FIVE MINUTES TO GET HOME - VAMOS !!
ZIP
ZIP
ZIP
I'LL DO IT IN FIVE SECONDS.
AND I'M GIVING YOU "RETS" JUST ONE FIFT OF A SECOND TO GET AWAY FROM HERE — NOW SKATTA !!!
FEAR NOT, "IGNATZ" THE "JEWELS" IS SAFE.
JEWELS, WHAT JEWELS ?
L'IL "ROMEO" HE'S GONNA MAKE LOVE TO HIS WIFE SO I'LL SNICK QUIETLY AWAY.
"TO THE MOST CHARMING OF CHARMERS" - WHO IS SHE ?
WHO BUT THEE DEAR WIFE.
AINT POPPA KIND TO MOMMA
SINCE WHEN HAS THAT HUSSY, MISS. PULLET KNOWN MR. PURP ?
HOW SHOULD I KNOW.
SURE THEY LIVED HEPPY FOR EVVA EFTA-WIDS.
HERRIMAN

December 8th, 1918.

OH-HO - SO "IGNATZ MICE" YOU IS A L'IL INFIDDLE HEH?
I DON'T BELIEVE IN "SANTA CLAUS" - I'M TOO BROAD-MINDED, AND ADVANCED FOR SUCH NONSENSE.
WE OPEN, WITH A SCENE, RIFE WITH SKEPTICISM, AND HERESY.
COSTUMES.
GOLLIX, YOU GOT NO IDA HOW THIS OUTFIT MAKES ME FEEL YULE-TIDISH, AND XMASY - IF ONLY IT CAN HAVE THE SAME EFFECT ON "IGNATZ MICE" L'IL UNBELIEVA -
YEZZA, IT'S THE BUNK OF THE AGES - I'D JUST AS SOON BELIEVE THE MOON IS MADE OF CHEESE, AS TO BELIEVE IN MR. S. CLAUS.
WE GET THIS FAR, AND YET THE ATMOSPHERE OF UNBELIEF AND INFIDELITY ABOUNDS IN COPIOUS AMPLITUDE.
IGNATZ MICE!! BEHOLD!!! I AM SENTA KLAWS -
FORGIVE ME FOR DOUBTING, MR. CLAUS; I REALLY DID NOT THINK YOU EXISTED.
ALL IS FIGGIVEN, I EXCEPT YOUR APOLOGY - A-RISE!!!
OH-HO - THAT TAIL.
IT WAS EASY.
L'IL REPENTINT SINNA HE THENX ME FOR DELIVERING HIM FROM INIQUITY.
POW!!
ZAB
I DON'T BELIEVE IN SANTA CLAUS, I'M TOO BROAD-MINDED, AND ADVANCED FOR SUCH NONSENSE.
WE CLOSE, WITH A SCENE, RIFE WITH SKEPTICISM, AND HERESY.
HERRIMAN

December 15th, 1918.

DAW-GUNNIT !! HERE IS A REGULAR PARADISE OF "DORNICKS" AND "BRICKS", AND YET ONLY THIS MORNING DID I OBSERVE THE CUSTOM OF THE NEW YEAR, AND RESOLVE TO REFRAIN FROM BEANING THAT "KRAZY KAT" !!! DAG-NABBIT !!
ONE.
OH, "RHUM" THAT I WAS TO MAKE SO RASH A RESOLUTION—
TWO.
HO, MANY A TRAIL, AND MANY A JAIL I'VE HIT IN OLD "AUSTRALE", BUT I'VE YET TO GET THE WORD Y'BET THAT'LL RHYME WITH—"KAN-GA-ROO"
I'VE TRAVELED BY RAIL, AND TRAVELED BY SAIL FAR AWAY FROM OLD AUSTRALE, BUT I'M HOPING YET THAT WORD TO GET. BOY! PAGE JIMMY JAY "MON-TA-GUE".
NEWLY ARRIVED, IS "JOE. BUSH" THE BUSHIEST BUSH RANGING BUSH-HOUND FROM THE AUSTRALIAN BUSH—FONDLY CARESSING THAT ANTIPODEAN INSTRUMENT OF DESTRUCTION, THE BOOMERANG
THREE.
WHAT'LL YOU TAKE FOR THAT ??
TWO BITS
FOUR.
YOU'RE ON !!!
KLINK
25
FIVE.
THEY TELL ME YOU HAVE A WONDERFUL PITCHING ARM, "KRAZY," I WONDER HOW FAR YOU COULD TOSS THIS ?
WELL "IGNATZ," I HATE TO BREG, BUT I GOT A IDA I COULD THROW IT A CONSIDDBLE DISTINCT—
SIX.
WONDERFUL !!!
UH-HAH UHH H
ZIP
SEVEN.
WUNDAFIL IS RIGHT, I TOSSED IT CLEAR OUT OF SIGHT.
EIGHT.
GOOD HUNTING !!
B-ZE-EE-E
POW
NINE.
HERRIMAN

December 22nd, 1918.

OH, WHAT A BOONS IT IS INDEED TO HAVE A GREAT "MORAL SENSE", OH, WHAT A GIFF IT IS TO PUZZESS THAT WUNDAFIL KNECK OF KNOWING RIGHT FROM WRONG -
WHAT MANNER OF PERSON IS THIS OF WHOM YOU PRATE, "KRAZY" WHO POSSESSES THIS GREAT GIFT, "MORAL SENSE" - OR, DO YOU DREAM ?
OH, OFFISSA PUPP" KNOW YOU NOT HE ? WHY WHO BUT "IGNATZ" IGNATZ MICE", HE IS THE LIL "MORAL SENSIST" OF WHO I PRATED. -YEZZA-
A AAH - QUIT YOUR LALLYGAGGING. THAT MOUSE HAS ABOUT AS MUCH "MORAL SENSE" AS HE HAS FUR ON HIS TAIL - TELL ME ANOTHER, "KRAZY"
B-BUT OFFISSA, I ASSURE YOU. -
BRICKS" !! CHOICE BRICKS !!! CHEAP TODAY - FRESH BRICKS !!!
HERE'S WHERE HE LOSES HIS MORAL SENSE.
KOLIN KELLY DEALER IN BRICKS
D'LIKE TO HAVE A NICE FRESH "BRICK" OR TWO MR. MOUSE - FRESH BAKED, JUST OUT OF THE OVEN, AND DERN CHEAP -
HE'LL FALL.
KOLIN KELLY DEALER IN BRICKS
NO, I DON'T WANT ANY "BRICKS" !!!
AH-H-
VERY WELL, SIR.
MAYBE I CAN TAKE YOUR ORDER FOR ONE, OR TWO "BRICKS", TO-MORROW HUH ?
NO, NONE TOMORROW, EITHER !!
M-M-M
KOLIN KELLY DEALER IN BRICKS
YOU SEE, OFFISSA "PUPP" ?
I DO-
HEY, "KELLY" !!!!
LIL JINYIS.
HERRIMAN

December 29th, 1918.

# A Genius of the

by Summerfield

LA CASA DE JOSÉ CIGUENO, OR IN OTHER WORDS THE HOUSE OF JOE. STORK ON THE CREST OF THE ENCHANTED MESA IN THE "DESIERTO PINTADO" = = HE'S ALWAYS LOOKING FOR A "CUSTOMER" =

THERE is a man named Herriman. All that I know of him is that he signs his name in curious letters to the most charming column of comic pictures that it has ever been my privilege to see. Do not recoil in horror before what you fear is going to be an apology for American vulgarism. The personalities that populate the world of Krazy Kat as they appear from day to day in the Hearst journals are not vulgar. They are rather the products of one of the most original and delicate of all contemporary American creative geniuses. It is my purpose to point out in the following pages wherein that genius is original and delicate, and in some measure to show that its indigenous nature is something of which Americans might well be proud. A person with a fancy for the comic section is ordinarily prone to be ashamed of it, to excuse it as a means of relaxation, as an escape from reality, as a thousand and one other foibles. The shame and the excuses are right and natural, save in this single instance. For to follow the adventures of Mr. Herriman's fantastic animals is a delight which no one should underestimate or fail to enjoy.

I am not sure exactly when the series started. It must have been at least six years ago. For a number of years the sole actors on Mr. Herriman's stage were Krazy Kat and Ignatz Mouse. The motif of the drama they enacted was the perpetual chastisement of the Kat by the Mouse, a chastisement usually performed by the hurling of a brick at the former's head, and usually incited by some particularly atrocious manifestation of idiocy on the former's part. The origin of this conception is obvious enough, and is based solely on a reversal of the normal relations of the feline to the rodent.

Now it is a distinguishing characteristic of the technique of the comic artist that with the exhaustion of the situations suggested by the original protagonists and their

AH-H- LIL AINJIL

"KRAZY KAT" NEVER WRONG, NEVER RIGHT = SO DOPE HIM OUT YOURSELF.

# Comic Page

Baldwin

primary raison d'être, the material may be enlarged in two ways: first, and to the greatest possible extent, by the development of new phases in the old characters; second, as a last resort, by the introduction of new personages. In this respect, Mr. Herriman's craftsmanship does not differ from that of his fellow-workers. While the original brick motif is still predominant, there has been introduced a minor motif which revolves around the indeterminate sex of the cat. The origin of this idea is again sufficiently obvious to need no explanation. That it contains the germ of a vast number of humorous situations must be equally clear. A third motif, of still more recent origin, is that of Krazy Kat's patient submission to, nay, actual delight in forever recurring maltreatment at the hands of his smaller fellow-denizen of the animal world.

Within the last two years Mr. Herriman has found it necessary to have recourse to the introduction of new characters. His enlarged dramatis personæ includes a dog, known as Officer Pupp, who protects the Kat (uncharacteristically enough) from the assaults of the Mouse. There are also a large number of other animals, who pass rapidly across the stage and serve largely as excuses for new vagaries on the part of the chief actors.

"KRAZY KAT" AS A "KRAZY KITTEN" IN THE "WASH-BOILA", THE SHRINE OF HIS NATIVITY.

SPEAKING OF "IGNATZ MOUSE", HERE'S
THE HOLE IN THE CORNER OF THE BATH ROOM, BACK OF THE OLD ZINC BATH TUB, THROUGH WHICH HE FIRST SAW THE LIGHT OF THE WORLD

WHERE Y'GOING WITH THAT "BRICK", AND WHAT ARE YOU GOING TO DO WITH IT, HUH?

"BRICK", OFFICER, "BRICK", WHAT "BRICK"?

WE ARE NOT DEALING IN "CONSCIENCES" BUT IF WE WERE, AH, IF WE WERE

**Drawn for Cartoons Magazine by George Herriman**

Mr. Herriman's medium is the pen and ink sketch. In the daily issues there are five of these. In the Sunday isues the form is less strictly limited. As a rule, each sketch contains an horizon line decorated with quaintly fantastic trees and houses. In the foreground the characters speak their lines and go through their business. Where speaking of lines predominates and the characters move little, the audience is entertained by a miraculous shift in the landscape from picture to picture. Such a shift is often made, indeed, where the movements of the protagonists are violent, but in these cases its value is not so great. I should like to speak at length of these charming landscapes, but they defy description. They consist almost exclusively of trees with extraordinarily large and bulging trunks crowned by the merest tuft of foliage (giving somewhat the effect of misshapen asparagus stalks) and of small, squat, one-storied houses with thatched roofs, evidently intended to suggest the hovels of Mexican peons.

The appearance of the actors themselves is also well-nigh incapable of reproduction in words. To be appreciated they must be seen. (I dare say few of my readers, however high their noses are, by this time, lifted, have failed to see them.) Krazy Kat is black, with a large body and short legs. His face is white, with two black dots for eyes, and a thick black line for a nose. His tail (also black) is a most remarkable creation, ending very squarely indeed, and almost always betraying one or two quite heart-rending kinks. Ignatz Mouse is done in line. His head and trunk are of approximately the same size. His legs and tail are single lines. His feet are made by a mere wiggle of the artist's pen. The other characters are also done in line, and are, if possible, of an appearance even more fantastic than that of Krazy and Ignatz. Officer Pupp, for example, is exceedingly stout in the waist, wears a policeman's hat, and a belt from which is suspended a billy. He suggests, to be sure, a humanized bulldog, but his attitudes are far from canine. All the actors, of course, walk on their hind legs, and in general assume human postures.

From the point of view of drawing, Mr. Herriman's work is distinguished by the simplicity of the means whereby he secures the utmost subtlety of effect, by the fantastic nature of his conceptions, and (what appeals to me most of all) by his ability to create kinæsthetic illusion. No better example of the simplicity of his means could be found than in the face of Krazy Kat. It consists, as I have said, of a white patch in which are two black dots for eyes, a thick black line for a rather protruding nose, and a thinner line for a mouth. By almost infinitesimal variations in the position of the eyes and of the corners of the mouth, Mr. Herriman contrives to run the whole gamut of the emotions on Krazy's excessively stupid countenance. Fear, affection, devotion, wonder, surprise, amusement, content, all find a place. Before me, at this moment, he is depicted (in the somewhat more elaborate Sunday edition) as sitting rapt at the feet of Mr. Stork, and hearing from him the circumstances of his birth and the birth of many of his intimates. He has drawn his knees up and holds them clasped in his forelegs. His eye dots are raised a trifle nearer than usual to his arching eyebrows, and are somewhat extended vertically. His mouth line, of which little is visible, suggests the close-pressed lips of a child fascinated by a fairy story. Again, on the same page, he is depicted asleep in his natal washtub. His eye dots are now horizontal—clearly shut. His mouth, again barely visible over the edge of the tub, has become relaxed into a small triangle. His face is essentially asleep.

Mr. Herriman's conception, unlike his execution, is rather complex. It is, as I have said, fantastic, and yet fantastic in a way more quaint than out and out grotesque. Having turned the relations of the animal world upside down, he must perforce distort the animals themselves. Krazy and Ignatz are marvelous enough representations of the cat and mouse, but they are not comparable in this respect to some of their fellow-performers. These last, I shall not attempt to describe. The bookworm with the pair of legs, the ostrich with the mittenlike feet, the turtle with the cigar, the duck with the shoes and the silk hat, the dog (not, in this case, Officer Pupp with the spectacles and the barroom posture), are all utterly inimitable, and, as a rule, so nonsensical as to transcend the vulgarity usually found in comic animals. Of his landscapes and trees, I have spoken. To those who would delve deeper, I can only say (as

Philip to Nathanael): "Come and see!"

The third phase of Mr. Herriman's craftsmanship is his ability to create kinæsthetic illusion. Here again his means are fairly simple. The "arms" and legs of Ignatz Mouse consist, as I have said, of single lines. With these crooked at various angles, the artist contrives to depict almost perfectly the posture assumed in throwing. Thus, in those pictures wherein chastisement is inflicted on the unfortunate Krazy, one can feel, as it were metaphysically, just the sensations of the mouse as he hurls the brick, or the stone, or (once most charmingly) the watermelon. The preposterous disproportion between the thrower and the missile lends added fascination. Somehow or other the tremendous physical exertion required is brought out in every line of Ignatz' body. More ingenious and elusive still is

WHAT'S THE MATTER, KRAZY.
I JUST GOT CHEATED.
1
HOW ?
WITH THIS WATER-MELON
2
OH-HOH- IT'S A GREEN ONE, HEH ?
OH, NO, IT'S RIPE ENOUGH =
3
THEN WHAT ARE YOU HOWLING ABOUT ?
IT'S DILUTED TOO MUCH =
4

Krazy Kat—He Likes His Watermelon Straight

the method by which the sense of Krazy's precipitation through space is conveyed. Sometimes, after being struck from behind, he comes hurtling directly at you. Again he moves along directly parallel with the horizon—moves, mark you, not merely hangs suspended in mid-air, as would inevitably be the effect were the artist's hand less skillful. I cannot speak in detail of other illusions of motion which Mr. Herriman conjures up. He understands perfectly how to depict slinking, hasty retreat, the walk of perfect indifference, the walk of those accustomed to ride, the walk of those with something on their minds, and heaven only knows what else. Follow his column for a week and you will realize his boundless versatility.

But Mr. Herriman's genius is almost as much manifested by his literary style as by his drawings. Krazy Kat, for example, indulges a vast variety of most engaging idiosyncracies of diction. The flat "a" of "Ignatz" becomes the "e" of "Ignetz." Singular and plural are not very clearly differentiated either. "Ignetz Mice" is usually Krazy's way of addressing his companion. On the page before me, I see such delightful specimens of Kat dialect as: "Wundafil, Mr. Stork, just simpfully wundafil," or, as Krazy renders a variation on a well-known ballad:

"How dear to my heart is the scene of my infinthood,
Where fond reckillection pr-e-e-e-zents tha-m-m-m to view.
The ole haunted house and the cellar undaneet it,
And the dear old wash-boila e-e-e-n which I was born. . . . .
And every loved spot whom my infinthood knew."

On the same page, we discover Mr. Herriman in an altogether different vein as he writes this almost beautiful explanation of the significance of the day's pictures:

"The clocks of the universe are striking the hour of now and Joe Stork, who dwells on the topside of the enchanted mesa in the desierto pintado, and who pilots princes and paupers, poets and peasants, puppies and pussycats across the river without any other side of the shore of here, is telling Krazy Kat a tale which must never be told, and yet which everyone knows."

One would like to see Mr. Herriman try his hand at writing fairy tales, for one has a feeling that he could do it in a most quaint and effective manner. "The river without any other side to the shore of here"—what a phrase! How miraculous in its suggestiveness! How steeped in that imagery which is always associated with childhood's notion of the origin of life.

Mesa and desierto pintado illustrate another feature of Mr. Herriman's verbiage. He is apparently well acquainted with Mexican dialect and employs it with startling frequency. I am myself ordinarily well-nigh unable to recall enough of my college Spanish to make out what he means. I am tempted to conclude that not a few of his phrases pass completely over the heads of a majority of his audience. I have a similar feeling with regard to his inexhaustible store of literary allusions. In one out of every five of his columns there occurs some indication that Mr. Herriman is by no means an unlettered man. Frequently, also, Krazy and Ignatz indulge in a sophistical hair-splitting that might have delighted the heart of a Socrates. Forgive me if, in all this, I seem to patronize. The experience of finding a genius in a comic section is novel enough to serve as excuse for any tactlessness.

Another charming feature of the conversations of his characters is their indiscriminate mingling of the choicest of diction with phrases scarcely in the best literary use. Thus on this single page to which I have referred so often, Mr. Ostrich speaks thus:

"There wasn't a grander castle in all the Kalahari than the one in which I was born. That was me starting life as a infant swathed in the purple of royalty, and a golden spoon in my mouth. Yizza-boy!"

Mr. Turtle goes on in the same vein as follows:

"Ha, you prate of castles and golden spoons, and you boast of the purple, but know you, my friends, that I, Terrapin Turtle, had all that stuff at my birth, and more, my swaddling clothes were diamonds. Segura Miguel!" which, being interpreted is, presumably, "Sure, Mike!"

I should like to add a few words in connection with the incidents to illustrate which Mr. Herriman draws his pictures. I am unfortunately altogether dependent on my memory in this matter, and consequently cannot perhaps make citations so apt as if

I had a number before me to choose from. One of the slightest and yet one of the most amusing series I recall is this: In the first picture, the artist has mixed his conversation. Krazy is made to say "Hello, Krazy," while Ignatz says "Hello, Ignatz." In the second picture, each glances at the other's remarks. In the third each has grasped the line which binds the words spoken to the lips of the speaker. In the fourth, we find these lines crossed, and in the fifth the remarks are arranged properly, while a look of contentment is writ large upon the features of both. This typifies that class of incident in which the artist in a manner introduces himself to his audience by emphasizing the limitations and general nature of his medium. Again I recall a series of which the first scene represents Krazy carrying a large framed picture. In

COME AWAY, "IGNATZ" COME AWAY: OH THEM "WASH-BOILA"; OH THEM WASH-BOILA"
1
WHAT WAS THE MATTER WITH THAT "WASH-BOILER" ?
IT MAKES ME SO SAD =
2
HOW CAN A WASH-BOILER MAKE YOU SAD ?
ITS THE MEMORIES "IGNATZ" IT'S THE MEMORIES
3
HOW, MEMORIES
YEP, "IGNATZ, I WAS BORN IN A "WASH-BOILA
4

How Dear to My Heart Is That L'il Ole Wash Boila

SKOBSH!!
ZIPS
HERRIMAN—

© International Feature Service

the next we discover him hanging it, the picture being a representation of himself. He is mounted on a box during the process. In the third the picture is hung, and Krazy is departing with the remark that Ignatz will be delighted to see it. In the fourth picture, Ignatz is on the box eyeing it quizzically. In the last, we find the picture utterly ruined, as if something had been hurled at it, while Krazy looks at it regretfully and shows by his remark that he knows that Ignatz has already seen it. This is essentially a series designed to throw light on Krazy's pitifully submissive character, and the brutal way in which Ignatz tramples on his feelings. Finally, one of the most delightful of the incidents I recall is an allegorical depiction of birth control. Krazy, the epicene, is now become a tabby cat, and is revealed standing outside her cottage. The second picture shows a stork winging its way in the far distance. In the third, Krazy is running to her house, while the stork draws nearer. In the fourth, Krazy is seen partly emerging from the chimney, over which she is spreading a sheet. In the final scene, the chimney is covered, the stork flies over the cottage, and Krazy from the window peeps out at it with an exceedingly mischievous twinkle in her eye.

Let me say one word more of Mr. Herriman's ingeniously onomatopoetic way of representing sound. The passage of a brick through the air is usually represented by the letters Z-I-Z-Z strewn in its wake. The concussion of the brick on Krazy's head is represented by the greatest variety of symbols. I recall one in particular where the missile happened to be a watermelon, and where the sound it was supposed to make was represented most appropriately by some such combination of letters as skobsh. Here as always, Mr. Herriman's art is rather designed to suggest than to imitate.

Oscar Wilde has somewhere written that the only literary forms not devised by the Greeks are the sonnet, the ballad written in sham Scotch dialect, and American journalism. For the sake of Hellenic reputation, one cannot but rejoice that American journalism, indeed, finds no prototype in the age of Pericles. But at the same time, it is an obvious fact that without American journalism we should not have American funny pages, and without American funny pages we should not have Mr. Herriman's Krazy Kat. And I hope I am not making myself too ridiculous in suggesting that even the age of Pericles need not have been ashamed to stand sponsor for this last.

In the foregoing pages, I have surveyed Mr. Herriman's work in an exceedingly cursory and careless fashion. I have endeavored to point out the poignant originality and innate delicacy of his drawings in respect to both their conception and execution. I have tried to cite illustrations of his delicious literary style, and of his ingenuity in devising plots in which to set his artistic and literary creations. I have been compelled to leave many things unsaid that I should have liked to say. I have been incompetent to devise any consistent critical theory that would do justice to his genius and vindicate his work of the charge of vulgarity so justly levied against that of many of his contemporaries.

My sole purpose has been to bring him to the attention of thinking people as a phase of American art well worth thinking about; in other words, to perform what is really the sole function of criticism, the function of discovering genius wheresoever it may be concealed. If I have in any measure accomplished my purpose or performed my function, I shall rest content.

# George Herriman, 1880–1944.

## by Bill Blackbeard

There was a lot of Dickens in him, a lot of Lewis Carroll, a lot of W.C. Fields and vaudeville and low-life comedy, and just as obviously a lot of Eliot and Joyce and Ubu Roi.

But George Herriman was ultimately a hundred and eighteen and a half coconino per cent his own man, a man who would have undoubtedly lifted his eyebrows at the mention of those names, all of which are much more present in our assessment of the artist than they probably were in his own view of himself — a view that seems to have been modest to the point of self-effacement.

Herriman would have certainly liked the Dickens and Carroll and Fields analogies — and he would have sparked a grin at the inclusion of Chaplin and Laurel and Hardy as well — but he might have boggled a bit at the others.

It is a strange thing to say about a cartoonist so revered and widely known in his own time, but Herriman's intellectuality remains still unplumbed.

We have sparkling letters from him to the lowest of risqué gag-cartoon magazines of the 1920s, comic reviews of Chaplin films in movie magazines (written as if by Krazy), but not a signed word by him in the heavyweight literary and artistic periodicals of his epochal period in the arts.

*Vanity Fair* put him in its Hall of Fame and got him to do a Sunday-style Kat page for one of its 1930s issues, but garnered not a line of non-comic prose or verse from this shy master.

The fine-tooth-comb research on the cartoonist's life set forth in the 1986 Harry Abrams *Krazy Kat* volume elicits no hint of his reading or visual interests.

We know he loved to visit the old Mack Sennett studios in Hollywood and put his feet up and gas with the directors and comics, but we don't know what galleries he frequented, or what books crammed his shelves.

We don't even know his response to the Armory Show — even though it contained a painting by Rudolph Dirks of *Katzenjammer Kids* fame.

All we have is *Krazy Kat* itself.

All we have, in short, is a universe of fantasy and poetry and the wildest comedy this side of Charley Chase and the Marx Brothers.

In the end, *Krazy Kat* tells us all we need to know about Herriman.

Herriman's father, variously a barber, a baker, and a tailor, had the foresight to move his family (including George, then six years old) from the creole poetry of New Orleans to the cinematic golden mean of sun-dappled Los Angeles in 1886.

As soon as he could, George skipped out of the apprenticeship to whichever of his father's Micawberish occupations was then turning up to pursue his own way with pen and ink and what was to become the most wholly individual comic graphic imagination of the twentieth century.

It seemed at first that there was nothing that Herriman could draw that wouldn't sell. One-shot comic-page layouts went into print at once in major newspapers; his gag cartoons garnered quick and welcome bucks from the *Judge* and *Life* humor magazines of the time.

George Herriman's tenative strip character ideas took hold and delighted readers on sight.

From *Professor Otto* and *Musical Mose* in 1902 he went on to *Lariat Pete* and *Two Jolly Jackies* in 1903, then to *Major Ozone* and *Bud Smith* and *Zoo Zoo* and *Baron Mooch* and *Alexander* and *The Dingbat Family* and there seemed to be no end. Even after he unknowingly entered into immortality with *Krazy Kat*, he spun out more graphic fancies in "Baron Bean" and "Stumble Inn" and *Us Husbands* through the 1910s and 1920s.

And all of this work, every bit of it right down to the most casual effort, is a visual delight and a dithyramb of ebullient, subtly offbeat fancy that is simply unlike anything else in comic art before or since his time.

It is, of course, the work of genius.

Biographically, there really isn't much more to say.

Herriman's life was largely quiet and devoted to his family and his work. He greatly enjoyed excursions to the great American desert he so deftly portrayed in his later work, in the company of such cartoonist buddies as Rudy Dirks, Jimmy Swinnerton, and "Rubbernose" Tom MacNamara.

He relished family life, and gloried in the considerable cartooning talent of his daughter, Bobbie.

He was tickled with Don Marquis' delirious *archy and mehitabel* books and wound up illustrating all three of them in a one-volume reissue edition that has now become a comic classic and a perfect wedding of author and artist talents.

He suffered through some poor film adaptions of *Krazy Kat* without being allowed to add the supervisory touch that might have made these films marvellous.

He corresponded a lot and bowled over friends and even first-time letter-writers with gifts of original watercolors, hand-tinted comic strip art he had had the good sense to retrieve from the syndicate slide-chutes to oblivion.

For George Herriman, it was a largely good and happy and obviously inspiring life.

# The IGNATZ MOUSE DEBAFFLER PAGE.

Herewith the Ignatz Mouse DeBaffler page from the *Coconino County Chronicle* for 1916, 1917, and 1918, devised to allay bafflement at occasional items in the *Krazy & Ignatz* pages reprinted here. Mr. Mouse, our Residential Rodent in the County, maintains the physical strength vital to his work by elevating bricks while humming his favorite song, "Old Zip Coon."

The reader should keep in mind that the U.S. was engaged in a war with Germany in 1918, a fact which supplied Herriman with subject material in the pages for 6/2/18, 6/30/18, 9/29/18, and 10/13/18. (The helmeted character in the 9/29 page is the Kaiser himself.)

—Bill Blackbeard

BY GOLLIX, MR HERBIT HOOVA 'IS RIGHT, AND AS I PERSINILLY KNOW A NUMBA OF HOGS I'LL ADOPT ONE.

**4/23/16:** In this first-ever Sunday-style Krazy Kat page we are granted the good fortune to meet a fair sample of the Coconino County gentry, whose names and personas will engagingly emerge in the pages to follow.

To Mrs Helen Dirks
with best wishes
from Geo Herriman May 1st 1916

**4/30/16:** The dedicatory inscription in panels 23 and 24 to Mrs. Helen Dirks is meant for the wife of Rudolph Dirks, cartoonist, creator of *The Captain and the Kids*, who received the original as inscribed here.

**5/7/16:** The book next to the volume on Plato in the third from last panel appears to be a bound collection of a then-popular dime novel series featuring a detective named Old Sleuth. Nothing else relating Herriman to dime novels is known to this commentator.

**5/14/16:** This is apparently the first use of the Minnie Mouse cognomen in continuity comics (12 years before the animated short Plane Crazy introduced her as Mickey's inamorata), while the Mickey Mouse name appeared initially (in tandem with a Minnie Mouse figure) in an all-mouse narrative written and drawn by Johnny Gruelle in *Good Housekeeping* Magazine for most of 1919. Gruelle, of course, made a children's book fortune with his Raggedy Ann and Raggedy Andy series.

**12/3/16:** This gorgeously mad daymare can be nothing more nor less than a Krazy Kat dream — brick-induced, of course.

**5/20/17:** America's nearing and final involvement in World War I, touched on frequently in these pages, is the clear motivation for the theme developed in this episode. See also later episodes for 7/22/17, 8/5/17 and 10/7/17.

ZIP
GREAT WORK, KRAZY, VERY, VERY ARTISTIC, — Y'GET .10¢ EXTRA FOR IT.
THENX MR. HENNIT.

**7/1/17:** "Ledda zzip zink wodda I care?": Igntaz's caustic comment on Officer Pupp's habit of wasting his time on minor matters instead of more important police duties. The phrase also reflects wartime poster warnings. Here Ignatz seems to see the coming national abolition of liquor as itself foolishly intoxicating, as goofy as the posturing of Halloween celebrants. (Note Krazy alone is shown as sober.)

**11/25/17:** Anticipating the national mood, by 1917 many states had already gone "dry," canceling all liquor sales. In those states, semi-clandestine locations where liquor was still available "with a buck and a wink" became known as "blind pigs" — a term which obviously tickled Herriman's volatile imagination.

**12/16/17:** "Jam closet" became a synonym for the abovementioned "blind pig."

**2/17/18:** In this page, where Krazy has his pick of Coconino's hogs, the "Herbit Hoova" referred to is, of course, the same Herbert Hoover who became President in the late 1920s. In 1918, he was President Wilson's choice to preside over a national program of food conservation, which advocated the raising of livestock in private homes.

**3/10/18:** Herriman probably visited the filmings of Mack Sennett film comedies at Paramount Picture's Astoria Studios outside Manhattan in 1917 and 1918; certainly he was a frequent Sennett Studios visitor in Hollywood after 1922. This page shows a more than casual familiarity with slapstick movie making at the time, and the original artwork probably went to Sennett. (O where izzit now?)

(In February 1916 through May 1918, the Hearst corporation animated a series of "Krazy Kat" cartoons as party of its Movietone newsreels, as a kind of silver screen comic strip following the main news content of each weekly newsreel, but Herriman had no control over the content of these generally poor cartoons, probably didn't like them much, and it is doubtful this page comments in any substantial way on Krazy's kareer in such flicks. Interested readers can find a number of these on YouTube: Use the search words "krazy," "kat," and "1916," and you can enjoy — or not — "Krazy Kat, Bugologist" or "Krazy Kat Goes A Wooing," among others.

**4/21/18:** "Cholly Kokonino." In the more meretriciously entertaining press of the early 1900s, society notices were written up with zest and color, their authors often signing their work with a continuing byline based on that originated by the New York American's "Cholly Knickerbocker," and, like that pseudonym, reflection he locus of the author's papers, i.e., "Cholly Chicago," "Cholly Angelino," etc.

**9/22/18:** Most of the noxious concoctions on Mr. Kaskara's exotic shelves are a panoply of jokes or obscure references that can be decoded by the resourceful reader: "Nux Vomica" (a genuine homeopathic remedy), "Tic Doolooroo" (a more-or-less phonetic spelling of *Tic Douloureux*, a neuropathic disorder also known as trigeminal neuralgia), "Habeas Corpus" (ha ha), and "Kasta Erl" (think about it). But "Gunbutus Hudsonia" is an in-joke in need of debaffling: In this panel Herriman is paying homage to "Gunboat Hudson," the legendary Hearst office boy whose daily chores once involved daily banter with the members of the old Hearst New York American "bullpen" of cartoonists — Winsor McCay, Ed Wheelan, Tad Dorgan, Walter Hoban and, of course, George Herriman *lui-même.*

BLIND